The
Ultimate
THREE
MINUTES

The nineteenth century preoccupation with the historical approach has been called historicism. . . . Mention must also be made of the application of systematic historical techniques to the Bible; the critical assessment of Biblical texts, their sources and authorship.

PETER H. NIDDITCH, University of Sussex (UNESCO "History of Mankind: Cultural and Scientific Development," Volume 5, "The Nineteenth Century," pp. 275–276)

The
Ultimate
THREE
MINUTES

The Story of Two Great Human Watersheds –
Their Preparation and Their Coinciding

William Cummings

sussex
ACADEMIC
PRESS
Brighton • Chicago • Toronto

2 4 6 8 10 9 7 5 3 1

First published 2015 in Great Britain by
SUSSEX ACADEMIC PRESS
PO Box 139
Eastbourne BN24 9BP

and in the United States of America by
SUSSEX ACADEMIC PRESS
Independent Publishers Group
814 N. Franklin Street, Chicago, IL 60610

and in Canada by
SUSSEX ACADEMIC PRESS (CANADA)

British Library Cataloguing in Publication Data
A CIP catalogue record for this book is available from the British Library.

Library of Congress Cataloging-in-Publication Data
Cummings, William.
The ultimate three minutes : the story of two great human watersheds
—their preparation and their coinciding / William Cummings.
   pages   cm
   ISBN 978-1-84519-734-6 (pbk : alk. paper)
   1. Salvation—Christianity. I. Title.
BT751.3.C86 2015
234—dc23

                                                                2015009158

Typeset and designed by Sussex Academic Press, Brighton & Eastbourne.
Printed by TJ International, Padstow, Cornwall.
This book is printed on acid-free paper.

Contents

Foreword by the
Rt. Revd. Nicholas Reade

I am struck by the extraordinary breadth of 'The Ultimate Three Minutes', though not surprised having, during his time as Dean of Battle, known William Cummings as a serious student, widely read, and above all as a fine conventional parish priest with a deep concern for the people in his care. His book takes an innovative look at the central tenets of the Christian Faith, focusing on those ultimate three minutes in the context of world history from earliest times, using both historical and scientific data to suggest that both history and science support the central Christian truths of the Incarnation and Saving Death and Resurrection of Jesus Christ.

The book follows the agricultural revolution of the Neolithic Period; the establishment of civilisation in the Bronze Age; the slow gathering of the whole of the West into the control of the Roman Empire, and then, above all the providential appearance and career of the Roman emperor Augustus at the time of the birth of Jesus Christ. When we reach the final summarising chapters we find some unusual parables involving a phenomenon of modern physics, and a poignantly personal dedication to the Gospel message.

In his time in office I always saw Dean Cummings as among the last of that breed of clergy committed to carrying on that great tradition, once quite common in the Church of England, of many parish clergy who regarded good learning and a scholarly approach as a priority in their ministry, and this is a strong reason why this book needs to be taken seriously. It will appeal to both the believer and those seeking the truth of the Christian message, and also those interested to know how a thoughtful Christian with a scientific background finds meaning and Divine disclosure through the processes by which things in this world happen.

Very fittingly the final section ends with the General Thanksgiving from the 1662 Book of Common Prayer. This prayer, said by generations of Christians in thanksgiving for our Creation and Redemption through Christ, is where the answers lie to Paul

Gauguin's three questions at the heart of this book, 'Where do we come from?' 'What are we?' 'Where are we going?' Most certainly this book will help us to answer those questions, and show us that every moment of our lives is filled with eternity, which is why it needs to be read widely.

List of Maps and Genealogy

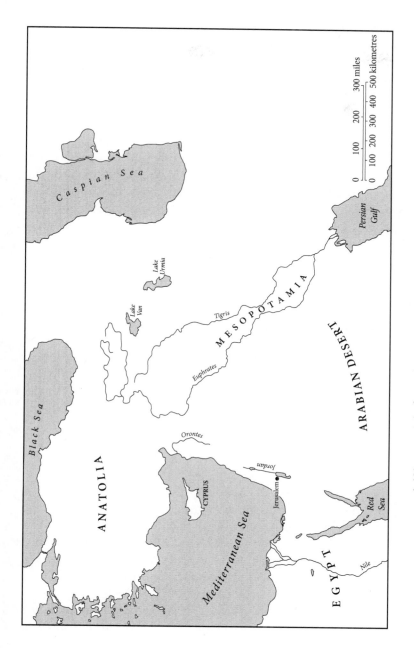

1 Western Asia from the Caspian Sea to Cyprus

(3,500–2,000 BC) when both Mesopotamians and Egyptians alike had to guard against the infiltrations of the "sand-dwellers."

There were two routes from Mesopotamia to Egypt. The less common was by sea, down the Persian Gulf, round the Arabian peninsula, and up the Red Sea, docking at Berenice.

The more well-travelled route was overland along the passage first named by Professor J.H. Breasted "The Fertile Crescent." Caravans would follow the Euphrates along its north-western course, and from its bend near Aleppo, hop across to the river Orontes and then towards Damascus. There they had a choice of two tracks. The King's Highway ran east of the Jordan and down to the Gulf of Aqabah. The Great Trunk Road led down towards the Mediterranean coast and then on through Gaza to the northern gateway to Egypt.

Egypt was a mysterious, awesome yet colourful civilisation. It stretched along the Nile from the Delta where it entered the Mediterranean (Lower Egypt) to, at its greatest extent under the Pharoah Tuthmosis III (1,482–1,450 BC), almost the Fourth Cataract (Upper Egypt). Egypt's majesty and its splendours stood, to outward appearances, inviolable and untouched for something like two and a half thousand years.

The coastlands of north Africa were more fertile than in modern times and less populated. Phoenicians colonised Carthage, and Greeks Cyrene, but the whole territory, from the Nile to the Atlantic Ocean, was only a secondary player in the development of human progress.

The Caspian Sea, and the Way to Europe

We return from the African Atlantic coast to the Caspian Sea. A couple of crows setting out south of the Caucasus mountains but north of the Fertile Crescent would fly, one of them north-westwards across Lake Urmia and Lake Van, and the other due west across the mountainous terrain of Armenia. Meeting over eastern Turkey they would then together cross the enormous high plateau of Anatolia. Anatolia, modern Turkey, reaches westwards like a giant tongue, the Mediterranean and Cyprus to its south, the Black Sea to the north, until it drops towards sea level and fronts the magical and historic sea called the Aegean. Studded with mountain tops, which appear above the water as small islands, the journey across the Aegean leads first to the peninsula of Greece, then across the Adriatic to Italy, and then across the Mediterranean to Spain/Portugal. The Mediterranean bears others islands apart from those of the Aegean – Minorca, Majorca, Corsica, Sardinia, Sicily, Malta, Cyprus and, astride the Mediterranean and the Aegean, the long, thin island of Crete.

From the north, the entrances into Greece, Italy and the Spanish peninsula are, none of them, easy. The mountainous country that descends from the Balkan peninsula into Greece is crazily steep and irregular. The greater part of the entrance to Italy is blocked by Alpine masses, rising at Mont Blanc, their highest summit, to 15,780 feet (4,708 metres). Spain is barred by the more tolerable but still exacting Pyrenees. Spain was, incidentally, found to possess great sources of mineral wealth, which were exploited by Augustus (27 BC–AD 14) and the magnates of the early Roman Empire.

The lands to the north and west of the Black Sea also came to play a part, later but permanently formative, in the history of the human race.

West of the Ural mountains (highest point 6,180 feet, 1,894 metres) stretched great plains and steppes, urging galloping explorers westwards, and interrupted only by the Carpathian mountains of Poland and Czechoslovakia. From a point near the Danube, vegetation began to rise, increasing in height until the whole of France, Germany and northern Europe up to Denmark was covered in thick deciduous and evergreen forest. From these millennia of ancient afforestation, out of several still living organisms, one still survives in the British Isles. The Fortingall Yew, Perthshire, Scotland, at an age of approximately 5,000 years, is still alive today!

The whole of this play-park, where astounding and historic human splendours rose and fell, was thus chiselled out of impressive and daunting features of mountains and plateaux; plains, lakes and deserts; seas and islands; rivers and forests.

Rivers and Roads

Six rivers and river systems in particular have left the mark of their influence upon the progress and development of the human race.

The Tigris and Euphrates meeting-points, at the north and south of Mesopotamia, fostered the earliest cities, their trading and eventually their writing, with which history, as opposed to prehistory, dawns.

The river Jordan, running down from the mountains of Lebanon to the Dead Sea, uniquely irrigated, and invited settlement, in Israel and Palestine. Alongside the Jordan to the west, in a fold of Sennonian chalk dating to the latter half of the Cretaceous Era (between a hundred million and sixty-five million years ago), lies a pinnacle of much earlier Cenomanian limestone dating from the early Cretaceous Era (between one hundred and thirty-six million and one hundred million years ago). On the platform of this pinnacle lies Jerusalem, one of the most historic and far-fabled locations in the history of the world.

In Africa the river Nile, steaming northwards from the impenetrable south, nourished the whole magnificent enterprise of ancient Egypt.

The Danube, the second longest river in Europe, (the longest is the Volga), rises to the east of the Black Forest and flows eastwards, making a sharp southerly turn just before Budapest. It turns east again as the Drave joins it, and passing through Belgrade and the plains of Roumania, dissipates through many mouths and deltas into the Black Sea. This river formed one part of the northern boundary of the Roman Empire, before the adventures beyond it of the emperor Trajan (AD 98–117).

The Rhine, running northwards from Switzerland and entering the North Sea via Rotterdam and the Hoek of Holland formed (for lack of security along the Weser and the Elbe) the other section of the northern Roman boundary. It is a matter of interest that at the very beginning of human history, all attention focuses upon the Tigris and the Euphrates, but that at the transition from the Ancient to the Medieval world, all eyes are upon the Danube and the Rhine. This is but one example, borne on the surface of a much deeper current, whereby between the years 3,500 BC and AD 500 the whole centre of gravity of human civilisation can be seen to drift gradually but relentlessly from east to west.

Travel across this entire territory was cheapest and easiest by sea or along the rivers. On land it had to be on foot or by pack animal, in Europe by tribes moving in concert, in the Asiatic parts (when not subject to the maraudings of invaders), by traders travelling in caravans. For literally thousands of years there were no roads. Even the King's Highway and the Great Trunk Road were enlarged and acknowledged tracks. The first real roads were built by the Persians in the sixth century BC (600–501 BC) for military purposes. The whole complex was finally knit together in an imperial ribbon-work of roads by the Romans in the third century AD (AD 201–300).

Roads, having existed for, say, two thousand six hundred years, are a relatively recent experience for the human race. For two thousand nine hundred years before then, we managed without them.

This glance at unfamiliar and mentally exhausting stretches of time, suggests that it is appropriate to move from the dancing floor to the dancing years – from a geographical to a historical preamble to the account leading up to "The Ultimate Three Minutes."

2

The Dancing Years

Prelude

Two million years – wheeling of the earth round the sun two million times! – is a long period for human form to emerge out of the mist.

The thirty million years prior to these two million years was a phenomenon of colliding land-mass, mountain building and volcanic eruption. The second million of the two million years was equally phenomenal for the surging of unprecedented ice. Four times bands of ice expanded out of the north and south polar regions and then contracted again. Adventurous bands of pre-human hominids trekked north out of Africa thinly populating eastwards and westwards. All this happened with a yawning, indescribable, slowness.

The Old Stone Age

The fourth encroachment of the ice, the Wurms Glaciation, withdrew itself only about 8,000 BC, ten thousand years ago, having begun its polar outreach some sixty thousand years ago. During this Ice Age, human beings of potential and passions equivalent to our own, had begun to roam the whole planet in small families and hunting groups, and to leave their traces behind.

The Wurms Ice Age did not cover the whole planet, but it buried the continents of the northern hemisphere beneath deep weights and heights of frozen moisture, locking up water and lowering the depths of the southern seas. When this Ice Age was "only" ten thousand years old – about fifty thousand years ago – conditions favoured pioneering human entry, somehow, into Australia.

About 28,000 years ago, in Hohlenstein-Stadel in Germany, late but still deep in the grip of the Wurms Ice Age, somebody carved a lion-man, with all the dexterity of modelling, the correspondence of anatomy and the adaptation of form to content which betoken entirely human observation, emotion, artistic intuition and artistic skills. The ice continued.

Seventeen thousand years ago, eleven thousand years after the Hohlenstein-Stadel lion-man (not eleven hundred, but eleven thousand, one hundred and ten centuries of painful, unimaginable, and indescribable interval) the Lascaux caves in southern France were penetrated by early, Aurignacian, man and exploited as galleries for animal painting.

About the same time, near Kimberley in north-west Australia, after resolute but unrecorded existence for thirty-three thousand years – the Dancing Years had not yet come – the anonymous and persistent descendants of the earliest pioneers into Australia left sophisticated "sash-paintings" on the walls of certain caves as, apparently, ritual decoration. The paintings are today named "Bradshaws" after Joseph Bradshaw who first discovered them.

For nine thousand years more of the Wurms Ice Age, some three hundred generations of the primitive human race endured the freezing conditions descending and ascending towards the tropics out of the north and south poles.

With laborious slowness the ice began to shrink back, the creaking continents to be relieved of their burdens, the rivers to run, the seas again to fill. Eight thousand years before Christ, events of a special order began to unfold. Following the Gunz (750,000 to 650,000 years ago), Mindel (450,000 to 400,000 years ago) and Riss (210,000 to 160,000 years ago) Glaciations, or "Ice Ages," of the last million years, no events like these had ever unfolded before.

The New Stone Age

Around the central Eurasian plains that stretch from the Caspian Sea to Jericho – largely the area later named the "Fertile Crescent" – were found from about 8,000 BC, accumulated in providential and fortuitous abundance, certain grasses and certain animals. With these the human beings of the transitional period between the retreat of the ice and the return of the warmer climates, began to experiment. Over a span of five thousand years from 8,000 to 3,000 BC, by breeding of plants and domestication and breeding of animals, these Fertile Crescent inhabitants settled down into a sedentary way of life in which the hunting and gathering practices of their distant Old Stone Age forefathers were long discontinued and forgotten. This was the new, farming, agricultural, Neolithic way of life, still illiterate, still ignorant of the use of metals, but forming a social revolution that, following the Gunz, Mindel and Riss Ice Ages, had never taken place before.

The Bronze Age

The new farming economy was spectacularly original. But there was more to follow. Somewhere between 4,000 and 3,000 BC, in south-eastern Anatolia, developments occurred which the Australian archaeologist V. Gordon Childe has called (not without justification) "the most dramatic leap in the history of mankind." The mysteries of metallurgy began to be reduced to formulae. The secret sorcery of smiths began to win for the human race an unprecedented mastery over certain metals.

So evolved an achievement in human progress which accelerated beyond all others. Chief of all, out of the alloy of tin and copper, craftsmen discovered the properties of bronze! From this beginning of the Bronze Age, perhaps about 3,400 BC at the earliest, followed not only metals, but trading (in products and ideas), writing, walled cities, ziggurat towers of baked brick which intruded presumptuously upon the heavens, and a dizzily widening circle of confidence and attainment such that the archaeologist Sir Leonard Woolley was able to say of it, "Almost all the branches of human Bronze Age activity might serve as a list of headings for the culture of our own time."

This Bronze Age (3,400–1,085 BC), deployed itself above all out of three distinct centres of activity, all bodies of water, two of fresh water fostering irrigation and agriculture, and one of salt water, favouring trade.

They were the valley ground between the rivers Tigris and Euphrates called Mesopotamia; the nurturing principle of all Egypt, the river Nile; and the island-studded stretch of sea at the eastern end of the Mediterranean, called the Aegean.

During nearly two and a half thousand years of their interaction, these three Bronze Age communities tended to be interrupted, harried and finally bankrupted by incursions from the jealous poor relations of the northern steppes – by such peoples as the Luwians, the Minyans, the Hittites, the Indo-Europeans, the Phrygians and the Peoples of the Sea.

The Tigris–Euphrates Valley

The first cities of Mesopotamia, with names like Uruk, Ur, Larsa, Kish or Shuruppak, engineered abundant excess of cereal crops. Wanting stone or timber in the Tigris–Euphrates valley, they were obliged to trade so far and wide with their surpluses, and so success-fully, that they were able to ascend to a sumptuous mode of living! Increasing friction between the city-states, breaking out into armed warfare, then began to drain their united strength; excessive infil-tration of salt into their irrigation systems reduced the quality of their barley. Natural disaster including (about 2,800 BC) a horren-dous flood of legendary proportions; increasing pressure of population from the Amorite "Sand-dwellers" of the deserts to their west, brought the great centuries of Mesopotamian civilisation to their knees – but not before they had imparted a spark of their dynamism to Egypt.

Egypt and the Nile

A handful of quality archaeological discoveries from the centuries between 3,400 and 3,100 BC suggests that Mesopotamia gave to Egypt something of an impulse towards a more advanced social and political level. But the land along the Nile was already of a stronger individual character, and more united, than the squabbling city-states of the Tigris–Euphrates valley. One suspects that already, during the long illiterate period before Narmer (also called Menes), founder of the First Dynasty of Egypt, first drew the people together in about 3,100 BC, the pre-Dynastic Egyptians had already begun to fall into the cultural distinctiveness and the governmental folds and formations of later generations.

Thereafter the Bronze Age in Egypt stretched out under twenty dynasties of Pharoahs, divided in later years into three convenient phases, the Old Kingdom, the Middle Kingdom and the New Kingdom, with Intermediate Periods between the Kingdoms.

Old Kingdom Egypt

Protodynastic and Old Kingdom Egypt (3,100–2,181 BC) traded in the eastern Mediterranean. With its wealth, the Pharoahs of the Fourth Dynasty erected the Sphinx and built the Great Pyramids of Egypt (2,600–2,500 BC) to mark their funeral resting-places. Through excess of centralisation and the revolt of over-mighty provincials the Sixth Dynasty, following the world-record reign of the Pharoah Phiops II (2,279–2,185 BC, ninety-four years) began to lose control of government and precipitate Egypt into the First Intermediate Period (2,181–2040 BC).

Middle Kingdom Egypt

The Middle Kingdom (2,040–1,674 BC) is largely monopolised by the illustrious Twelfth Dynasty of Egypt (1,991–1,786 BC), whose seven successive generations of Pharoahs seem one by one to have been unfolding a secret family plan for the state, sweeping Egypt, unimpeded, to the highest levels of prosperity.

The founder of the Twelfth Dynasty, Ammenemes I (1,991–1,962 BC) is applauded as the first thinking politician in the whole history of human governance. The Dynasty which he founded was comparable in length to the First Dynasty (3,100–2,890 BC) by which Narmer had first created the unity of Egypt, but the Twelfth Dynasty enlarged and sustained itself in an international climate vastly more crowded and competitive.

Under the Twelfth Dynasty the north-eastern corner of Egypt where Africa passed into western Asia became a cosmopolitan centre of international movement and trade, exchange and infiltration. Under the weight of such cosmopolitanism and instrusiveness, access was opened to the invasion of the Hyksos (1,674 BC) – invasion which brought the Middle Kingdom to its close.

Middle Kingdom Egypt also fostered the appearance of a genre of literature, the Middle Kingdom novel, which, admired and praised by Tolstoy, has become an early, ancient contribution to the catalogue of literature that is world class. The Second Intermediate Period between the Middle Kingdom and the New lasted from 1,674 to 1,567 BC.

New Kingdom Egypt

The New Kingdom of Egypt (1,567–1,085 BC) saw a revival of native Egyptian resistance against the northern Hyksos invaders and, under two Pharoahs of the Eighteenth Dynasty, Tuthmosis I (1,525–1,512 BC) and his grandson Tuthmosis III (1,503–1,450 BC), a restatement, reclaiming and an extension to their furthest limits of the economic and military might of Egypt.

Their descendants and successors Amenophis III (1,417–1,379) and the fourteenth century Amenophis IV (1,379–1,362 BC) who preferred to be called Akhenaton, introduced an over-confidence and a complacent relaxation into the governing psychology of Egypt from which, in spite of the military prowess of the last Pharoah of the Eighteenth Dynasty, Horemheb (1,348–1,320 BC), the Eighteenth Dynasty never recovered.

Akhenaton on the other hand was also the author of a "Hymn to the Sun," which, somewhat edited, still re-echoes today as Psalm 104; and the initiator of an international correspondence, the Amarna letters, which mention a subservient foreign element in the population, the "Habiru," and which refer to a prominent city of Canaan called "Aru-salim," ("City of Peace").

In spite of robust and determined leadership by many of the Pharoahs of the Nineteenth (1,320–1,223 BC) and Twentieth (1,223–1,085 BC) Dynasties, times were changing, and from the misguided order of governing priorities of Amenophis III and Akhenaton, Egypt could find no way back. Besides, in the century of the handover between the Nineteenth and Twentieth Dynasties (1,300–1,201 BC) uncomfortable rumblings were beginning to threaten the whole of the old order, accompanied by rise, yet further, in population numbers throughout the Middle East and Greece.

The Aegean

For the third body of water nurturing civilised progression, the salt Aegean, had now begun to arrive within political reach. Under Old Kingdom Egypt, already a cluster of Aegean islands, the Cyclades, had begun to experience the exciting tremors of prosperity. The renewed economy of Middle Kingdom Egypt began about 1,900 BC to stimulate the delicate and winsome merchant civilisation of Crete.

Some time in the sixteenth or fifteenth centuries (1,600–1,401 BC), a volcanic eruption on the Aegean island of Thera, followed by the only tsunami in Mediterranean history, seems to have destroyed Knossos, the leading city of Crete. Some time in the same era, whether in consequence of the tsunami or not, Mediterranean prosperity passed over from Crete into the hands of the swiftly-learning Mycenaeans.

As therefore the Old Kingdom of Egypt had prospered the Cyclades and the Middle Kingdom, Crete, so the New Kingdom of Egypt became one among many of the sponsors of the trade of Mycenae, the most eminent city of Greece.

Greece had had its aboriginal inhabitants from Old Stone Age times, but in the Bronze Age successive groups of northern invaders, of whom the Mycenaeans, who materialised somewhere before 1,600 BC, were neither the first nor the last, had expunged or expelled them.

The Mycenaean mercantile climax, when the Mycenaeans had taken over from Crete and from Knossos, was the most satisfying and prosperous era of the whole Bronze Age. Resting upon accumulated wealth and culture, untroubled by pirates or Phoenician competition, increasing in unimpeded opulence derived in the east from the Levantine sea coasts and the ports of the Aegean, and in the west from the Lipari Islands and Sicily, Mycenaean merchant craft ranged serenely over the century 1,400–1,301 BC from sea to sea.

But these enviable conditions were breaking up. Increasing populations and increasing discontents were beginnng to press upon the closing centuries of the Bronze Age from the north. The Peoples of the Sea came sweeping down to the coasts of Egypt. The Twentieth Dynasty Pharoah Ramesses III (1,187–1,156 BC) defeated and dispersed them, but, plunged into physical, economic and creative exhaustion, the Bronze Age itself sank from 1,100 onwards into irretrievable Dark Ages.

The Mycenaeans left behind one spark which would, after centuries of recuperation, ignite itself once again when the Mediterranean world would struggle to its feet again in a new order. Burning fitfully through the Dark Ages, this single spark was the Mycenaean colony at Athens.

The People of Israel

Bronze Age Egypt incubated unwittingly within it one other contribution to the distant and dynamic vistas of the future.

The visit of Abraham to an unnamed Pharoah who sent him home with wealthy gifts (Genesis 12.10–13.2); the account of Joseph and his Coat of Many Colours (also called his "Technicolour Dreamcoat") (Genesis chapters 37–50); the descent of Joseph's father Jacob with all his family into Egypt (Genesis chapters 46–47), all fit the confident and cosmopolitan prosperity of Egypt of the late Middle Kingdom (1,800–1,701 BC).

The Exodus of Moses and the Israelites from Egypt (Exodus 14), that rare invasion of Bronze Age times that came not from the north upon the central territories and trade-routes of Syria-Palestine, but from the south, fits the nervous and dissolving atmosphere of the early thirteenth century (1,300–1,201 BC) Following the Exodus, the siege and fall of Troy (1,250–1,240 BC) could just be fitted in before sea-faring in the whole Aegean and eastern Mediterranean became a matter of peril. The latest generation of the Hittites had been imploding and the Peoples of the Sea were impending.

Israel's Exile in Egypt ran four hundred and thirty years from Jacob to Moses (Exodus 12.41). When it started it seemed to fit the profile of late Middle Kingdom Egypt, especially of the border town of Hutwaret (modern Tell el Dab'a); and to fit the profile of early thirteenth century Hutwaret, re-named Per-Ramesses, and Pithom (modern Tell el-Maskhuta), whence, under the dramatic leadership of Moses, the Exile ended.

3

The Century of the Crescent Quiescent (900–801 BC)

The Ninth Century BC

The weary nations repaired from the Dancing Floor. During an interval of some two hundred years the Athenians and other beneficiaries of the Mycenaean legacy shifted some of the scenery. As the lights rose again at the beginning of the ninth century BC, Mesopotamia stayed by the side-tables. Egypt was content to dance a shadow role. Prepared to present a lithe, graceful and robust performance alone, the civilisation and peoples of the Aegean Sea advanced to the centre of the floor.

The ninth century BC (900–801 BC) was like a reprise of the late Bronze Age, without the evening shadows and with eyes attracted toward a new dawn. The life-blood of the whole Bronze Age had been trade, trade in goods and trade in ideas, trade between Mesopotamia and Afghanistan and trade between Mesopotamia and Roumania; trade in the Fertile Crescent; trade between Egypt and Byblos, trade between Egypt and the Cyclades, Egypt and Crete, Egypt and the Aegean; sweeping trade by the Mycenaeans. The busy, flourishing markets of the Middle East had slowed to a demoralised crawl following the collapse of the Bronze Age. In the darkness that followed, the Athenians had colonised Ionia, central parts of the eastern Aegean; Aeolian speaking Greeks had sent out communities to the north of Ionia and speakers of the Doric dialect, adventurers to the south; the markets of the once colourful world ticked over. Then, in the new era that followed the Dark Ages (1,085–900 BC), the anaemic economy of the former Bronze Age was revived with an injection of Iron. Such revival of the life of the markets was also like an overture to the new lyric and choral dance that was about to sound from the Aegean.

The Fertile Crescent

For the first ten years of the ninth century BC, the kings of Babylonia and Assyria were engaged in a duel, until both kings died in the same year, 891 BC. Babylonia then subsided for the rest of the century into relative obscurity and stillness.

Assyria through the centuries has enjoyed a reputation for cruel and invincible warfare. It is in fact a reputation somewhat inflated. In general the Assyrians' brilliant flashes of energy and power occurred only when there were no other states nearby with vigour to match or resist them. Thus in the ninth century BC in the absence of Babylonia or any other state with international ambition or vision, Assyria was able to institute a policy of westward expansion. Its king Shalmaneser III (858–824 BC) made laborious progress to Carchemish (849 BC), to Israel (841 BC), and to the Syro-Hittite states of Que and the Taurus mountains (840–831 BC). A period of decline and internal revolution beset the last years (831–824 BC) of Shalmaneser III, and following his death, Assyria withdrew again into a period of self-effacing quiescence.

The sea-going Phoenicians, whose mentality was always set on pioneering voyages to the west, were set in the northern part of that segment of the Fertile Crescent which runs along the Mediterranean coast.

Bringing down in quantity from the inland mountains behind them the best and stoutest specimens of timber from the forests of Lebanon, they built strong ocean-going vessels which carried them westwards wherever exploration, trade and adventure took them. Already they had in the previous century established a commercial centre at Citium on Cyprus, and sailed on from there along the coasts of Africa to found a base at Utica. Continuing further from Utica, they were searching out and exploiting new commercial routes, enterprises and markets in Spain.

Even more influential, the Phoenicians carried with them an alphabet of 22 letters, which was to be seized upon with spectacular consequences by the Greeks. To the south of Phoenicia, in Jerusalem, Solomon's Temple of the tenth century was still arguably the largest building for public worship in the whole of the ninth century BC world. The peoples themselves had divided after Solomon's death into two kingdoms, the northern kingdom of Israel and the southern kingdom of Judah.

The existence of two such small and squabbling kingdoms was itself evidence of the lack of energy among the greater nations of the Fertile Crescent, to police their smaller neighbours. Locked into petty and perpetual rivalry between themselves, Israel and Judah were still able to survive and prosper through tolls imposed on the trading caravans that passed along the two great commercial highways through their territories.

Ninth century BC songs composed for the Temple in Jerusalem, Psalms 20, 45, 72 and the core of Psalm 2, still ring in a monthly cycle through cathedrals to this day.

The World-Wide Market

If through all these lands from the Fertile Crescent and beyond – from Assyria in the north-east to Egypt in the deep south – political movement was at a virtual standstill, the tempo of commercial life was quite the opposite. The phenomenon really worthy of attention in the ninth century BC, was that which was moving towards a climax in the economic ventures of the world. From the beginning of the Iron Age (1,085 BC), technology, agriculture, transport and the provision of exportable goods had begun a process of steady but momentous increase along the Fertile Crescent.

Agricultural processes had begun to take further tentative but effective steps forwards, with the growing recourse to the use of iron. Iron ploughshares were introduced in this century for the working of the heavier or more resistant types of soil. The survival among archaeological remains of double yokes for oxen and horses indicates that ploughs and carts were being drawn by teams of two.

Rotation of crops seems to have been discovered along with more masterful command of the plough, and in some advanced quarters, harvests were even gathered with scythes and the grain ground in mills.

Communication buzzed mightily, and the whole theatre began to shape itself, falling into individual areas with distinctive rates of progress and typical characteristic exports. An Assyrian eastern contact, Persia, found it profitable to export horticultural and cereal products.

In Assyria the mule, which had been in use since at least 2,500 BC, was replaced by the horse and the camel.

Babylonia, as from remotest antiquity, still produced some grain for export. Moving along the Euphrates, northern Syria traded barley, olives, grapes, figs and stock. Coastal Syria produced cedar, vines and olives.

Both Syria and the Aegean exerted increasing trading influence on Cyprus. The camel, spreading west via Syria following its adoption by the Assyrians and by the Ionians penetrating from the west, met and opened extended trade routes and new means of carriage across Anatolia.

Egypt exported wheat, barley, millet, hemp, flax and vegetables. Its temples grew rich on monopoly exports of papyrus and textiles.

Further west, the infant Greek states imported foodstuffs and began early exports of wine, oil, handicrafts and pottery of progressive styles.

From Persian gardeners to Phoenician pioneers by way of Anatolian camel-drovers and Greek potters, all the Fertile Crescent and Mediterranean peoples of the early Iron Age, lightly governed, economically inventive, adventurous and robust, were by the end of the ninth century BC, straining to ascend to new levels of international prosperity.

The Aegean and Apollo

A portent of a precocious future for Greece lies in the fact that conditions about the Aegean in the ninth century BC can be spoken of in four languages.

In the poetic language of Homer it might be said that just beyond the eastern hills and horizon a "rosy-fingered dawn" was awaiting.

In the language of myth it was announced that the god Apollo had been born.

Translated into the language of prosaic reality, poetry and myth might be claimed to mean that in this century was stirring the pre-dawn of the phenomenon of Hellas!

In the realm and language of practical evidence, all this is symbolised in the bold enterprise of Euboean merchants in sailing south, out of the Aegean, and setting up a trading centre in Phoenician country at Al Mina on the mouth of the river Orontes.

By the floating nature of myth, whether the myth of the birth of Apollo dates from the ninth or any other century BC, is immaterial. It is appropriate to refer to it in this context, before the earliest Greek sunrise appears.

In the Aegean basin a woman, Leto, who had been made pregnant by the great god Zeus, fled as her time approached to the island of Delos. There, leaning against a palm-tree, she gave birth to twins, first a goddess, Artemis, and then a god, Apollo. Being the children of Zeus these two immediately shot up to adult stature and assumed the splendour of Greek godhead.

Apollo was the shepherd god of pastoralism, protector of both flocks, crops and harvests. He was god of archery, music and healing, god of building, navigation, marine expedition and colonisation. All the qualities attributed to the god Apollo seem to be projections of the rising virtuosity of the Greeks themselves.

Apollo was the god of oracular prophecy, who before long was to establish his shrine and worship at Delphi. Above all, Apollo was "Phoebus Apollo," the god of light. He was not the god of the sun, but a god of illumination and of intense and dancing light. He was the most popular god of Greece; he was the most respected son of Zeus within the assembly of the gods. One may suspect that the Greeks of the ninth and eighth centuries saw all their noblest activities and highest aspirations encapsulated and reflected in the attributes of the god Apollo.

Such was Apollo and the myth of his birth upon Delos. Interpreted, the myth seems to mean that in the alchemy of the Aegean, some vigour entirely unprecedented and brilliant, was struggling for expression. Out of the Aegean atmosphere of sea and island, breeze and billow, challenge and response, sunlight and sparkle, a new magic was emerging.

Scattered about their small city-states on the mainland and among the islands of the Aegean, lodged in Ionia and other cities on the eastern coast, sailing, trading, inter-relating, singing, potting, exploring, cohering, increasing in population, expanding geographically, socially, spiritually, the Greeks were beginning to discover their racial unity and establish their identity. More than frogs around a pond, they were the audacious and adventurous offspring of a young and radiant god!

The archaeology of the ninth century BC supports this vision. Corinth began to grow in exports of pottery and in parallel influences. In Athens, the Peloponnese and the Cyclades transitions in pottery styles built up pace. A growing impression appears of an enlarging population and more settled social conditions. Burials of between 900–850 BC in and around Athens show a wealthier appearance. Agriculture, trade and art register reviving prosperity.

In the second half of the century the merchant mariners of Euboea established their trading foot-hold at Al Mina. Also at Al Mina archaeologists have found a deposit of liquid mercury dating from the ninth century BC. It was here that the Greek merchants came into abrupt daily contact with the older and even more adventurous commerce and practices of the Phoenicians. From them they would take home to Aegean ports new lessons about navigation and, above all, use of the alphabet.

Three Waters

By the end of the ninth century BC, the great bulk of inland Anatolia lay in comparative silence; the whole length of the Fertile Crescent was politically quiescent; the nations nourished by the great rivers, the Tigris–Euphrates basin and the valley of the Nile, were in a state of suspension.

The bustling peoples shaped and challenged by the Aegean were champing to exert fresh energies.

4

The Century of the First European Miracle (800–701 BC)

The Eighth Century BC

In the face of the valiant splendours and exploits of prehistory and the Bronze Age, there is a sense of awe which is heightened by reflection on the slow pace and patient tempo of development.

70,000 years since human foot first stood beside the Aegean; 60,000 years of the flowing of the Nile; 50,000 years of the Jordan river system; 12,000 years since the retreat of the last (Wurms) Ice Age; 10,000 years since the first experiments with agriculture; 450 years sovereignty of Crete over the Aegean; 450 years of Crete's successor, Mycenae, until it vanished into the dark; 300 years recovery (following the end of the Bronze Age) before economic enterprise began to make headway again.

At the end of the Bronze Age, the catastrophic climax of the Peoples of the Sea, followed by the invasion of Greece by the Dorians produced a reaction of deep exhaustion throughout the Aegean, Egypt and the Near East, a natural interval in the programme of minuets on the Dancing-Floor.

During this interval the only initiative came from Greece.Speakers of one of its dialects migrated to the central areas of western Anatolia, speakers of another to the southern plains, and speakers of the Ionic dialect occupied the lands in between. From 1,085–776 BC, the name given to this interval is the "Dark Ages." But the "Dark Ages" was also a period of incubation.

In the ninth century BC, new life began to stir and unfold. Notably, during the continuing exhaustion of Egypt and Assyria, smaller states, and especially the kingdoms of Israel and Judah, were able to extend and prosper. The pace of human history was about to quicken. Its centre of gravity was to begin a shift to the west. All this was to be propelled by two European miracles and one Asiatic phenomenon.

Compared with the hosts that write about the twentieth century AD, there are few historians who explore the eighth century BC – yet such as there are come back from their researches with smiles like lottery winners. They have witnessed one of the few great, earth-shaking transformations of human history.

So numerous and so dynamic were the unexpected political responses of the eighth century BC to the economic and market stimuli of the previous one, that each influence bloc has to be considered individually in its own right, first Assyria; then Palestine, including Israel and Phoenicia; and finally Greek entrepreneurship in Italy and the west.

Assyria

From the declining years of the previously highly effective Shalmaneser III (858–824 BC), Assyria and the newly-established empire it governed to its west had suffered internal turmoil due to the competition and rivalry existing between over-mighty provincial governors. Then Tiglath-Pileser III (744–726 BC) came to power.

He put down those officials and governors of the Assyrian provinces who had profited from the fragility of the previous regimes. He campaigned against the Medes and against Urartu and undertook a programme of aggressive expansion into Babylonia in 731 BC. In 729 BC he actually moved to reign in Babylonia, but there he died in 726 BC. However, by the time of his death, Tiglath-Pileser III had succeeded in instituting a tradition of strong, centralised Assyrian rule, which was cemented by a succession of further powerful Assyrian eighth century monarchs, Shalmaneser V (726–722 BC), Sargon II (722–705 BC) and Sennacherib (705–681 BC). These successors extended the Assyrian empire of the upper Euphrates in a westerly direction, terminating the independence of the surviving, largely Hittite, western states. In 722 BC, falling upon Israel, the northern division of the once unified kingdom of David (1,000–960 BC) and Solomon (960–931 BC), Shalmaneser V carried ten out of the twelve tribes of the full kingdom away into exile, from which no individual was ever known to return.

Israel

The unit during the eighth century BC which went more through the mincing machine and the wringer than any other, was the people of Israel.

The prophet Amos reveals that during the period of Assyrian ineffectualness (right down to 744 BC) Israel and its neighbours showed all the delinquencies of small states left to their own devices without any greater or imperial authority to police them.

Still the tenth-century division between the ten northern tribes of Israel and the two southern tribes of Judah prevailed.

On the eastern and southern borders bitter conflicts were continually breaking out between the states of Ammon, Edom, Moab and Gaza. Small nations can only afford the luxury of such squabbles and squandering when they do not need to maintain defences against more menacing authorities.

Worst of all, in the view of the prophet, were the symptoms of the social damage inflicted by a successful and prosperous market – the corruption; the immorality; the debased luxuries; the materialist mentality; the social divisions; the vast economic gap between the multitude of the exploited poor and the obscene wealth of the exploiting few.

The prophets Hosea (745 BC), Micah (740 BC) and Isaiah (740–700 BC) were at one with Amos in their catalogue of the sins and injustices of the people, the moral deterioration and infidelities of the nation, the abandonment by the Chosen People of their obedience to the God of Abraham, their idolatrous straying from the observance (commanded by Moses) of the monotheistic faith in one sole Creator, the living God.

In reflecting these pessimistic moral consequences of the thriving market economy of the Near East, Amos foresaw that one day would follow punishment and disaster. Looking round for some political *force majeure* which would descend upon Israel with deserved vengeance, Amos could see only one state that would have the vigour to enforce it, an adversary from the north-east, beyond Hamath and beyond Damascus. In 722 BC the foresight of Amos was confirmed when Shalmaneser V fell upon the ten tribes of Israel in the north and carried them away to the north-east to Assyrian exile.

For the rest of the century Assyrian might was a permanent threat and discomfort to the remaining minuscule population of Judah and

Jerusalem. Sargon II and Sennacherib were always close by, poised to throttle them.

Phoenicia

At the same time in another quarter in Palestine a completely different culture was surviving and thriving.

The Canaanite Phoenicians had established themselves on the north-west coast opposite Cyprus some 300–400 years before. Their sailing and trading enterprise westward into the Mediterranean was valorous and legendary. Their outposts stretched from Cyprus to Carthage, to Utica, to Motya, Panormus, Sardinia, Massilia and southern Spain.

Less well appreciated at that period, though vastly more explosive in its cultural consequences, was their 22-letter alphabet. At Al Mina on the mouth of the river Orontes the Phoenicians and their alphabet began to mingle with exploratory traders from Euboea in Greece.

The Olympic Games

In this century, the real miracle is the miracle reaching out from Ionia across the Aegean to touch Europe in mainland Greece.

In its language, its trade and its expansion; in it artifacts, its poetry and its competitiveness; in the constitutions of its emerging city-states and generally in its total spirit of unlimited enterprise, the Aegean, on its east coast, on its west coast and in its islands was evolving a categorically different and unfettered mode of new civilisation. This emerging phenomenon owed nothing to the ancient Near East, except its alphabet, which, from 750 BC onwards, it began, momentously, to adopt and adapt from the Phoenicians.

The critical date of the emergence of Greece was the year 776 BC, the date of the first celebration of the Olympic Games at Elis in the Peloponnese.

These first Olympic Games presuppose prior decades, if not centuries, of the establishment of identity by the participating city-states. Of their growing together as entities with individual character but collective unity, the foundation of the shrine and worship of Apollo on Delos in the ninth century BC was both the initiation and the continuing symbol. In the Olympic Games of 776 BC, the Greek city-states first came overtly together as a demonstrable unity in their own instinctive time of ripeness.

The City-States and their Colonies

Cutting themselves off from the monarchical political principle alike of the Near East and of their own Mycenaean ancestry, the Greek city-states now began to banish hereditary monarchy. The search then by independent groups of fiercesomely intelligent aristocrats and townsfolk for alternative principles of harmonious living, produced the city-state or *polis* system, each city preserving its own constitution, independence and customs, choosing its own tutelary god and evolving its own method of self-government. This lively gestation on the Greek mainland was accompanied by comparable adventurous mercantile enterprise overseas.

Already by the first Olympic Games, colonists sent out by Euboea in 780 BC had anchored and settled as far west as Pithecusa (Ischia) in the Bay of Naples. Some Euboeans went home from these very Games only to thrust out again less than a year later in a colonising expedition to Al Mina.

Other Greek city-states, on both sides of the Aegean, were at the same moment also on the point of sending out commercial outposts, Phoenician-style, and consolidating them into standing colonies in Italy, Sicily and the Black Sea. Sinope, for example, was established from Miletus in 758 BC; Syracuse from Corinth in 733 BC. There were many others.

Homer

The most lasting monument of this whole explosive burst of eighth century BC Greek prosperity, population growth and self-discovery, is what is celebrated today as the epic poetry of Homer. The highest standards of European literature are set by epic poetry, the "Iliad" and the "Odyssey," which appeared in writing some 2,750 years ago and which still endures to set the pace today.

The formation, transmission and ultimate reduction to writing of these most human, sublime and evocative works, are still surrounded with mystery and curiosity. For six hundred years the component myths and heroic fables seem to have been composed, enlarged, embroidered and sung by specialist bards who committed lines in their thousands to memory – the feat explained by certain stock repetitions, but above all (apart from native talent) by the facility of the dactylic hexameter metre to engrave itself upon the mind.

When the adaptation of the Phoenician development of the alphabet meant that these epics, 24 books each in the "Iliad" and the "Odyssey," could be displayed to the world in writing, the Greeks began to see there a captivating outline of their history and traditions, which became also a mirror and exemplar for their future aspirations and self-understanding.

Greeks in the West

Greek arrival in Sicily, at the foot of Italy, and in the Bay of Naples also had its quickening effect upon the west.

Half way up the western side of the Italian peninsula lay a hilly site on the river Tiber, where a scattered people of Iron Age pedigree, the Italians or Latins, gave way to and merged with a Bronze Age culture, the Etruscans. In the second quarter of the eighth century BC, merchant ships, reaching out from Greek Euboea and Phoenician Tyre, began to produce a quiet, aesthetic, economic and intellectual revolution. The site on the Seven Hills began to develop as a small trading emporium. Certain families within it began to achieve aristocratic pre-eminence.

From this cultural and commercial blend there finally swirled together, towards mid-century, an unparalleled process from which emerged, in 753 BC, as tradition maintains it, one Romulus, founder of the city of Rome. On the death of Romulus in 714 BC, succession in kingship to the enlarging community and city of Rome passed to Numa Pompilius, the second of the seven kings.

Review of the Century

The influences and control of the eighth century BC are with us today, in the Olympian heights of the poet Homer; in the summons of the poet Amos, "Let judgement run down as water and righteousness as a mighty stream;" but above all in the 26-letter western alphabet, the simple tool with which children, from their first day at school, are taught to read every printed or electronically transmitted word.

Underappreciated generally, the eighth century BC is like a secret adventure park of pristine energy and infinite fascination. Those who have stumbled across the eighth century BC, its budding genius and its outburst of every kind of fresh enterprise, tend to celebrate it as something of a garden of dynamic amazement and unlimited attractiveness.

5

The Century of the Fall of Assyria (700–601 BC)

The Seventh Century BC

For countless centuries peoples living on the great land masses of Anatolia, Egypt and the Fertile Crescent had been conditioned into expecting that they would be corralled, one after the other, into the empire-grabbing ambitions of their most imperial neighbour. For them this was the normal course of political events.

Greeks living in the towns of Ionia, the islands of the Aegean and the sparse valleys of mainland Greece had no such conditioning or expectation. For them, the normal form of human government was a federation of small, independent, self-governing units; no king, but a common language and a common religion were the unifying force.

There was no reason why these two conceptions of government should ever come into confrontation against one another, except for the insatiable lust for empire of the former. By the beginning of the seventh century BC such confrontation was still over 200 years away.

Indeed, in the land mass of western Asia, Esarhaddon (681–669 BC) and Ashurbanipal (669–627 BC) continued the tradition instituted by Tiglath-Pileser III (744–726 BC) of strong and fearsome warrior Assyrian kings. Under them, for the first three quarters of the seventh century BC, the arms and expansion of Assyria eclipsed anything stirring in Egypt, Palestine, Babylon or Anatolia.

Esarhaddon, successor of Sennacherib (705–681 BC), even, in 676 BC, repulsed a dangerous invasion of the Cimmerians from the north-east. In all quarters only one minor reverse was experienced by the Assyrians in the time of Esarhaddon – at Melid in Anatolia in 675 BC.

The Fall of Assyria

In 673 BC Esarhaddon designated one of his two sons, Ashurbanipal, as heir to the kingdom of Assyria, and the other, Shamash-shuma-ukin, as heir to Babylonia. He called his subjects to swear allegiance to these heirs in 672 BC. He invaded Egypt and sacked Memphis in 671 BC, and then died, two years later.

Esarhaddon had put his finger on the essential weakness of Assyria – its inability to govern both Assyria and Babylonia simultaneously and effectively. His attempted solution of the problem was bold and novel, but fated to fail.

In Assyria Ashurbanipal spent six years extending final imperial control over Egypt. Nevertheless, he was only able to hold this distant southern frontier for three years (663–660 BC).

In 652 BC, his brother Shamash-shuma-ukin of Babylonia went into revolt, and a draining civil war broke out between the two sons of Esarhaddon. The revolt ended in 648 BC, with the fall of Babylon and the flight of Shamash-shuma-ukin. The victorious Ashurbanipal went on for 21 years more to complete a glorious and opulent reign in Assyria. These uncontested years were to outward appearance the height of Assyrian imperial prestige and luxury. But never, since its first appearance in 2,040 BC, had Assyria been able to devise a successful policy towards Babylonia.

With the death of Ashurbanipal in 627 BC, and the accession in Babylonia of the vigorous soldier of Chaldaean origin, Nabopolassar, fortunes became completely reversed. The seat of energy was now in the subject kingdom rather than in the former dominant one. In the very year of Nabopolassar's enthronement, for the first time ever an Assyrian army was plundered by Babylonia.

In 608 BC Assyria was gone. Its fall was swift, dramatic and historic. In the Near East, at least Egypt, Babylonia and Syria/Palestine remained as entities. Assyria was, for ever, swept from the board.

Full of significance by now, for the century to come, was the death in 605 BC of the Babylonian ruler Nabopolassar, the accession of his son Nebuchadnezzar, and the destruction by Nebuchadnezzar of the army of Egypt at Carchemish in the same year. To the problem of governing Assyria and Babylonia in tandem, Cyrus the Great would find an answer when in the next century (the sixth century BC) his new invention would begin to tighten the world.

Egypt and Judah

In Egypt the Twenty-sixth (Nubian) Dynasty maintained itself competently in Upper Egypt, and with patience withstood the attempts of Ashurbanipal to penetrate south below Memphis. The dynasty brought a slight stir of new life and energy into the fading, ancient civilisation of the Nile and its Delta, but the fall of its army to Nebuchadnezzar at Carchemish was no surprise.

In Judah the apostate Manasseh, the worst of all her kings, reigned from 686 to 642 BC. The traditional faith, worship and literature of the people was meanwhile assembled and preserved within the capsule of Temple life.

After a brief interval of instability (642–640 BC) the good king Josiah (640–609 BC) came to the throne. He died in battle at Megiddo against the Egyptian Pharoah Necho, just one year before the final climactic fall of Assyria.

Religious reforms by Josiah nurtured the vocations of the prophets Jeremiah (627–580 BC), Zephaniah (625 BC), Nahum (616 BC) and Habakkuk (605 BC). By the time of the death of Josiah, Assyria was on the brink of falling, Babylonia was in the ascendant, and instability was breaking in throughout the Near East. The call of the Hebrew prophet Ezekiel dates to about 602 BC

Greece in the Seventh Century BC

Archaeological and literary remains from seventh century BC Greece are fewer and less exotic than those of the eighth century. Homer, for example, was hard to follow.

The gradual transformation of the Olympic Games into an institution had many advantages for the scattered Greek city-states, colonies and islands. By becoming a fixed four-yearly reference point, the Games sharpened the unity and identity of the disparate Greek entities. By adding competitions not only in athletics but also in poetry, dance and song, they defined and protected a common culture of religion, language and competitive temperament.

The Greeks further tightened their bond of common national fellowship by using the Olympic Games as their unversal system of dating. Our "seventh century BC" became for them the period between the twentieth and the eve of the forty-fifth Olympiad. Among the traditions guarding the Olympic Games was the selection of a song composed by the seventh century BC poet Archilochus, as the victors' song.

Colonisation and its Consequences

Meanwhile for the merchants and businessmen, the aristocrats and farmers, the law-givers and the soldiers, the adventurers, the explorers, the colonists, the politicians and the artisans of seventh century BC Greece, it was business as usual – but business on such a scale as to produce great social transformations.

During a certain confined belt of time around the 660s BC, although colonies continued to be sent out, law-givers appeared in some of the mainland Greek city-states, suggesting that a certain consistency in civil affairs had been reached, and that the intuition had been generated that this stage or level needed to be made formal. Thus this novel and glittering facet of European culture, the Greek city-state, came to be stabilised by the application of codes of law.

Stabilisation was needed. In the increasingly prosperous cities, islands and colonies, wealth and trade were producing new social challenges never experienced before.

Colonies began to increase the surplus of their harvests to such a degree as to open up a thriving export trade. The former colonising cities in their turn traded back with luxury items.

The whole Greek complex from Ionia to Sicily began to grow rich. For a people unfamiliar with any kind of economic science or control, wealth began to produce shifts and problems.

The old aristocratic families of the eighth century and earlier began to find their position in society challenged by *nouveaux riches* mariners and mechants. A second challenge came from farmers and producers who likewise grew rich by their own wits and industry while remaining at home.

The so-called "hoplite" revolution of the seventh century BC in Greece was set in motion by local businessmen and farmers who became wealthy enough to arm themselves as hoplite soldiers, and to demand for themselves some sort of status equivalent to that of the long-established aristocrats.

Such flux and upheaval, reinforced by the invention and introduction of coined money late in the century, culminated in the development of a group of so-called "tyrants." In city after city throughout Greece, ambitious individuals, taking advantage of bubbling confusion and discontent, made a successful bid for sole rule in their home town – Megara, Sicyon or Corinth.

Produced through the unstable circumstances of wealth, class rivalry and political fluidity with the Greek city-states, the tyrant-system reached its climax in the seventh and sixth centuries BC, but in Sicily continued as an institution or viable political alternative for almost 400 years. Against all this background, the delights of Greek off-duty life during the seventh century BC should never be under-valued. Mere droplets from the Homeric thunderstorm were enough to produce, in consequence of their life-giving irrigation, a vivid and sparkling creativity in every art–poetry, music, dance, sculpture, architecture and painting.

One Mutant Organism

In what was, in those days, the far west, the trend in Rome seemed to be for the continuing consolidation of the political, religious and social institutions that had, in the previous century, begun sponta-neously to gather in the amenable location served by the Tiber; but for a city-state with a Greek contribution to its foundation, Rome was starting to sprout unusual features.

Instead of aristocrats, it was governed still by kings: Tullus Hostilius (672–640 BC), Ancus Marcius (640–616 BC), Lucius Tarquinius Priscus (616–578 BC). Instead of seafaring, Rome remained obstinately on land. Instead of trading, it built up its army. Instead of maintaining its boundaries, it was pressing always to extend them. Instead of living with its neighbours in relative peace, it set out to conquer them.

The influence of the impenetrable Etruscans and the indepen-dently-minded Latins was throwing traditional Greek development off course. This colony (if it ever was a colony) was beginning to develop into an unconventional mutant.

6

The Century of the Tightening World (600–501 BC)

The Sixth Century BC

All through the length of the Bronze Age, some 2,500 years, through the Century of the Great Market (900 801 BC) and on down as far as the fall of Assyria in 608 BC, experiments in communal and even in imperial living had been attempted in six different geographical quarters. As well as Mesopotamia, Egypt and the Aegean, there had been Assyria to the far north-east, Anatolia to the north and Syria/Palestine in the centre. The Dancing-Floor had seen sometimes one competitor swirl into prominence, sometimes another, but no contender had ever left the floor. The disappearance of Assyria in 608 BC was both a sign that times were changing and, above all, that the pace of change was accelerating.

It had taken fourteen centuries of gyration, interchange and balance, from about 2,040 to 608 BC, for one nation to be wiped out entirely. It was now to take only one century, the sixth century BC, the Century of the Tightening World, for four more communities to be relegated to insignificance. By the end of the century, only two powers remained: Persia, swallowing up all previous international boundaries, and the Aegean community of Greece.

Where Assyria had failed in fourteen centuries to devise ways to govern together the two eastern civilisations of Babylonia and Assyria as one, from 560 BC Persia had appeared, risen and achieved a tight domination over Egypt, over every population of western Asia, and even, in certain districts of Thrace, over a segment of Europe.

All this was really the work of two men, Cyrus the Great (559–529 BC) and his younger son Darius (522–486 BC). Before Cyrus the Great, however, was the final flourishing of Nebuchadnezzar's Babylon.

The Coming of the Medes and the Persians

Nabopolassar (626–605 BC), assisted and succeeded by his even more renowned son, Nebuchadnezzar (605–562 BC), had by the end of the seventh century BC taken under Babylonian control almost everything that had been Assyrian.

Nebuchadnezzar began the sixth century BC with the capture in 597 BC of Jerusalem. He deposed the king, Jehoiachin, and replaced him with his own nominee, Zedekaiah. Zedekaiah was to be the last king of Judah. Following a revolt by him, Nebuchadnezzar fell upon Jerusalem again, and on 16th July 586 BC finally captured the city after an eleven-month siege, and brought the population of the city back with him to Babylon to suffer exile. In a relatively obscure phase of history, Nebuchadnezzar continued to campaign westwards in Palestine and Egypt until his death in 562 BC. The following kings of Babylonia lacked both fire and energy. Between 562 and 556 BC reigned the short-lived rulers Evil-merodach, Neriglissar and Labashi-Marduk in swift succession. The longer-surviving Nabonidus (556–539 BC) spent the greater part of his reign in retreat in Teima among the oases of northern Arabia.

The return of Nabonidus to Babylon in 541 BC signalled an emergency. Within two years his empire had fallen to Cyrus the Persian, also called Cyrus the Great. The tomb of this Cyrus may still be visited today on the Iranian plains of Pasargadae.

Throughout the history of the Bronze Age and the Iron Age in the Near East, hardly anything had been heard about the Medes and the Persians. Existing further to the east, beyond the Zagros mountains, perhaps of Indo-European stock, originally entering in the twentieth century BC at the end of the Early Bronze Age, they began to come into notice only in the late seventh century, the Persians absorbing the Medes and penetrating through Anatolia across territory that had formerly been Assyrian.

They had allied with the Babylonians and the Scythians in the destruction of the Assyrian capital of Nineveh in 612 BC. Now, in the year after Jerusalem fell to Babylon, they conquered Mannaea and Urartu. In the same year, 585 BC, they came to an agreement with the kingdom of Lydia.

In 559 BC Cyrus the Great came to the throne. By the vigour of Cyrus and his successors Cambyses and Darius, aided, no doubt, by the languour of the later Babylonian kings, Persia came by the end of the sixth century to dominate the whole of ancient western Asia and some parts of Macedonia and Thrace. Persia had come to conquer and control the widest territorial empire ever, so far, in the history of the world!

By 549 BC Cyrus had captured the Median capital of Ecbatana. By 546 BC he had over-run the whole of western Anatolia, destroying Sardis and the Lydian kingdom of Croesus. Falling now upon the remaining kernel of the Middle East, he attacked and conquered Babylonia in 539 BC. His death occurred in 529 BC. His son Cambyses (529–522 BC) fell upon Egypt in 525 BC. He died in 522 BC, and for the rest of the sixth century his younger brother Darius (522–486 BC) consolidated all the former territories of Babylonia, Assyria, Anatolia, Syria/Palestine and Egypt under the Persians.

In a mere half century, by a process of unprecedented administration, which included above all the visionary inspiration of the building of military roads, Cyrus and Darius were able to draw together the whole of the ancient Near East including Anatolia and Egypt; to spread eastwards; and to venture westwards into Scythia, Macedonia and Thrace. This was a new vigour, unknown ever before in the thousands of years of the ancient orient. The conquests and consolidation of Cyrus and Darius were the greatest so far that the world had ever seen!

Meanwhile the Jews, in exile in Babylonia throughout the time of Nebuchadnezzar, his successors and Nabonidus, completed the two Books of Kings in about 560 BC and were sustained by the prophets Ezekiel and Second Isaiah. Released from Babylonian Exile by the command of Cyrus the Great in 538 BC, and their release confirmed and renewed by Darius in 520 BC, they rebuilt Jerusalem in partial measure, and consecrated the Second Temple, on the site of Solomon's former Temple, in about 515 BC.

Persia Rises on the Greeks' Horizon

For the first half of the sixth century BC, while Nebuchadnezzar still bestrode the near east and before the rise of Cyrus, the history of the Aegean area and westwards remained a swirl of trade relationships, artistic movements and battles, with only the name of Solon of Athens standing out prominent. In Egypt, on a statue of Ramesses II, Greek mercenaries who went on an expeditionto Nubia in 591 BC left their graffiti.

In 585 BC Thales of Miletus foretold the eclipse of the sun of 28th May. The citizens of Ephesus began, in about 550 BC, the construction of their temple of Artemis (Diana). Both in Ionia and at Delphi other temples and treasuries began to rise.

Attic black figure vases ("Attic" means "made in Athens") began to seize the pottery market.

During the first half of the sixth century, Nebuchadnezzar of Babylon was balanced at the heart of the Greek world by the Dorian states of the Peloponnese. There Sparta consolidated her individual way of life and unique constitution.

Suddenly, about the time of the rise of Cyrus, the figure of the tyrant Pisistratus appeared in Athens (560 BC). Like all Greek tyrants of this era, Pisistratus is not to be visualised as a "tyrant" in any modern sense, but as the practitioner of a personal sovereignty of a novel kind, often public-spirited and benign. After a chequered start, Pisistratus began a policy of the architectural beautification of Athens, the standardisation of the revered text of Homer, and a thorough-going reorganisation of the Athenian festival called the "Great Panathenaea." With this enlightened influence stemming from the house of Pisistratus, began a shift of the centre of gravity of the Greek world away from the Peloponnese towards Athens.

With the sparkling intellectual achievements of the philosophers of Ionia; with the appearance of distinct personalities in the city-states and islands; with the development of coinage; with the pottery of Exekias of Athens; and ultimately, following the expulsion of the sons of Pisistratus from Athens (510 BC), with the new democractic constitution of Cleisthenes making its way in the city of Athens, an unprecedented and dazzling brilliance began to pulse out from the east and west coasts of the Aegean. In the second half of the sixth century BC new levels of loftiness were being attained in the Aegean at the same time as new and extensive tightening of political control was being exerted in the east!

After the fall of Sardis in 546 BC the Persian took the whole coast of Ionia and reduced it under the governance of officials whom they called "satraps." They tried then to take to the sea, and were successful at least in the capture and crucifixion of Polycrates, tyrant of Samos, in about 523 BC.

After the death of Cyrus the Great's older son and successor Cambyses, Darius, the younger son, during the period 522–521 BC, had to face down enormous revolts against his authority. After he had settled the throne, he succeeded in putting together an expedition to Scythia. The expedition failed, because in the vast wastes of their territory the Scythians simply disappeared, refusing even to give battle. The Persians were however successful in over-running and establishing satrapies in Macedonia and in Thrace. They were thus now pressing hard upon the Greek residents to the north, and on the east coast of the Aegean.

The energies of Cyrus the Great and of Darius had been so irresistible that Persian government now held sway, in a pincer movement, over the northern territories of Macedonia and Thrace, the coasts of Egypt and Africa to the south, and in the east, not only the Anatolian coast-line of the Aegean, but further territories and tribes in a deep easterly direction towards such previously untouched regions as Sogdiana and Bactria. For the ingenious and mercurial Greeks, there was no way out of this potential bear-hug, except to the west.

A Different Destiny

In the west the evolution of Rome seems to have continued as smoothly as it had done for almost two centuries. Greek, Phoenician and Etruscan influences continued to play over an enlarging community of Latins and other native Italians.

The aristocracy of Rome was content to observe a monarchical constitution and to submit itself to Servius Tullius (578–534 BC), the sixth king, and to Tarquinius Superbus (534–509 BC), the seventh and last. The energies of the mixed peoples of Rome were satisfied in consolidating their military expansion outside, and their urban inclinations at home.

Upon this sixth century texture, later historians in the ancient world seem to have projected their own assumptions and vision about the parallel destinies of Greece and Rome. For example, an organisation of the Roman population by Servius Tullius into three tribes, thirty "curiae" and into "comitia centuriata," was equated with the constitutional reforms of Solon in Athens in 594 BC.

Similarly, the ejection of the Pisistratids from Athens in 510 BC was assimilated to the expulsion of the Etruscan monarch Tarquinius Superbus from Rome in 509 BC; and the Roman republican constitution of 509 BC, in which power was vested, by annual election, in two equal consular colleagues with a one-year tenure of office, was presented as a parallel to the democratic reforms of Cleisthenes in Athens in 508 BC.

Historical research into the expulsion of Tarquinius Superbus suggests that the circumstances were less glorious and more complex than they are made out to be. It would seem however to have been convenient to later generations to visualise the events of 509 BC as a seamless transition from monarchy to republic, and the birth of a new Rome, weighty with a different destiny.

7

An Underestimated Contribution
(546–538 BC)

The Prophet of the Exile

In 586 BC the ruler and conqueror Nebuchadnezzar captured Jerusalem and took away into exile in his own city of Babylon all the most prominent and dynamic of the Jews. In 539 BC Babylon itself, and Nebuchadnezzar's inferior successor Nabonidus, fell to the even wider-conquering Cyrus the Great, the Persian, and the exiles were set free to return home.

The unusual circumstance of this elite enclave of Jews – detached from their homeland for almost two generations, teaching, praying, adhering faithfully to their traditional culture in a sealed community in alien surroundings – nurtured a prophetic voice of unusual power and insight, the name of whose owner remains a mystery to this present day.

Hiding within the chapters of the prophet Isaiah, the scholarship of the nineteenth century discovered a unique individual of intelligence, perception and artistic gifts far above and beyond the commonplace. His work covers Isaiah chapters 40 to 55 and some elements of chapters 56 to 66. To him, for want of any other, were given the names "Second Isaiah" or, alternatively, "The Prophet of the Exile."

Among the prophets of ancient Israel, the Prophet of the Exile stands out by virtue of the positive nature of his message.

Other prophets condemned Israel because of the nation's materialism, fickleness, idolatries and infidelities. Second Isaiah echoes such condemnations in his chapter 48, but the great bulk of his writing is inspired by joyful anticipation of the people's deliverance from Babylon. He looks back more than any other prophet to the triumphant Exodus of the Israelites from Egypt under Moses some

750 years before. His vision of this dynamic historical prototype supercharges his expectation of Return.

Second Isaiah's chosen medium of expression was poetry. As in the light of the discovery of his separate identity his prophecies were explored, realisation dawned in the twentieth century that here was one of the greatest among the poets of the human race, and here was one of the most polished and accomplished minds of the Old Testament. The boldness of Second Isaiah's embrace of his prophetic calling, marked still with traces of an adolescent dash and buoyancy, suggests that at the time of writing (546–538 BC) he was a little below middle age. The range and confidence of his religious grasp imply a precocious maturity. The daring and variety of his poetical techniques testify to his artistic gifts; his nature similes register the acuteness of his powers of observation.

If the Babylonian Exile lasted 48 years, in all likelihood Second Isaiah was born early on, or lived all the time of his childhood, formation and early maturity, in the Exile.

From his ghetto surroundings he would have grown up learning that Jerusalem was his proper home and that his own birth and upbringing in Babylon were unusual. He would have heard speculation that the exile in Babylon was punishment upon his people for their idolatries and infidelity to God. In all likelihood the Jewish capsule into which he was born was careful to maintain scrupulously, and as best they would in discouraging circumstances, the annual, and perhaps daily, cycle of religious observances and Festivals.

In contrast with these, the future prophet would also become familiar with the parades of idols which were the high points of the Babylonian New Year Festival, and with the astrology, palmistry and sooth-saying of down-town Babylon. Yet as he grew, he was taught the tradition of Abraham, Moses and the escape from Egypt. He participated in the Passover. He learned of his people's unique belief that there was not a plurality of gods, but one sole God, the universe's Creator. He absorbed from those among whom he grew up that they and their race were God's Chosen People – chosen for blessing if they were faithful vehicles of his messages, but, if they abandoned them, for punishment.

From the Psalms that he learned to sing, he discovered that God the Creator is both transcendent and immanent; he realised that the same God was both God of nature and God of history. He accepted, digested, reshaped and sharpened these articles of belief in such a way that his own poetry became in its turn an inspiration for those who in generations after him were to compose other Psalms worthy of inclusion in the final Psalter.

It is this Prophet of the Exile, the man who first absorbed his people's traditional faith and culture and who then in his own turn re-expressed and celebrated it in new forms of clarity and exultation, who remained the great undiscovered and underestimated genius virtually to this day.

Second Isaiah's First Lesson in Monotheism

The primary influence upon this prophet's mind and teaching was the clash between the monotheism (or belief in only one Creator) of his own people, and the polytheism (or belief in a multitude of gods) of the Babylonian populace. This was impressed the more deeply upon Second Isaiah by the contrast between his own people's inherited tradition of forbidding the representation of God in any sculpted form or painted image, and the brazen practice of their Babylonian captors in creating lifeless idols, parading them, consulting them as oracles, and worshipping them. Juvenile puzzling over this contradiction resolved itself in his adult mind in verses against Babylonian idolatry created and expressed in a mood of towering scorn.

In consequence, his surviving sixteen chapters present two lessons in the essence of Israelite monotheism:

There is one God only, the Creator, and none other than he, at one and the same time exalted in the heavens and yet present in all the transactions on earth; by virtue of this latter, he underlies all the wonders of nature and observes and guides the paths of destiny and history.

Second Isaiah's two great "Lessons in Monotheism" occur in his chapters 41 and 45.

Chapter 41 begins with a typical arresting opening built up of five imperative verbs enforcing consideration of a wide range of geography and of aspiration. The chapter concludes with a gesture of dismissal towards Babylonian idolatry, built up, like the opening of the chapter, with a grammatical list, not this time of imperative verbs, but of nouns, mostly abstract, evocative of the utmost folly and spiritual destitution.

44

The poem of chapter 41 seems to envisage the approach of Cyrus, who is shortly to capture Babylon and set at liberty the captive exiles held within the city. God therefore is presented with a breathless excitement as God of history (verses 2–4); within human history, Abraham is the "friend of God" (verse 8) and the people of Israel are his Chosen People (verses 8–20). The economical portrait of abundant, fertile and refreshing nature in verses 18–20 is inspired by the prophet's belief in God, the God of nature.

Verse 21 seems to open a new poem. Suddenly the prophet transfers his readers to the Babylonian New Year Festival and to the consultation of idols for oracles and lots for the year ahead. The irony of verse 22–23, assuming that lifeless images of wood or stone can have any influence upon human destiny, leads up to the magisterial dismissal of verse 24. Verses 25 to 28 rest upon the assumption that the God of Abraham, who has chosen the people of Israel, is the only living God. It is he that disposes nations and history. Beside him other usurping claimants to influence within human affairs are valueless and pretentious.

Of profound but hidden significance for both "Lessons in Monotheism" are the expressions "the first and the last" in verse 4 and the name, descending from the vision of Moses at the Burning Bush, "I am," introduced as the final words at the end of the same verse.

Second Isaiah's Second Lesson in Monotheism

For the opening of chapter 45, Second Isaiah has crafted another succinct and sovereign statement of his vision of the majesty of God. Again he ends the chapter with an economical up-beat flourish that reverberates with his patriotism.

The futility of Babylonian idols (verses 16, 20–22); the God of history (verses 1–4, 14–15); the God of nature (verses 7, 12, 18); the God of the Chosen People (verses 3, 4, 11, 13–15) are all presented again; but there is special emphasis upon the use of the word translated "else" (verses 5, 6, 18, 22) and upon the repetition of the formula, derived from Moses' "I am that I am," the simpler and shortened "I am," the divine name.

This "I am" is first taken up in verse 3 confined to the "God of Israel." Its universal application is then almost immediately stated in verse 5, "I am the Lord and there is none else, there is no God beside me," and verse 6, "I am the Lord, and there is none else." God's material creativity or "Makerhood" are emphasised in verses 11–12 and 18. His moral creativity is expressed in verses 7–8, 17 and 22.

At the head of both "Lessons in Monotheism" there stands a phrase, placed by the prophet in chapter 41, verse 4, "the first and the last," which governs all that he teaches in both chapters. This phrase is to be understood not only in terms of being "first and last" in time, but in a wider sense; not only chronologically but logically.

The name "I am that I am" implies not only the God of Creation, nature and history who has chosen, and who works through, Israel, but also a single, personal principle behind all existence – the "hand" in the Lady Julian of Norwich, which holds the hazelnut, the "noumenal" of Immanuel Kant.

At its logical conclusion, this name and this vision presuppose God in Creation not "finding" the stray material of the universe and "organising" it with commanding power, but rather himself "bodying out" the universe, both observable and unobservable, as an intrinsic expression of his own inner being and creative will. The transcendent God far "beyond" the created universe is also the immanent God permanently present "within" his universe, under-lying its sub-atomic sub-structure, supporting every ripple and motion of nature throughout; and establishing also, within the world of man, the principles and objectives of moral creativity.

Second Isaiah's knowledge of the expanding universe or of particle phsyics was zero, but his mind and its categories were suffi-ciently flexible for him to take them, if he had heard of them, in his stride. Stretched by comprehension of Moses' formula and by the teaching of the Psalms on Israel's God, the mind of the Prophet of the Exile was agile enough to embrace all the discoveries of modern physics and to accept and digest them all.

The "Servant" in Second Isaiah

In almost every chapter of Isaiah 40–55 one can hear the tread of Cyrus the Persian, king, conqueror and liberator, drawing closer month by month to Babylon. In the later chapters one can imagine the Jews who respond to Isaiah's poetry jostling and assembling themselves outside the Ishtar Gate, forming the caravan in which they will journey home. Every chapter is three-dimensional and full of colour – except one!

There is one chapter devoid of all historical or geographical reference, without local colour, graven, as it were, with an iron pen and in rock for ever. The unique and bleak style of this chapter suggests that it is meant to be a universal, monumental statement, an archetype of human experience. It teaches of suffering and relief, anguish and redemption, based upon the experience of Israel and/or of the prophet Second Isaiah himself, but applicable to every form of human vicissitude, every revolution of the wheel of human fortune. This is chapter 53.

Chapter 53 of Second Isaiah describes the fate of an unnamed Servant who suffers vicariously for others (verses 4–6), descends to death (verses 8–9) and yet who ultimately, beyond contradiction or peradventure, is vindicated and justified. It commands attention with an opening pair of rhetorical questions and it concludes with an irreversible triumph, beyond death, celebrated with a restrained dignity and tranquil poise.

Who is the "Servant" who in this icy and isolated narrative suffers but so signally succeeds? To seek for an explicit identification is labour in vain. This archetype embraces all innocent suffering, all suffering for the protection or defence of others, all vicarious and unjust misfortune, all ultimate justification and restitution. One particular and poignant feature of the Servant's suffering, which finds an echo in later chapters of the prophecies, is the Servant's aloneness.

This emphasis on the lonesomeness of one who is ultimately the Redeemer resounds in chapter 53 with a hollow mournfulness. It occurs again in chapter 59, verse 16, in an atmosphere of bewildered wonderment, and then in chapter 63, verse 1–6 in a spirit of indignant self-help. The Servant is so categorically unique that he alone can succeed in the necessary work of redemption, and his destiny is, first, to be condemned, but ultimately to be privileged, to strive heroically and alone.

The image of the Suffering Servant/Redeemer of Second Isaiah stands on the pinnacle of his chapter 53 in a terrifying yet majestic isolation. He is manifestly far above the immediate market-place of Babylonian/Israelite politics. To him all instances and examples of unjust suffering correspond and may turn their eyes, whether from the past, from the prophet's own sixth century BC present – or with reference to one who is to come.

8

The Century of the Second European Miracle (500–401 BC)

The Fifth Century BC

Either by coincidence, or by a symmetry devised by later historians, the years 509–508 BC stand out as among the most significant in world history.

In 508 BC, Cleisthenes of Athens, in response to popular request in his city, drew up the first firm outlines of Athenian democracy. According to a later commentator, the "Old Oligarch," the Athenians did not know at first how to exploit the full possibilities of the constitution drawn up for them. It took them time to ease their way into it.

Meanwhile, in 509 BC Rome had expelled Tarquinius Superbus, the last of its seven kings, and by common aristocratic consent had formed out of the Italian variations and Etruscan options open to it the "res publica," the "public matter," the Roman Republic, governed by a Senate and, above it, by two annually elected consuls.

The Athenian democracy and the Roman Republic bear in their names the very marks of their original foundation. One hardly ever speaks of the "Athenian Republic," never of the "Roman Democracy." The "democracy" was the gift of a single law-giver, responding to a request by the people of Athens. The "Republic" evolved spontaneously from a selection of the best ideas proposed in the public square in Rome.

Two revolts or "Secessions" by the unrepresented common people (the "plebs") forced on the evolution of the Republic in Rome. First in 494–493 BC, and again in 449 BC, direct action by the plebs resulted in the acquisition of their own officers or representatives, the "tribunes," and the publication, in the form of the Twelve Tables, of the provisions of common law. This venture in publication represents a legal interest and mentality innate in republican Rome. Almost half a millennium later, the office of "tribune of the plebs" was to operate with the most resounding consequences.

Economically and externally the fifth century BC was a hard testing-ground for Rome.

From 490 BC for almost fifty years the city was plunged into inexorable annual guerilla campaigning against the tribes of the Aequi, the Volsci, and the Sabines. In 460 BC, the Sabine Appius Herdonius, in an attempt to seize Rome, actually captured and for a few days held the Capitol before being ejected and killed.

No new buildings or temples were erected. Economic recession set in. Nevertheless, if in the second half of the century Rome began to achieve some small economic surplus, the expenditure continued to go on military campaigning. The three wars of this century, against Veii (483–474 BC; 437–426 BC; 405–396 BC) were not undertaken, like the Aequi and the Volsci campaigns, reactively, but as a matter of deliberate expansionist policy; and the third of these wars hints at improvement, at last, in the grindingly poor economic status of fifth century Rome.

A Western Offshoot

350 miles to the south in Sicily, it was a very different climate. Here was no future prodigy struggling to its feet, but an organic offshoot of a dynamic civilisation already established for three hundred years.

The fortunes of Sicily in the fifth century BC – steady upward economic, cultural and political progress, not without rivalries, reversals and much human suffering – are best exemplified in the history of Syracuse.

Syracuse and the Greek Sicilian cities associated with it had at the beginning of the fifth century BC three local alien peoples in potential oppposition to them, the Carthaginians, the Etruscans and the Sicels.

The Carthaginians were despatched by the Syracusan tyrant Gelon in 480 BC. (Constitutionally Syracuse at the beginning of the fifth century BC lagged behind mainland Greece in that it had not shaken off the archaic system of government by a single ruler or "tyrant" and his family.) Hiero of the Deinomenid dynasty became "tyrant" of Syracuse on the death of his brother Gelon in 478–7 BC.

The following year, in 476 BC, Hiero won over the Etruscans, at the naval battle of Cumae, a victory which can be seen in retrospect to be the event from which the Etruscans never recovered.

With the death of Hiero in 466 BC and effective revolt against his successor Thrasybulus, the archaic system of rule by "tyranny" came to an end, and five individual states formed in the place of the erstwhile Deinomenid dynasty and its dominion–Syracuse, Catana, Naxus, Leontini and Camarina.

The native peoples of Sicily itself were separate from the Carthaginians and the Etruscans.

Under an enterprising leader, Ducetius, the Sicels, as they were called, tried between 461 and 440 BC to bid for their own independence. This effort was in vain. In the decades following the death of Ducetius in 440 BC, even the native dialects of the aboriginal Sicels were swallowed up and submerged in the Greek tongue. As the Sicilian city-states which were the successors of the "tyranny" consolidated and the Sicels declined, in Athens in about 443 BC the policy of Pericles became to ally with Leontini and the far southerly Italian state of Rhegium, possibly as a counterbalance to the rising power of Syracuse – for Syracuse at this later stage of the fifth century was now becoming the most populated and powerful state of the Greek west, and the most prominent repository and representative there of Greek culture.

A lover of Greek poetry, and host, in the time of Hiero, to the poets Pindar and Simonides and to the dramatists Aeschylus and Phrynichus, Syracuse was, by mid-century, along with other Sicilian cities, exploring the development of persuasive prose as an effective method of public speaking.

This was the standing of Syracuse when in 427–424 BC post-Periclean Athens, following the request of Gorgias of Leontini, first came into material confrontation with her.

For the real glory and continuing miracle of the fifth century BC had been the trajectory of the city of Athens. By many ironies the splendour of fifth century BC Athens was to eclipse the squalid poverty of fifth century BC Rome; but ultimately, by a rashly miscalculated expedition against Syracuse in the final fifth of the fifth century BC, Athens' own vanity was to be exemplarily and viciously punctured.

The Trajectory of Athens

For her culture and her constitution Athens was already the most prominent and the most promising of all the Greek city-states as, at the opening of the fifth century BC, those states all began tentatively to edge beyond the adventurous, yet still limited, boundaries of the preceding "archaic" age. It was the precocity of Athens in sending twenty ships to contend against the empire of Persia in 498 BC, that thrust her far ahead of all her contemporaries.

For at that time Persia was governing with firm discipline the most vast territory and the largest number of subject peoples that any world empire had hitherto seen. Darius, the implacable Persian king, was determined that his combined forces should be concentrated on the deserved punishment of the single city of Athens.

In the summer of 490 BC he sent his fleet directly across the Aegean from Samos to the coast of Attica. In a battle at Marathon, possibly the most formative battle in human history, the phenomenon and prodigy of Athens, under its general Miltiades, defeated the assault of the combined forces of Persia!

The Athenian statesman Themistocles foresaw that this would not be the end. In 485 BC Darius died, but his son Xerxes in 480 BC took up Darius's crusade of punishment. He marched into Greece with a multitudinous army, supported by a covering fleet. He descended southwards and attacked Athens. But he was finally outwitted by the versatile strategems of Themistocles.

In September 480 BC his impetus was broken at the sea battle of Salamis and Xerxes fled. The following year, 479 BC, the military commander Mardonius, whom Xerxes had left behind as his representative, was routed at the land battle of Plataea. No Persian invader ever again set foot upon European soil.

From the critical year 478 BC onwards Athenian enterprise, having now in the Greek mind eclipsed Sparta as the natural leader of the city-states and islands, saw no reason any longer to be content with the mere defeat of the Persians and their flight.

The move to follow the Persians up and drive all their fleets and forces from the whole of the Aegean and beyond, saw Athens increase in respect and renown; the Greek states unite comprehensively under her generalship; and, with the destruction of the Persian fleet at Eurymedon in about 465 BC, the achievement of a complete Greek dominance, with attendant euphoria, throughout all their seascapes and territories.

With the spirit of democracy gaining the edge in 462 BC over the declining vigour of the aristocratic movement in Athens, the city was set to consolidate her supremacy over the Aegean world as no state had ever done before. Guided by the visionary Pericles, who grasped all the political verities of the day – the retreat of Persia, the fading of Sparta, the waxing of the Athenian empire, the force of democratic politics in his own city, the open and unimpeded possibilities of her future – Athens set out to assert for herself a supremacy no longer only by sea, but also on land and in the arts.

Almost exactly about the middle of the fifth century BC the movement of the great and golden years of Pericles produced momentous changes both in Athens and in Greece. These changes were accompanied by four unanticipated consequences.

The first was a rise of hubristic arrogance within the city itself, provoking as a second consequence the corresponding resentment of the subordinate Greeks. The third was the flow towards Athens of cultural admirers and contributors, coming from all corners of the Greek world but possessing, some of them, unconventional and subversive ideas. The fourth and most damaging of all, was the problem of succession to Pericles.

Resentment against Athenian arrogance broke out into practical expression with the Archidamian War (431–421 BC). With the death of Pericles early on in this war it became clear that the triumphs of Athenian democracy in the central decades of the century had in fact been the triumphs of a democracy under firm, visionary, but discreet control. The democracy (that is, the Athenian people) could find no successor to Pericles. The decisions of the misgoverned and unguided post-Periclean democracy descended from the erratic to the wayward to the capricious.

The Archidamian War shaped itself into a ten-year struggle of the stolid Sparta and her land allies against the mercurial Athens and her sea empire. After attrition had reduced both sides to an exhausted truce in 421 BC, there was a pause with many regroupments. In 415 BC the frenetic Athenian democracy voted to undertake an expedition by sea against Syracuse.

The expedition went out as the most fearsome and splendidly equipped of any fleet ever seen in Greek waters. The expeditionary force was after three years of semi-paralysed leadership, humiliatingly defeated. Barely a single prisoner escaped the Syracusan stone-quarries to stow away home.

The Peloponnesian War, as is the name of all hostilities from 431 BC involving Sparta and Athens, resumed. As its first part was called the "Archidamian War," so its second bitter part was called the "Decelean War." Athenian fleets were hunted down both by Sparta and by Syracuse.

Persia returned to play a hidden supporting role behind Sparta.

The end came when the Spartan general Lysander swooped in an unexpected lunch-break raid on the Athenian fleet drawn up on the beach at Aegospotami in 405 BC. Devoid of her fleet, Athens lost command both of the seas and of the sea routes which conveyed her provisions to the port of Piraeus from the bread basket of the Black Sea. With Athenian surrender, the Peloponnesian War was brought to a final grim close.

Thus the century of the Second European Miracle ended for Athens in five great ironies. The city which had destroyed a reckless eastern invader became herself a reckless eastern invader destroyed. The western city which had sent out Cimon, son of Miltiades, against the Persians, became the city against whom western Syracuse sent out her general Hermocrates. The city which had hunted Persian fleets in the eastern Aegean had her own fleets hunted in the same quarter. The city which had destroyed the Persian fleet at Eurymedon became the city whose own fleet was destroyed at Aegospotami.

Running through everything and most perverse of all was the supreme irony that the free sovereign western democracy was seen to be no less rash, reckless and arbitrary than the sovereign oriental monarchy of Persia which it had trounced at the beginning of the century.

Yet the significance of fifth century BC Athens and of its whole wheel of fortune lies not only in the military and political vicissitudes of the century. It is impossible to follow the remarkable trajectory described by Athens in this distant era without being struck by the moral analogies and political parallels with modern times. For in fifth century BC Athens, at last a distinct crowd of personalities begins to emerge beside the odd distinguishable individual whom the previous misty centuries had disclosed.

The most obvious and the most simplistic example is that of Pheidippides, the long distance runner and messenger, whose arrival in Athens in 490 BC with the news that the Persian invasion had been defeated, is indirectly commemorated on every occasion that a Marathon race is run.

Other heroes of the Persian Wars have left similar secular examples behind: Miltiades and his son Cimon, the unbending, patriotic soldiers; Themistocles, whose detailed preparation left nothing to chance; the Athenian Aristides the Just; the Spartan Pausanias, too easily victim to those temptations of luxury against which an austere upbringing has no innoculation. In the middle years of the century, Pericles is the supreme example of the visionary statesman diverting every resource, every current, even every breeze of the political climate to the advantage of his own people and city. The later years provide less heroic exemplars: Cleon the tabloid entertainer; the uncomfortable Nicias, square peg in a round hole; Alcibiades, feckless product of a feckless age. Within the politics of the century every observer of Athens, Sparta and their contrasts can find their favourite stereotypes.

There are however at least forty other facets by means of which this "Century of the Second European Miracle" can be explored. Among them are the Olympic and other four-yearly sets of Games and the competitive spirit which sustained them; the changing tastes of the century in its costume, style, thought, aesthetics and specialisations; its economics, geography, travel, medicine and communications; its discovery of freedom and internationalism; its intellect, philosophy, religion, warfare, ethics and self-understanding; its pottery, architecture, sculpture, historians and dramatists; their investigations of the contours of humanity and their treatment of the agonies, anguishes and aspirations of the human condition; the history and contributions of each city-state apart from Athens; the features of each individual Aegean island and the reflection of their fortunes on the Athenian tribute lists.

Greece in the fifth century BC is an astounding, majestic, mercurial movement, held in permanent admiration and astonishment. It is an elevation of cultural splendour and an intensity of human intellect never to be re-attained in the history of Greece, Europe, or of all mankind. It is a phenomenon of unbelievable yet meteoric maturity. Following the eighth century BC, it was the second, and alongside other proposed competitors, the most outstripping, the most amazing and most abiding of all European miracles.

A Glance Further East

Yet for all this, it would be a mistake to overlook what was taking place in contemporary Jerusalem. Nearly a hundred years after the liberation of the Jews from Babylon and their Exile there, the Temple in Jerusalem had been rebuilt, but little more. A blunt and fiery individual, Nehemiah by name, sent out as governor in 444 BC by the Persian king Artaxerxes I, forcefully galvanised the listless population not only into rebuilding its walls but also into the restoration of its institutions, its literature, its religion and, harnessing something of the fervour of Second Isaiah, its Temple worship and its Psalms.

Yet although, through the mind of Second Isaiah, the theological insights of Abraham and Moses had been concentrated into a compact, indeed exultant, system of comprehensive monotheism, still the prophet's work remained a theology so far ahead of it time that all its full implications had not yet dawned upon the exiles returned to Jerusalem, or even upon their descendants.

9

The Century of Farewell to the Aegean (400–301 BC)

The Fourth Century BC

The land battle of Marathon (490 BC) and the sea battle of Salamis (480 BC) have become part of European folklore. They were miraculous victories by small armies over large; by intelligence over numbers; by defending Europeans over aggressive eastern invaders. They focused attention upon Athens and upon the start of her spectacular progress to become both imperial and intellectual mistress of the Aegean world.

The sea battle of Amorgos (322 BC) and the land battle of Crannon (August 322 BC) were remembered only by a few specialists even in the ancient world, let alone today – for in them Athens was defeated; her final fleet was sunk; her constitution amended; and old Greece, the dynamic Aegean world of drama, history, philosophy, poetry and oratory; of architecture, sculpture, trade, travel and military adventurism was for ever eclipsed.

In this doleful contrast lies the greatest mental adjustment in the history of the world hitherto – the opening of the mind to frontiers far beyond the Aegean fringes. Suddenly in the fourth century BC, vision was stretched, in the east to Afghanistan and north India, in the west to Rome. From this century onwards the informed intellect took in not merely the Aegean hub, but the lands extending eastwards from it, and the Mediterranean to the west, as well.

The Prising Open of the Mind

The rearrangement and enlargement of the geographical picture within the mind of civilised society did not occur like the flick of a switch. Even by the end of the century it had not come to prevail completely in the minds of prominent political figures on the late fourth century stage.

Nevertheless, this was the irreversible drift of the common, communal and corporate mind.

In the early decades of the fourth century the city-states of Greece, as though vying for some sort of succession to the pre-eminent political and cultural superiority of fifth century BC Athens, continued to compete against one another. There was however, from the beginning, a sense that that Athenian model and paradeigm could never be reproduced. The ambition to achieve it was growing out of fashion.

Athens had been an incomparable, concentrated phenomenon. With her fall, not just the city, but the whole Aegean world as its fifth century BC inhabitants had envisaged it, imploded. 2,400 years later, even we can still feel the bursting of the dam. From the moment of that fall, the long-standing Aegean rivalries lost their urgency. The river of Greek influence began to spread out over a broader and a flatter plain. This realisation was less obvious to contemporaries. Into the power vacuum that followed crowded, first, Sparta, then Corinth, Thebes, Argos, a restored Persia and even, later, a revived Athens. From their skirmishes no Greek state or party emerged with enduring supremacy.

In the battle of Cnidos (394 BC) in the so-called "Corinthian War,"Spartan sea-power was destroyed. Eventurally Sparta's powers were irrecoverably smashed at the battle of Leuctra (371 BC). If any people emerged from these early decades of the fourth century BC with any edge of advantage, it was the Persians! In 386 BC they took advantage of the war-weariness of the era by persuading the Greek states to sign the "King's Peace." It did not solve Greek problems for long, but it began to prise open in the Greek mind a readiness to incline to a more international dimension.

In the decade 370–361 BC Sparta, Athens and Thebes jostled one another for some sort of supremacy. The battle of Mantinea (362 BC) brought something like peace and conclusion to the forty year period of confusion following the fall of the world order of 405 BC. Thebes stood in the ascendant, Sparta on the decline and Athens in a useful and international flexible position. The sensation remains, however, that their rivalries were becoming irredeemably out-dated and small-town. This was the juncture at which appeared one vigorous ruler and fresh thinker to whose original mind all this preoccupation with the Aegean theatre now seemed hopelessly unambitious and provincial.

An International World

In 360 BC, two years after the battle of Mantinea, the Macedonian king Perdiccas III was killed in battle. His successor was a young man born in 382 BC, Philip II.

Steadily year by year, from his accession in 360 BC to his assassination in 336 BC, by fearless personal courage, by ingenious military engineering (for the fourth century BC was a century of increasing military sophistication and violence), and by a ruthless political guile unhindered by treaties or promises, Philip II of Macedon brought the whole of the Greek mainland, with all its proud, individualist, Aegean-minded city-states, under his personal governance.

This rise to power over the whole of Greece was a phenomenon unprecedented in the whole of Greek experience. It presaged a tectonic movement in the whole of the irregular evolution of Greek history – an international vision. By the time of his death, Philip was already eyeing the vulnerable Persian empire.

Philip's son Alexander (known to history as "the Great") acted in direct continuity with the radical ambitions of his father. Pausing briefly to establish his authority after his succession in 336 BC, Alexander embarked in 334 BC for Asia, never to return to Europe again.

In eleven years of vigorous, sometimes reckless (some observers have suggested drunken) campaigning until his death in 323 BC, Alexander spread Greek arms, government and culture steadily through Anatolia, Syria, Egypt, Babylonia, and far beyond to Bactria and northern India. In the year 332 BC he set foot in Jerusalem.

Following his death, it took only two years (323–321 BC) for the empire of Alexander the Great to collapse; but it took 42 years before a completely settled order could be established in its place. Approximately only half of this period fell in the later part of the fourth century BC.

An International Conference

Across the broad land masses of Anatolia and western Asia, eastern conquerors ever since the end of the Bronze Age (1,085 BC) had been spreading wider and wider empires.

There had been the Assyrian Tiglath-Pileser III (744–726 BC); the Babylonian Nebuchadnezzar (605–562 BC); and the Persian Cyrus the Great (559–529 BC) and his second son Darius (522–486 BC). All of them, having fought for their kingdoms, had then organised and ruled over them. Alexander the Great had by 333 BC, over-run a territory more extensive than them all; but instead of surviving to organise and rule it, he died.

At Triparadisus in north Syria in 321 BC, there assembled the four Successors of Alexander the Great to debate and share between themselves at the first ever international conference on government in the history of the world.

To the conference came first the aged Antipater, regent of Macedonia, a loyal henchman to Alexander's father Philip II, who by swift action following the death of Philip II had assured the succession to Alexander.

To Triparadisus came second, Antigonus-with-the-One-Eye (Antigonus Monophthalmus), appointed by Alexander the Great in 333 BC to be satrap of Phrygia. His son Demetrius Sacker-of-Cities (Demetrius Poliorketes) was to become prominent early in the third century BC. Both Antipater and Antigonus Monophthalmus brought to the Conference the assumption that the conquests of Alexander the Great were to be preserved as a single unitary empire under one sovereign.

Third at the conference of Triparadisus was Ptolemy, a boyhood friend of Alexander the Great, educated with him from 342 BC in Macedonia under Aristotle. Colourfully, shortly before the conference, he had hi-jacked Alexander's funeral cortege as it passed through Syria and transferred the corpse to Egypt.

Seleucus, who claimed to be the son of the god Apollo, had in 324 BC married Apame in a mass wedding of Greeks and Persians organised by Alexander the Great. Following the death of Alexander he had arranged the colonisation of the Persian Gulf. He was the fourth prominent and powerful participant at the conference of Triparadisus.

Ptolemy and Seleucus, more realistic than Antipater or Antigonus Monophthalmus, understood that the empire conquered by Alexander was so vast that political prudence and logistical expediency demanded that it be divided among his successors. Although however, two different points of view faced each other across the table at Triparadisus, a nostalgic centralising of the Aegean was common to the unconscious minds of all four parties at the conference.

It would be pleasant to report that at Triparadisus the voice of political realism prevailed, and that the allocated spheres of influence – Europe and Anatolia to Antigonus Monophthalmus; Egypt to Ptolemy; the Babylonian satrapy to Seleucus; the senior Antipater as regent and arbiter over the whole – was agreed and peaceably established. Human life and human history are not so uncomplicated.

Antipater died only two years later in 319 BC. Antigonus Monophthalmus immediately set out to realise his own vision of one vast empire under his own control. The peoples of Anatolia and north Syria had to endure nearly fifteen years of the ambitious trampling of his armies to and fro.

Ptolemy and Seleucus were not prepared to co-operate. The issue was finally decided at the battle of Ipsus (301 BC) where Antigonus Monophthalmus was both defeated and killed.

Then at last the three-fold division of Alexander's inheritance was confirmed. Egypt continued to be the realm of Ptolemy, Syria/Babylonia that of Seleucus. In Macedonia and Anatolia there remained unfinished business, the heir to which, following the death of Antigonus Monophthalmus at Ipsus, was his son Demetrius Poliorketes. But the Aegean-centred vision of all four survivors was now fading as the Hellenistic empire stretched and scattered itself far to the east, and a fast new dynamism began to command attention in the west. Having begun the fourth century BC as an archaic Italian society desperately struggling out of the depths of poverty, Rome ended the same century dabbling in that form of later Greek culture known as "Hellenism."

A Ferocious Arrival

In 390 BC Rome was sacked by the Gauls. The speed of Rome's recovery suggests, however, that somehow in the dark recesses of the ill-favoured fifth century BC, there had developed a social and an economic momentum that no temporary misfortune would derail.

In 400 BC the area of Roman territory ("ager Romanus"), was measured at 822 square kilometres. By 329 BC, after the annexation of Tusculum (381 BC) and Velitrae (367 BC); after subsequent successful campaigns against the Hernici and against the old, fifth century BC, opponents, the Aequi and the Volsci; after the conquest of the whole of Campania from the Tiber to the Bay of Naples, the "ager Romanus" stood enlarged by tenfold at a total of 8,505 square kilometres.

Unobserved in Triparadisus, and barely even noted at Syracuse, Rome had become a ferocious military phenomenon. No other community of the fourth century BC (or of many other centuries) had been able to extend its territory tenfold while still remaining a compact city.

This so-called "commonwealth" movement has been seen as the turning-point of Roman and of all Italian history. A severe, but not fatal, reversal of fortune at the hands of the Samnites at the battle of the Caudine Forks (321 BC) set Roman aggression back; but hostilities were resumed, ultimately bringing to Rome political control over the whole of central Italy by 302 BC.

Before 318 BC, a constitutional law, the "Lex Ovinia" had instituted senatorial membership for life, thereby establishing at the heart of republican government in Rome, a small, but potentially self-interested and self-perpetuating clique of wealthy, aristocratic oligarchs.

The end of the fourth century BC saw in Rome the beginning of a great new temple-building period. Rome's first coinage was issued in 326 BC, suggestive of the first gleam of an ambition to link up with the glittering promises of Hellenistic culture. Internally the population of Rome seemed to be in a state of coherent and developing anticipation. The archaic society of the Twelve Tables (449 BC) had passed through a dramatic series of ferocious transformations.

On the world stage it was "Farewell to the Aegean" as the age-old centrality of the importance of that bustling body of water evaporated away.

10

The Century of the Intermeshing (300–201 BC)

The Third Century BC

The division of the empire of Alexander the Great into three parts should have been confirmed in 301 BC with the death at the battle of Ipsus of its most resolute opponent, Antigonus One-Eye (Antigonus Monophthalmus). The empire as a total unit however remained an object of fantasy and desire as long as Antigonus's son Demetrius Poliorketes was alive. Only after his death, in 283 BC, was the realistic separation out of Egypt, Asia and Europe irreversibly assured.

The Successors to Alexander: (1) Egypt and the Ptolemies

The kingdom of Egypt was ruled in the third century by five kings named Ptolemy. It consisted of the ancient kingdoms of Egypt along the Nile and its Delta, governed from the newly constructed city of Alexandria.

Egypt was basically a native peasant population living in a Bronze Age culture, irrigated by the Nile, governed from this time onwards by a Greek dynasty and kept in order by Greek mercenaries and veterans to whom land-holdings were allocated by the Ptolemies. The population was docile and its boundaries definable. The Ptolemies fixed their capital in Alexandria as the expression of their lingering interest in affairs in and around the Aegean. In the early years of the century, the Ptolemies were able to take advantage of the confusion of the era of Demetrius Poliorketes to annex Cyprus and the Aegean islands. Towards the end of the century, Ptolemy IV Philopator (221–204 BC), who was not necessarily the greatest

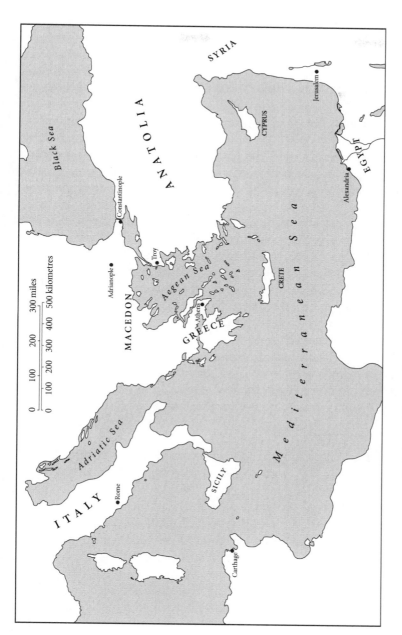

2 Asia and Europe from Cyprus to Italy

of the Ptolemies, neverthless by his victory over the Seleucid monarch Antiochus III Megas at the battle of Raphia in 271 BC, opened the way to maximum penetration of Coele-Syria and Anatolia.

The Successors to Alexander: (2) Asia and the Seleucids

By contrast with Egypt, the Asian section of Alexander the Great's empire, ruled by the Seleucid dynasty, covered the whole of Anatolia, Syria/Palestine, Mesopotamia and eastwards beyond. It was the largest fragment of Alexander's original realm, and for that reason too vast for Hellenistic governing techniques to keep under control.

Individual territories in Anatolia steadily leaked away: Bithynia and Pontus as early in the century as 297–296 BC; Pergamum in 283 BC; Cappadocia in 250 BC; Phrygia in 200 BC. Certain cities, preeminently the island of Rhodes, enjoyed unrestricted freedom. In the east, Parthia began to slip away in 256 BC; by 250 BC Parthia was, with Bactria, independent.

Wide open to the Black Sea and the Caucasus, the Seleucid kingdom was vulnerable to the incursions from the north of nomadic Gauls and Celts. The invasions in 237 BC of Lutarius and Leonnorius made the most permanent impact of these. In four Syrian Wars in this century certain Seleucid monarchs found themselves in intermittent conflict with the Ptolemies of Egypt.

The Successors to Alexander: (3) Macedonia and the Antigonids

The third kingdom, the ancient and original heartland of Greece and Macedonia, abutting on the western Aegean, remained mired in the squabbling inter-state mind-set of the fifth century BC. The main development beyond the city-state mentality was the tendency to form federations.

The Peloponnesian states, except Sparta, allied with one another in the Achaean League: the states north of the Gulf of Corinth combined into an Aetolian League. Through much toil and distraction the sovereignty over these thankless territories was finally won in 272 BC by Antigonus Gonatas from Macedonia. During this period one Pyrrhus (295–272 BC), was also able to gain the mastery as ruler of Epirus.

Until he died in 239 BC Antigonus Gonatas fought to maintain stability and security in Greece, and to his great credit was able to hold some form of balance between the competing animosities of the Achaean and Aetolian Leagues, and over an attempted resurgence by Sparta.

This pattern of the ungoverned rivalries between the Aetolian and Achaean Leagues and attempted control by Macedonia continued following the death of Antigonas Gonatas, but in 229 BC. Antigonus Doson came to the throne as guardian to the proper heir, Philip V.

In 225 BC Antigonus Doson absorbed the faltering Achaean League and crushed Cleomenes in Sparta, thereby completely restoring Macedonian authority over the unruly Greek peninsula. When he died in 221 BC Antigonus Doson handed over a compact situation to his young ward, Philip V of Macedon.

Thus in these various ways the Aegean inheritance of Alexander the Great was scattered all across the easten horizon. Meanwhile in the west, this slow dispersal of a mature culture was to be contrasted with the precocious military progress of an irresistible adolescent force. Indeed, by now the momentum of Republican Rome had become so powerful that no opposition could weary it or slow it down.

The Rise of Rome

Mesopotamia and Egypt, the two great engines of earliest civilisation, had materialised out of their two great river systems – the Tigris and the Euphrates enclosing Mesopotamia, and the Nile inundating Egypt.

Athens had shone almost by accident, through the dust of a successful conflict with Persia and the consequent clear skies of versatile attainment and prestige. The significance of Israel's contribution to society and civilisation remained at this time underestimated and unappreciated.

Rome, the fifth, and last, and the greatest political influence enduring from the ancient world seems to have propelled itself forward by conscious effort; by arms and conquest; by a central governing elite, the Senate, resolved upon ruthless expansion; by bitter losses sustained and even more cruel victories won; by enrolling into its martial policies a higher proportion of its own population than any other state or city in the pre-industrial era.

In the "Latin Wars" of the previous century (406–338 BC) Rome had expanded prodigiously from a large archaic city into a fighting force that was in control of the whole of central Italy.

By 300 BC Rome was half way through the "Italian Wars" (338–264 BC) which had already added Campania to her holdings and which were eventually to make her the mistress of all Italy. The figures of the two battles of Sentinum (295 BC) and Aquilonia (293 BC) give some idea of the ruthless ferocity of Roman expansion. At Sentinum, 27,000 Samnites and Gauls were killed, although with the loss of 8,700 Roman lives. At Aquilonia, a Samnite army of over 36,000 men was defeated.

In return, there were also to be defeats for Rome in the course of the third century BC, at the hands of Hannibal in Lake Trasimene in 217 BC, and most resoundingly at Cannae in 216 BC They were indeed bitter, disgraceful and dire disasters. Nevertheless, not even these catastrophes could hold back for long the onrush of Rome's third century BC career.

By 264 BC Rome had achieved the conquest of all Italy, arriving thereby face to face with Carthaginian domination in Sicily. The friction brought on the First Punic War (264–240 BC). By its end, after fierce see-sawing warfare in which storm at sea played a significant part, Rome emerged victorious over Carthage and, to her surprise, with the capture and government of Sicily as her further reward and obligation.

Next, just as the First Punic War drew Rome permanently into Sicily, so the Second Punic War (218–202 BC), inducted her, inextricably, into the full web of eastern Mediterranean politics.

The "Intermeshing" (220–216 BC)

Our ears are accustomed today to the two great cliches, "the glory that was Greece," and "the grandeur that was Rome." The "glory that was Greece" was accumulated century by century from Homer (750 BC) to Demosthenes (385–322 BC), during a time when Rome was still barbarous and virtually unobserved. The "grandeur that was Rome" was eventually to follow. Now in the third century BC there was to be a slow drawing together of autumnal Greece and the hard-fought springtime of Rome, until there finally occurred, in the 140th Olympiad of Greek calculation (220–216 BC) that historic engagement between the "glory" and the "grandeur" which was named by the historian Polybius (200–118 BC) "The Intermeshing."

Rome's first ever brush with Greece had been, inevitably, military. Pyrrhus of Epirus, a ruler from the Greek mainland brought in by Tarentum to defend the city, Greek by foundation, from Roman encroachment, engaged in war with Rome between 281 and 275 BC. After two expensive successes, Pyrrhus was defeated by Rome at the battle of Beneventum (275 BC). Contact between Rome and Greece then lapsed.

Then in 228 BC Rome sent competitors to Corinth to participate in the Isthmian Games. By the last third of the third century BC the Roman Senate seems to have been making tentative explorations in the direction of a Mediterranean role for Rome. Shortly after, rolling change occurred at an unexpected pace. There were four sudden changes of kingship in the four empires of the world eastwards from Rome, in the Olympiad leading up before the "Intermeshing" – in the years 224–221 BC.

In 223 BC Antiochus III Megas became king of the Seleucid empire. In 221 BC Ptolemy IV Philopator became Pharoah in Egypt; in the same year Philip V took up his inheritance as ruler of Macedonia. From Carthage, Hannibal was appointed as commander-in-chief of the Carthaginian forces in Spain and in 218 BC the Second Punic War broke out.

On 22nd June 217 BC Ptolemy Philopator defeated Antiochus III Megas at the battle of Raphia. Only sixteen days later Hannibal, on 8th July 217 BC, trounced the Roman forces at the battle of Lake Trasimene.

In fact, two years later, in 215 BC, Hannibal surrendered the initiative against Rome, and although the Second Punic War was not to finish until 202 BC, from 215 BC slowly but relentlessly Roman force pressed Hannibal further and further away from the area of danger.

It was however the Roman posture towards Greece, even more than the eventual fall of Carthage, which made the 140th Olympiad, and with it the last twenty years of the third century BC, portentously influential in the history of the world. For the defeat of Rome by Hannibal at Lake Trasimene in 217 BC had aroused in Macedonia the fateful curiosity of Philip V.

Rome and Greece: The Point of No Return

Friction arose between Philip V of Macedon and Rome over the person of Demetrius of Pharos, advisor to Philip. It broke out into the full First Macedonian War of 214–205 BC, with the Adriatic and its eastern coastline as the battle-ground.

Philip was easily beaten back in the first campaigning season, 214 BC, but in 213 BC returned in a strong resurgence. The Roman commander Marcus Valerius Laevinus was obliged to enter in 212 BC into an alliance with the only Greek complex strong enough to contend with Philip – the Aetolian League of states north of the Isthmus of Corinth. From the moment of this alliance, Rome was of necessity sucked into the complexities and internal tensions of the Greek city-states.

The First Macedonian War ended in 205 BC and Roman forces evacuated Greece entirely-but nine years of military contact had formed a relationship that now proved to be indissoluble. By the experience of the First Macedonian War, Rome had developed a much deeper intimacy with, and interest in, Greece than ever before.

In 200 BC, free of Carthage, and responsive to clamorous petitions against Philip V made not only from the Greek but also from the Asiatic seaboard – from both sides, therefore, of the Aegean! – Rome declared war again.

The Second Macedonian War ended with the Roman victory of Cynoscephalae in 197 BC. But a process was now engaged which was to lead militarily to the conquest of the whole of Greece by Rome – and culturally to Rome being led by the nose entirely by the conquered Greeks!

11

The Century of Creaks, Cracks and Contradictions (200–101 BC)

The Second Century BC

Athens in the fifth century BC sprang up like a wild flower, defiant of the Persian invasive storms; blossomed in mid-century under Pericles, and withered and died under the Decelean War.

The Roman organism was longer in germinating and correspondingly slower in decay. Indeed, once it so fought off fate that the Roman Empire (30 BC–AD 476) proved even more enduring than the Roman Republic (509–30 BC). Nevertheless, the short decline of Athens and the long and lingering expiry of the Roman Republic were both lined with similar ironies.

For both states their virtues became their Achilles heel. Seeds of destruction planted long before came to calamitous fruition. Contradictions produced their own wry patterns. Traps that had once ensnared enemies the Romans, like the Athenians, themselves slipped into. Prophetic moments came to uncomfortable self-fulfilment. Providence kept unforeseen patterns or strokes of misfortune close to her chest.

Contradictions of this sort, which had sprung up rapidly to destroy Athens, began in the second century BC to foreshadow long-term erosive consequences for Rome. Yet Providence also had up her sleeve two totally unanticipated and unparalleled phenomena.

The First Contradiction

The First Macedonian War had been fought between 214–205 BC. The Second Macedonian War of 200–197 BC belonged to the second century BC; so did the Third, from 171–168 BC. The confrontations switched on between the two cultures a current of magnetic attraction which was irresistible and irreversible. The contradictory and paradoxical consequence was that by these three wars Rome and Greece were brought into more inextricable and lasting rapprochement with one another than would have been possible if they had entered into any alliance or treaty of peace!

True, the Roman armies withdrew entirely from Greece following the First Macedonian War. Nevertheless, through this war a focus of interest, a body of knowledge, and a nucleus of Roman early experts on Greece came into existence. More materially, there came also an alliance with the Aetolian League, and ties of friendship with numerous city-states of southern Greece and even Asia Minor (formerly "Anatolia"), including Bithynia and Pergamum.

It was not long before the Romans were back again. The Second Macedonian War of 200–197 BC triggered in Rome a new and wider outburst of interest in Hellenism (Greek culture), which was followed by steady social and cultural change.

Rome was by this time a city of some 250,000 inhabitants, and admiration for Greek superiority began to catch light in it. Innumerable works of Greek art were paraded in 194 BC at the triumph of Titus Quinctius Flamininus, victor in the Second Macedonian War, and one of Rome's new specialists on Greece. Among other hostages who settled in Rome was Demetrius, son of Philip V of Macedon, himself.

The Second Contradiction

Philiop V of Macedon died in 179 BC His successor's name was Perseus. It was against Perseus that the Third Macedonian War (171–168 BC) was waged. On 22nd June 168 BC Perseus was defeated by Lucius Aemilius Paulus at the battle of Pydna. Now one thousand Greek hostages, including the historian Polybius (born 200 BC), were carried back to Rome. So also were the king of Illyria, Genthius; the family of Genthius; the royal family of Macedonia; and the library of Macedonia.

With all these, a new and stronger tide of Hellenistic influence broke on the shores of Italy and over the population of Rome. The conquest of Rome by Greece, even more than the simultaneous military conquest of Greece by Rome, was well advanced.

The Third Contradiction

In 146 BC Lucius Mummius sacked Corinth and the Romans finally declared Greece "free." In fact the year 146 BC was, in the calendars of universal history, the date of the final extinguishing of the independence of Greece. No further dates or events of any significance are recorded in any account of the history of Greece following the proclamation of this ironical "freedom."

The Fourth Contradiction

The Hellenistic spell was however weaving its hypnotic enchantments over the generation whose predecessors had fought the Latin Wars (406–338 BC), the Italian Wars (338–264 BC) and the Punic Wars (264–202 BC). Greek luxury and culture were preparing to dissolve the stern rigidities and seduce the unbending rectitudes of those ancient heroes.

Contemptuously overwhelming the resistance of Marcus Porcius Cato, the Lex Oppia of 215 BC, a law restraining Roman enthusiasm for luxuries, was repealed in 195 BC – the very year of Cato's own consulship – on the grounds that it dated from obsolete austerities applicable only to the times of the Punic Wars.

The Fifth Contradiction

Also from this period onwards, the increased characterisation of Roman individuals, and the increased amount of tabloid gossip about Roman personalities, suggest than a spot-light operated by Greek entertainment-mongers is beginning to be shone! Thus, Marcus Aemilius Lepidus is caught out at the beginning of the Second Macedonian War (200 BC) treating Philip V with an unseemly arrogance. At the end of this war (196 BC), Lucius Cornelius Lentulus is revealed in Asia Minor in a similar posture towards Antiochus III.

In 168 BC, Gaius Popillius Laenas was no less diplomatically disrespectful of Antiochus IV; and in the same year the Senate peremptorily turned its back upon a long-standing friend and ally, Eumenes II of Pergamum. In 164 BC it even sent out Gaius Sulpicius Galus in a deliberate move to undermine him. Roman government had scarcely come in touch with Greece, than it was showing itself avaricious, cruel, capricious and tyrannical.

Similar exposures from the first third of the second century BC, stretching across the Mediterranean from Spain to Rhodes, reveal the inexpertise of Rome in governing abroad; Rome's stumbling into the gaffes of arbitrary dictatorship and the personal will-to-power of certain individual governors; and the state's ignorance in the fine art of establishing just and legitimate rule over free and grateful populations.

The Greek riposte, in the enthralment of Greece's conquerors, had to be more surreptitious. Marcus Fulvius Nobilior, consul of 189 BC, is a good example. Nobilior used to take with him on military campaigns in Greece, the poet Ennius, somewhat in the way that Alexander the Great had taken poets with him on his eastern conquests. On his own estates, Nobilior also built a temple of Hercules and the Muses; from Ambracia he carried off almost all the works of art in the city and adorned his home-made temple of Hercules with statues of the Muses from this looted lot.

But the few works of art that he has left behind revealed the lack of refinement of his education or taste; and a "Temple of Hercules and the Muses" is a conjoined concept as bizarre as the parallel modern incongruity of the "elephant dancing among the chickens."

The Sixth Contradiction

In 154 BC Rome began to build a theatre on the Greek model. Hardly had it begun, than an opposing point of view, maintaining that the principles of theatre-going were Greek, imported and degenerate, prevailed and successfully had it destroyed.

Nevertheless, in the following century, Pompey built a theatre in Rome and Julius Caesar planned another; and finally, just as the theatre had been a hall-mark of Hellenisation (Greek cultural supremacy) eastwards in Asia, so in the time of the Roman Empire (30 BC–AD 476), the theatre was to become a hallmark of Romanisation (Roman political supremacy) westwards in Spain, France and Germany.

Multiple Contradictions

Greek gossip about Roman overbearing, tyranny, hypocrisy, self-contradiction and avarice however, really highlighted only superficial symptoms of deeper and barely diagnosed sociological problems in the second century BC Roman Republic. From 193 BC the aristocratic Roman families began to grow restive and irritable, expressing discontents in competitive tendencies, rivalries, wranglings and even law-suits and prosecutions against one another.

In 169 BC there arose problems in recruiting man-power for the Third Macedonian War; in 168 BC there began to appear a decline in military standards and the first stirrings of a mood of opposition to the Senate. The writings of Cato demonstrate that agricultural and economic problems were beginning to come to the surface from about 167 BC. They included the depopulation of the countryside of southern Italy; the growth of large estates in the hands of absentee landlords; the displacement of small-holders by slave labour; drifts to the city; desertion of villages and general deep economic discontent.

In the realm of international government too, the Romans were still amateurs. The irresistible Roman current that in the fourth and third centuries BC had surged dramatically through the Italian peninsula was beginning to break up upon its contact with the more challenging cross-currents of the Mediterranean. As the demands of the second century BC progressed and grew weightier, Rome began to fall into the perils of over-extension – over-extension of governing techniques, energies, man-power and, now distance.

The Supreme Contradiction

The year 146 BC in which both Corinth and Carthage were destroyed (and Greece at the same time "liberated"), was the high water-mark of the Roman Republic's ironical and self-contradictory destiny. There was now on the Roman horizon no military or political force capable of sustaining opposition to the might of Rome. There was no curb therefore, upon her greed, arrogance and violence abroad. But there was also no reversal of her decline in military man-power and governing calibre at Rome.

In the final third of the second century BC the brothers Tiberius and Gaius Gracchus (died 132 BC and 121 BC respectively) represented the realisation by some thoughtful Roman observers that something needed to be done. In each case, however, the attempts of the brothers at agricultural reform met with violence and their own deaths. The death of Tiberius Gracchus was provoked most immediately by his attempt, contrary to Roman law, to stand for election to the same office twice. There was irony here – for before the second century was out, the Roman general Marius was to serve as consul no less than five times!

The symptoms were there of a political organism in turmoil. The Roman Republic was a colossus by any measurement, and her steep downhill decline was also desperate, blood-thirsty and colossal. The Greeks had the mental power to analyse any phenomenon, political or natural, but no analyst came forward with any formula to arrest or reverse Rome's late second century BC slide, decline and fall. With increasing acceleration Roman internal rivalries and bitter-nesses, Roman external arrogance and cruelties continued to sweep the fortunes of the Republic onwards into the first century BC, and downwards in the manner of a slow train crash.

12

The "Century" of Accelerating Discontents (100–50 BC)

The First Century BC

Most people believe that history is the records of events, battles, deeds, personalities, dates and places. Nor are they wrong. Nevertheless, below the surface of such records lie currents, customs, trends, traditions and national characteristics passed along, often unspoken, by and through generations. Sometimes a feature or an idea introduced at an early time can come to fruition with novel or startling consequence after an incubation of centuries. Twice in the history of Rome, such a process worked with metamorphosing effect. The second time was when, in the fifth century AD, the western empire "morphed" into the seed-bed of diverse and larger civilisations. The first time was when the Roman Republic "morphed" into the Roman Empire at the end of the first century BC. There were outstanding personalities in first century BC Rome – Marius, Sulla, Cicero, Pompey, Crassus, Catullus, Lucretius and Julius Caesar – but these personalities were at the same time the creatures, victims or name-tags of trends. Seldom in human history has an era been so obviously dominated, less by events and personalities, more by undercurrents and converging trends than in the first century BC.

The era is dominated by numerous conflicting currents and motivations – by discord between the nobles, the knights and the common people; by the clamour for recognition of the Italian allies; by the creeping corruption of Greek lubricity and luxury – but two trends especially colour the period and contrive the downfall of the late Republican period of Rome. These were the absence at the heart of government of any concept of a loyal opposition; and the passage of the army out of senatorial control and into the hands of powerful individual generals and leaders.

Together these features in particular were destined to run the Roman Republic (509–30 BC) into exhaustion – but then to transfer it into the guardianship of a most unparalleled and a most unforeseen providence.

The Power of the Veto

At no time did the Romans, not even in the period of their most majestic Senatorial ascendancy (261–146 BC) achieve the idea of debate in the central chamber of government between a ruling party and a loyal opposition.

What they had experienced was the danger of power falling into the hands of one particularly forceful individual, or of one small and irresistible group of determined men. The Romans were therefore, from the day of the Republic's foundation in 509 BC, fully aware of the needs of checks and balances in a healthy state. For this reason they placed supreme power into the possession of two men, their consuls, elected annually for service for a single, unrepeatable, year.

An equal partner in the highest office was generally sufficient to prevent abuse of supreme power by one individual consul or the other; but lest any consul should set out on a delinquent trip fuelled by offensive will-to-power, the one magistrate in the Republic who had the right to oppose him was his consular colleague. He could do so by interposing his veto, which at once brought any controversial initiative to a summary end.

Following the secessions of the plebs (494–3 BC, and 449 BC) during the arduous fifth century BC in Rome, the most lasting constitutional consequence was the election annually of ten "tribuni plebis," ("tribunes of the people"), with significant powers and privileges in protection of the interests of the common people. Among these powers were the right to propose business in the Senate, and the right to impose, at their discretion, a veto upon senatorial business.

The veto was the only form of opposition that the Roman state could devise, but, as in all political arrangements, the price paid for any measure of liberty had to be decline in governmental efficiency. The veto was found to be, in later times, a measure bristling with potential obstruction and mischief.

During the early centuries of magisterial Roman conquest of Campania and Italy, unity of purpose within the state guaranteed little, or responsible, use of the veto. From the late second century BC onwards, increased use of the veto became a prime symptom of disjointment and disorder within the state. In the early first century BC the tribunes began to use their veto with increasing frequency in order to hinder efficient business.

The teeth of the tribunes were in effect drawn by Lucius Cornelius Sulla during the period of his ascendancy (82–76 BC), but their powers were restored following Sulla's retirement and death.

The most notorious case of the use of the veto for irresponsible blocking by a consul came in 59 BC, when almost every initiative of the consul Julius Caesar was vetoed by his colleague Bibulus. The most notorious case of the same by a tribune came at the climax of the period of animosity between powerful men on the eve of the Civil War (49–45 BC). In 50 BC the tribune Caius Scribonius Curio, ostensibly a supporter of Pompey, but secretly in the pay of Julius Caesar (who had settled all his debts), perpetually exercised his veto in the Senate in the interests of Caesar.

The veto was the first of the institutions of the ancient Roman Republic which, like a political acid, poured out of the bottle in the first century BC to begin eating away traditional respect for the Senate.

The Decline of the Senate

Alongside the veto however, the one further solvent which hastened the most confusing changes in the Roman state was the gradual transition away from the Senate and into the control of individual magnates, of all the springs of power. The magisterial Senate of the fourth and third centuries BC had by the late first century (30 BC) dwindled in status to a pathetic and despicable rump. The whole process was carried chiefly on the backs of the army.

In the great days of expansion across Italy, membership of the army had been by means of conscription senatorially controlled; farmer-soldiers themselves supplied their own weapons and armour and came out temporarily, when required, to fight. Then came the threats and emergencies of the years 107–101 BC, which brought to the fore the Roman general Marius and his military reforms.

During the years 107–101 BC Rome was menaced, as it had not been menaced for 300 years, by two German tribes, the Cimbri and the Teutones, descending from the north. Only the low-born but militarily gifted Marius was capable of saving the nation. Upon him, by virtue of the emergency of the times, and contrary to all normal rules of Roman magistracy, was the award of the consulship conferred on five occasions.

Marius achieved his victories not only in the field, but by the imposition in parallel of radical military reforms. Legions were recruited no longer by conscription but through volunteers; all sustenance and military equipment were state-supplied; and from being an occasional citizen army, the whole body became a standing professional concern. Through these reforms and through the resistance of Marius to the Cimbri and the Teutones, Rome recovered externally; but internally the mechanisms of the state became now permanently changed.

There had been one great omission in Marius's plans for a standing army. What of retirement provision, homesteads and agricultural holdings for military veterans? The shortage of such provision left open the devastating possibility that volunteer, full-time professional soldiers would line up, no longer behind an increasingly dithering Senate, but behind powerful individuals, whose offers of terms of service would come as a firm and deliverable promise.

Such proved to be the developing military current of the first century BC. Increasingly the wretched Senate went through the motions of government, although all substantial executive power was draining away. First Sulla, then Pompey, Crassus and Julius Caesar took over command of private armies of their own.

There were many other desperate and seething discontents in the steaming caldron of first century BC Rome – corruption in the law-courts; abuse of power by provincial governors; problems associated with agrarian possession, debt and slaves; antipathies; frictions; jealousies; the status of tribunes; polarisation; incompetence; aggressive short-sightedness in all classes of the population; over-extension of Roman Republican ambitions – but foremost among them all were the veto and the withering of the Senate as the command of standing armies passed over into the hands of individual powerful men.

The two consuls for 70 BC, Pompey and Crassus, were such men. Yet at the same time they too and their contemporaries were tempest-tossed by the stormy inheritance which was reaching out from ancient times to savage and to sink them.

The Fourth Decade of the First Century, 70–61 BC

Pompey and Crassus in their year of office were successful in reforming the law-courts. They did nothing about the abuse of power by provincial governors; but they did restore all full rights and prerogatives to the tribunes of the people.

This last move was a disaster. The aggressive and selfish ambition displayed by the representatives of the common people was no better than the passions that motivated the nobles in the Senate. Pompey, appointed to the eastern command in 66 BC brought home unprecedented booty, glory and power to Rome, but remorselessly the ancient Republican constitution was becoming unworkable.

For all the inflowing splendours, how could a metropolis, increasingly torn and scandalised by conspiracy, mob-violence, corruption and decline in senatorial authority sustain the responsibilities of governing a wide and wealthy empire? Ambitious individuals increasingly shamelessly broke the surface – Catiline and Clodius, Cato and Cicero, but above all Pompey, Crassus and Julius Caesar.

Within this whirlpool of animosity and immorality, one detail passed unnoticed. On 23rd September 63 BC, there was born in the household of Julius Caesar to his sister Julia, a grandson, Gaius Julius Octavius.

The Fifth Decade of the First Century, 60–51 BC

So Rome entered the last decade before its Civil War. Alternative competitors dropped away; the Senate continued to mount fading resistance; power began to concentrate into the hands of three determined individuals. Under the initiative of Julius Caesar, Crassus and Pompey agreed to an informal association of mutual self-interest known to history as the "First Triumvirate," or "Body of Three Men." (A Second Triumvirate, senatorially and constitutionally established, was to follow some twenty years later.) The emergence of these "Triumvirates" was the prime symptom of the manner in which senatorial power was flowing progressively away from the main body and into individual control.

In the elections for 59 BC the First Triumvirate was not entirely successful. Julius Caesar was elected, but his colleague M. Calpurnius Bibulus, was a protegé of Caesar's senatorial opponents. Caesar's programme of legislation, far-seeing and potentially effective, was perpetually hampered procedurally by Bibulus's veto. It was the custom, after a consul had completed his year of office, for him to receive a senior or "proconsular" command outside Rome. From 59–58 BC Caesar was able to acquire as his proconsular command, the unconquered territories of Cisalpine Gaul, Transalpine Gaul and Illyricum. He spent the 50s reducing them to senatorial Roman control. At the same time, from this proconsular proximity he was able to watch more closely, as he needed to, the progress of events in Italy.

The continual ascendancy within the Republic of the First Triumvirate was signalled by the conference in 56 BC of these three commanders at Luca. Caesar used the occasion to repair relationships with the other members of the Triumvirate, and the three together took it upon themselves to nominate the consular officers and the proconsular commands for some years ahead. The First Triumvirate however, soon dissolved. Crassus died in warfare in 53 BC, and Pompey and Caesar drifted further and further apart.

Julius Caesar from his position as proconsul of Gaul and Illyricum now resolved to campaign again for election to the consulship for the year 49 BC. Under Roman law, it was not until after he had resigned his post, that a proconsul could be prosecuted for any misdemeanour that might have stained his period of office. But also a candidate could not present himself for election to a new office without first laying down his former one. Constitutionally, this practice threw open a window of vulnerability for any candidate seeking a new office – and for that candidate's opponents, a window of opportunity!

With regard to the consular elections for 49 BC, Caesar's determination to evade this constitutional death-trap became the flash-point between himself and the rest of the increasingly estranged establishment. In the previous century there may have been many a disagreement between members of the governing circles in Rome, and many a murder committed – but now Julius Caesar's deliberate calculation brought the great Republic, for the first time ever, to the brink of Civil War, and into it!

In 51 BC, Julius Caesar's sister, Julia, died. Her funeral eulogy was delivered by her precocious grandson, Gaius Julius Octavius, who at the same time was promoted to a place in the college of priests. This prodigious twelve-year old was destined for only six years more to enjoy the blessings of a tranquil and modest obscurity.

13

Thirteen Centuries of Song
(1,370–103 BC)

Meanwhile in Jerusalem

Just over thirteen years before the outbreak of Civil War in Rome, in the October of 63 BC, the Roman general Pompey had, with his army, entered Jerusalem. Thus the descendants of Abraham (eighteenth century BC), and the successors of Moses (1,280 BC), Solomon (960 BC) and Second Isaiah (538 BC) came to be governed by the unstable late Republic of Rome.

Knowing nothing of the Jews' ancestry, Pompey found them focused upon their Temple, the Second Temple, rebuilt upon the site of the Temple of Solomon following their Return from Babylonian Exile in 538 BC. Three times a year the Jews would descend upon Jerusalem to celebrate their three great Festivals, the Passover in March, the Feast of Weeks in May, and the Feast of Tabernacles as September passed into October.

Their culture, history and beliefs, as reflected in their song, had been brought into shape at an unknown time before, but certainly no later than, 103 BC,when five inherited collections of poetry had been assembled, edited and re-issued as a single anthology, in the 150 compositions which are still known today as the Book of Psalms.

Although the Psalms were sung by the Jews throughout the year, they show signs of having been used with special intensity, fervour and concentration at the fortnight-long autumn Feast of Tabernacles. They demonstrate that the religious ideas first pioneered seventeen centuries before by Abraham had, by the time of the crisis of the Roman Republic, coalesced into a devout and coherent system, embraced and practised uniquely and entirely by the Jewish nation.

Abraham had discarded all the mythologies of the ancient civilisations he had known – Mesopotamia, Egypt and all Fertile Crescent options in between – and had put his faith in, worshipped and obeyed one single God only, as Creator of all things. This belief had been taken over, examined, advanced and refined by later generations to such an extent that, by the time of the fall of their city to Pompey in the mid-first century BC, the Jews were making the uncompromising claims that there was one God who was by definition the only God of creation, nature and history; and that their Temple in Jerusalem was the one place to worship him.

God of Creation and Nature

Their collection of Psalms included one, Psalm 104, which was a daring correction of a speculative hymn of the Egyptian Pharoah Akhenaton (1,379–1,364 BC), and which laid out the whole panorama of nature, not, as the Pharoah had supposed, as the creation of the sun's disc, but as the work of Abraham's and Israel's God.

This belief in God as God of creation and nature was also summarised in the sophisticated formula of Psalm 33, verse 7: "By the word of the Lord were the heavens made: and all the hosts of them by the breath of his mouth." Psalm 148 carried this belief throughout the known universe from sun, moon and stars (verse 3) to "Beasts and all cattle: worms and feathered fowls" (verse 10).

God of History

The Psalms were not only a vehicle of the Jews' belief in God as God of creation and nature. They also proclaimed belief in God as Creator of mankind and disposer of all his ways. God was for the Jews not only God of nature, but God of history. By the first century BC, at the Feast of Tabernacles every autumn, his work as God of history was especially celebrated in the singing of Psalms 78, 105 and 106. These "history Psalms" laid out ideas which were summarised also in the earlier Psalms 60, verses 6–12, and 67.

"Thou shalt judge the folk righteously: and govern the nations upon earth" sings Psalm 67, verse 4. "When the Lord turned again the captivity of Sion: then were we like unto them that dream" was the ringing opening of Psalm 126. In particular, there peals through the Psalms the belief that God in his capacity as God of history, had shown to the descendants of Abraham, the people of Israel, special favour by setting them aside in the privileged position of his Chosen People.

The Chosen People status is affirmed, for example, in that compendium of systematic theology which is Psalm 89, at verses 16–19. The Chosen People were set aside, formed and established, according to Psalm 132, verses 11–19, by covenant (verse 11), law (verse 13), and by geographical and historical signs such as the city of Jerusalem (verse 14) and the kingship of David (verses 11, 18–19).

The Chosen People status is also claimed in Psalm 147: "He hath not so dealt with any nation: neither have the heathen knowledge of his laws" (verse 20), and in Psalm 81, verse 11, justified by the Exodus motif: "I am the Lord thy God: who brought thee out of the land of Egypt."

This is not, however, to present the Psalms as a mere propagandist pronouncement of Jewish nationalism. Following the Return from Babylonian Exile in 538 BC, there was a strong body of influential Jews who were willing to endorse the view of Second Isaiah that the commission and destiny of the Chosen People was to commend the powers and consolations of their God to the ends of the earth:

"All nations whom thou hast made: shall come and worship thee, O Lord" (Psalm 86, verse 9). "He hath remembered his mercy and truth towards the house of Israel: and all the ends of the earth have seen the salvation of our God" (Psalm 98, verse 4).

To these may be added the strong international flavour of the Psalmic fragment which appears as Psalm 117.

God the Communicator

Thus on the cosmic level the Psalms worship Israel's God as Creator; and on the international level they proclaim him Lord of history and selector of the Jews to be his Chosen People with a commission to all nations.

The Psalms however are not only for the nations. They are also for individuals. They minister to the subjective anxiety which haunts the created and Angst-ridden self which is always conscious of its own mortality.

The Psalter's leading evaluation of man is condensed into one single, uncomplicated and uncomplimentary term: "vanity." By this single punch-word are penetrated, punctured and pinned down all the attention-seeking devices, all the self-advertising denial with which the individual mortal human being tries to disguise his hollowness and elude his transient fate.

" . . . every man living is altogether vanity.
"For man walketh in a vain shadow and disquieteth himself in vain: he heapeth up riches and cannot tell who shall gather them."   (Psalm 39, verses 6–7)

In the first book of the Psalter (Psalms 1–41) occur no less than thirty-five unflattering epithets in which are summed up the basic bleakness of humanity, our essential meaninglessness, vulnerability, sinfulness, transience, futility, idolatries and folly. However, with the individual, even in this doleful and pessimistic condition, the Almighty and sole Creator desires to communicate! In this respect the Psalms endorse resoundingly the original gamble of Abraham.

God who is both transcendent on high, yet immanent in the smallest interstices of the created world, is not only able in theory, but also in practice willing, to enter into dialogue with human beings within it.

They tell him of their distress:

"Lord, how are they increased that trouble me: many are they that rise against me."   (Psalm 3, verse 1)
"My life is waxen old with heaviness: and my years with mourning."   (Psalm 31, verse 11)

The Psalms also speak to God of their penitence:

"Have mercy upon me, O God, after thy great goodness: according to the multitude of thy mercies, do away mine offences."   (Psalm 51, verse 1)

God reveals his grace:

"O taste and see how gracious the Lord is: blessed is the man that trusteth in him." (Psalm 34, verse 8)

God also reveals his mercy and his redemption:

"The earth, O Lord, is full of thy mercy." (Psalm 119, verse 64)
"O Israel, trust in the Lord, for with the Lord there is mercy: and with him is plenteous redemption.
And he shall redeem Israel from all his sins." (Psalm 130, verses 7–8)

Especially significant in the dialogue between God and man is the word "thy." The regular use in the Psalms of the intimate "thou," "thy," is found nowhere else in the profiles of any other system. It is the most eloquent, yet also the most concise, affirmation of Chosen People status.

The Good Shepherd

In their eternal dialogue with him, whether appealing on behalf of the nation (Psalm 44, verses 10–26) or on the Psalmist's own individual behalf (Psalm 139, verse 5), the Psalmists often found God's ways to be inscrutable. All would endorse the sentiment of the author of Psalm 77:

"Thy way is in the sea and thy paths are in the great waters: and thy footsteps are not known." (Psalm 77, verse 19)

But although God's ways were inscrutable, God's final character always showed itself in grace, mercy and redemption.

In spite of slavery in Egypt, God had led his chosen people to deliverance (Psalms 78, 81,105). Out of Babylonian Exile (Psalm 137) God had engineered the Return (Psalm 126). In spite of deserved punishment because of the Chosen People's idolatries (Psalm 78, verses 57–65; Psalm 106, verses 34–43), in the last resort God's mercies had prevailed (Psalm 78, verses 66–73; Psalm 106, verses 44–45).

The final and most appropriate image with which this agrarian people would therefore characterise their relationship with God was as a flock of dumb sheep under the feeding and guiding protection of a knowing and merciful shepherd.

"He is the Lord our God: and we are the people of his pasture, and the sheep of his hand."   (Psalm 95, verse 7)
"We are his people: and the sheep of his pasture"   (Psalm 100, verse 2)

With a sure instinct, later imagination has seized upon Psalm 23 as encapsulating the relationship between the nations, the individual, Israel and Israel's God. Essentially his purposes and being are beyond human understanding. He leads sometimes through perils, disasters and the valley of the shadow of death. Nevertheless, he is his people's Shepherd, and their good and their vindication are his final objective.

His "way may be in the sea and his paths in the great waters." His "footsteps may not be known"   (Psalm 77, verse 19).

Even so:

"Thou leddest thy people like sheep: by the hand of Moses and Aaron"   (Psalm 77, verse 20)

An Awesome Future

In October 63 BC, had the Roman general Pompey penetrated the Jerusalem Temple and its surroundings; had he observed the Jewish Feast of Tabernacles and found opportunity to acquaint himself with the Psalter; had he, furthermore, been endowed, like the Sibyl of Cumae, with visions of prophecy, he would have gazed with speechless and uncontrolled amazement upon the events of the seventeen decades that were shortly to follow, "by the hands of" Augustus and Trajan!

The Dates of the Psalms

Nowadays, many people no longer believe that all the Psalms were written by David (1,000–960 BC). Attempts to discover the dates of individual Psalms are however, wildly controversial, often whisking from century to century. The suggestions offered in this Appendix can only be approximate. The left-hand column shows the number of each Psalm quoted in the chapter "Thirteen Centuries of Song;" the right-hand column is the suggested date.

3	700–601 BC
23	400–301 BC
31	200–120 BC
33	520–320 BC
34	200–120 BC
39	300–201 BC
44	200–120 BC
51	500–401 BC
60	800–701 BC
67	520–320 BC
77	300–201 BC
78	200–120 BC
81	700–601 BC
86	520–320 BC
89	620 BC
95	520–501 BC
98	520–501 BC
100	520–501 BC
104	1,370 BC
105	200–120 BC
106	200–120 BC
117	200–120 BC
119	300–201 BC
126	520–501 BC
130	200–120 BC
132, verses 1–10	1,000–960 BC
132, verses 11–19	200–120 BC
137	600–550 BC
139	300–120 BC
147	200–120 BC
148	200–120 BC

14–32
(A)–(S)

The "Long" First Century AD
(50 BC–AD 120)

14

(A)

The "Decade" of the Assassination of Julius Caesar (50–43 BC)

The Law of Unintended Consequences

Prominent among the reasons for the faltering of the late Roman Republic in the second and first centuries BC had been the outbreak among the noble or powerful families of Rome of internal contention for single dominance over the whole state and its empire. By 50 BC, there were left in supreme competition only two sets of families and supporters, those surrounding Gnaeus Pompeius Magnus (Pompey), and those surrounding Julius Caesar.

The 50s BC had been spent by Julius Caesar in Gaul, adding by conquest to the domain of Rome's widening territories, realms as far off as the shores of the North Sea. Pompey meanwhile, having returned from the East, remained in Rome, even closer than Julius Caesar to the levers of power.

As the year 49 BC approached, Julius Caesar made a decision to stand again for election to the consulship. This produced however what would in modern times be called a "Catch 22" situation.

Julius Caesar held proconsular office as governor of Cisalpine Gaul, Gaul and Illyricum. But under the Roman constitution, every candidate for election to any office had to present himself before the electorate as a private citizen. Caesar knew that as soon as he surrendered the governorship of Gaul and reverted, for purposes of election, to private citizen status, he would lose political immunity and be open to prosecution by Pompey or other enemies upon whatever charge they might choose to contrive.

It was therefore imperative for Caesar to stand for election without reverting to private citizen status; and for his opponents to insist that, unless he accepted relegation to private citizen status, in conformity with constitutional law, he could and should not stand for election.

Julius Caesar therefore made another momentous decision. Rather than sacrifice the governorship of Gaul and his proconsular standing (thereby forfeiting his immunity to prosecution), on 10th January 49 BC he crossed the river Rubicon and thereby declared war on the Senate and People of Rome – Civil War! Never in the whole of ancient time was the law of unintended consequences so dramatically and fatefully fulfilled.

Caesar's action on 10th January 49 BC led to the Civil War; his victory; his Dictatorship; his assassination; to the fall of the late Republic and the republican constitution; to the transition to the Roman Empire; to the Roman imperial conquest of Spain, Germany, Britain, the Balkans and the Danube; to the clamping of Roman authority upon Greece, Asia, Syria, Egypt and North Africa; to the establishment of Roman ways and civilisation by the Roman army, by imperial religion, by urbanisation, by literature, by building, by architecture and by political peace. All this, unforeseen by Julius Caesar, developed in the 170 years following 50 BC – the "long" first century AD. There was also one other thing that Julius Caesar did not foresee. Impressed as he was by his young great-nephew Gaius Julius Octavius, he did not foresee that this native Italian talent, born into and being nurtured within his own family, would mature into one of the most consummate, phenomenal and effective political geniuses in the history of the whole world.

The Assassination of Julius Caesar

In the first moves of the Civil War, during the years 49–48 BC, the consuls and Pompey fled in March 49 BC from Italy to Greece. Instead of pursuing, Julius Caesar turned unexpectedly westwards to Spain. In August 49 BC, having superficially subdued Spain, he returned to Rome and presided over consular elections, at which he was himself elected. Only then did he set off to Epirus in western Greece in pursuit of Pompey.

Greece became the theatre of Civil War in the following year, 48 BC. First Caesar surrounded Pompey on the west coast of Greece at Dyrrachium. When Pompey eluded the encirclement, Caesar defeated him finally and comprehensively on 9th August 48 BC at Pharsalus. Pompey fled to Egypt, where he was murdered. Upon the defeat and death of Pompey the Senate in Rome were left with little other choice than to elect Julius Caesar to the post of Dictator for a year.

The ancient, early Republican practice of electing a Dictator only occurred in extreme emergency, when it was generally considered expedient to lay the destiny of the whole city in peril into the hands of a single talented and trusted leader. It was the custom also for the Dictator to nominate his own second-in-command, or "Master of the Horse." Upon being elected Dictator, Julius Caesar nominated his existing lieutenant, Mark Antony, as "Master of the Horse" and then sailed for Egypt. He arrived at the port of Alexandria on 2nd October 48 BC. Egypt would hardly seem to be the place for a Dictator elected for purposes of emergency in Rome. In fact, the period of Julius Caesar's Dictatorship was unlike any other example of this ancient and rare office. He was suppposed to remain Dictator from October 48 BC to October 47 BC, but instead he held the post almost for the rest of his life.

Six months after his first Dictatorship ended, he was again elected, in April 46 BC, Dictator this time for ten years. This time he appointed Marcus Aemilius Lepidus as his "Master of the Horse." He was assassinated before he could celebrate the second anniversary of this, his second, ten-year, Dictatorship.

During this time he was seldom in Rome, but was instead in all corners of the Roman Republic's domain. In fact, the amount of time spent in Rome during his second Dictatorship was only from July to December 46 BC, and from October 45 BC until his assassination on the Ides (15th) March 44 BC – fractionally over one half of the total period. His exploits during the years of his two Dictatorships need to be summed up in diary form:

OCTOBER 48 BC to MARCH (or JUNE) 47 BC
Caesar in Egypt. His liaison with Cleopatra. The Alexandrian War or "Bellum Alexandrinum" in which part of the great Library of Alexandria, nearly three hundred years old, was burned to the ground (March 47 BC)

MARCH (or JUNE) 47 BC to SEPTEMBER 47 BC

Caesar in Pontus. His defeat of Pharnaces II, king of the Cimmerian Bosporus at the battle of Zela, scene of the famous throw-away line "Venit, vidi, vici" – "I came, I saw, I conquered." Birth to Cleopatra at the end of June 47 BC of her son by Julius Caesar; his naming "Caesarion."

SEPTEMBER to DECEMBER 47 BC

Caesar in Rome. His first Dictatorship ends in October.

25th DECEMBER 47 BC to JULY 46 BC

Renewed attention to the Civil War. Caesar in Africa for the African War or "Bellum Africanum." At the battle of Thapsus (February 46 BC) enemy resistance is broken. Caesar elected Dictator for ten years in the April of 46 BC

JULY to DECEMBER 46 BC

Caesar in Rome. His triumph, in September, over Gaul, Egypt, Pontus and Africa. Arrival in Rome of Cleopatra and Caesarion.

DECEMBER 46 BC to OCTOBER 45 BC

Caesar in Spain for the final stages of the Civil War. His victory at Munda in March 45 BC marks the formal closure of the Civil War, which had begun with the crossing of the Rubicon on 10th January 49 BC

In the course of this phase, in SEPTEMBER 45 BC, Caesar writes a will making his great-nephew Gaius Julius Octavius (born 20th September 63 BC), his heir. Octavius sent off about this time with M. Vipsanius Agrippa and other friends to military finishing academy in Apollonia, Greece. Caesar returns to Rome via Narbo and north Italy. Although already Dictator, elected, with Mark Antony, consul for the year 44 BC

OCTOBER 45 BC to 15th MARCH 44 BC

Caesar in Rome. He is assassinated on the Ides (15th) March, 44 BC by a conspiracy of republican die-hards. Cleopatra and Caesarion flee to Egypt.

In this bald diary of events is reflected to this day, in fact, the distant resumée of a collapsing thunder. Among other remarkable feats and events of the times, Julius Caesar proved to be the only one with a time-table sufficiently crowded for it to be conveniently presented in diary form; and the only Roman Republican to stand as far west as the shores of Britain, and as far east as Zela in Pontus.

The Second Triumvirate

Following the assassination of Julius Caesar, it was the mother of Octavius who sent first news of the event to the 18-year old heir in Apollonia. Without delay, Octavius set out for Rome to claim his inheritance and to avenge the great-uncle who was also his father by adoption.

He arrived early in May 44 BC. There seems little doubt that behind his overt objective to assert his legal claim to Julius Caesar's bequest, there was also in his mind some ambition to claim also Caesar's political inheritance. In pursuing this, he was destined also to inherit Caesar's travelling, fighting, and eventually governing, agenda.

Octavius arrived in Rome as an unknown quantity, and stepped into the turmoil of a situation where neither the Senate, nor consul, official, nor magisrate nor even the assassins of Julius Caesar knew where next to turn. But Octavius was, at 18, already politically perceptive and mature, ambitious and energetic, a consummate propagandist and a ruthless manager, political operator and concealer of his own motives, plans and intentions. He alone of all the Romans had in his mind at that time a clear programme for seizing the initiative within the prevailing confusion.

He began by persuading the Senate to validate formally his own right to Caesar's inheritance and his status under Caesar's will as his legitimate heir. It was a natural and sensible legal platform, but it was also the strategic stroke of an opportunist and an intuitive practitioner of propaganda.

In consequence of the Senatorial co-operation and declaration, Octavius took by right the name "Caesar," and with it all its favourable and positive associations in the popular mind. His new name was Gaius Julius Caesar Octavianus. Modern historians observe the formality of calling him no longer "Octavius" but "Octavian," from the moment of his assuming this name in 44 BC, until his adoption of a new propagandist title in 27 BC. Opportunist propaganda and a good admixture of adroitness outwitting all other competitors continued to roll out the red carpet of good fortune. The ascendancy of this mature and subtle youth continued during the rest of the year 44 BC to assert itself – even over the senior magistrate in Rome, the remaining consul of the year, Julius Caesar's constitutional partner and survivor, Mark Antony! By August the following year (43 BC), Octavian was now the consul, and Mark Antony a public enemy!

Under another seismic shift in that unstable era, by November 43 BC the constitution of the late Roman Republic had collapsed, the Late Republic had fallen, and Rome was governed by a Triumvirate.

This Triumvirate was not the informal arrangement of the First Triumvirate of 56 BC, some thirteen years before, but a body of three men constitutionally installed by the Senate to govern the state following the expiry of the Republican constitution. The mandate laid by the Senate upon these three men was to restore the Republic. The three men were Marcus Aemilius Lepidus, Mark Antony and Octavian.

Mark Antony had been "Master of the Horse" to Julius Caesar in his first Dictatorship of October 48 to October 47 BC. Lepidus had been "Master of the Horse" in Caesar's second Dictatorship, beginning April 46 BC. Octavian had been nominated by Julius Caesar in his will as his legitimate beneficiary and heir. Nineteen months after the assassination of Julius Caesar there was little opportunity to doubt who had won, not only the Civil War, but also the consequent peace!

15

(B)

The "Decade" of the Second Triumvirate (43–30 BC)

The Contenders

The Fathers of Rome went home from the Senate House on 27th November 43 BC having decreed, by the Lex Titia, that the constitution of the Roman Republic was for the next five years in the hands of "Tresviri Reipublicae Constitutendae" – "A Triumvirate Appointed to Restore the Republic."

The measure was merely a despairing cosmetic. Some Senators may have thought that by a clever act of constitutionalism they had resolved Rome's problems and achieved a final and lasting peace. The fact was that behind an accommodating facade, the struggle for supreme individual power over Rome was now about to rise to its climax. The detrimental dynamic of the whole first century BC was simply animating now, new and different personalities. Now that Pompey was dead, Caesar was dead and the Republic in abeyance, the number of contenders over the remnants of former glory in the next generation was no longer two, as in 50 BC, before the Civil War, but three and a half!

It is important to know the names and resources of the contenders in this ultimate competition, but above all to note where possible (as seldom in any other historical narrative), their ages!

Marcus Aemilius Lepidus was possibly the oldest of the four. He had served as city praetor (i.e. governor) in Rome, as a provincial governor in Spain, as consul in 46 BC, and in Caesar's second Dictatorship as his "Master of the Horse." In the surroundings of the Second Triumvirate however, lacking vision or any spirited ferocity, he was out of his depth. In the final eliminating rounds for the mastery of the Roman state and empire, he was the half-contender.

Mark Antony (b. 83 BC) was forty years old, and, outside the family, Julius Caesar's most favoured and able supporter. He was a strong military commander, although lacking the vision for long-term strategy, whether military or civil. He was also too ready to succumb to short-term material distractions. In his early middle age he was comfortable, established, and not without a touch of complacency and sun-baked somnolence.

Octavian (b.63 BC) was, at twenty, half Mark Antony's age. His resources included his nomination as legitimate heir of Julius Caesar and the very name "Caesar;" his sister Octavia; and two loyal friends, M. Vipsanius Agrippa and Gaius Maecenas, whose supporting qualities and acceptance of self-effacement made them arguably two of the most capable and reliable lieutenants that any leader has ever enjoyed in the annals of political history. Octavian's personal resources were also formidable. He was a long-distance strategist with an unwavering eye upon the far future and the route toward it. He had a computer-like gift of political assessment and adaptation, and a mind as calculating and ruthless as the circumstances of the era demanded. Time and again, during the decade of the Second Triumvirate, his perception, initiative and ingenuity, his judgement and improvisation, were original enough to outwit the sluggish reactions of his competitors.

Cleopatra (b. 69 BC) was 26 years old and Queen of Egypt. She was the fourth, constitutionally unrecognised, contender for the imperial crown and throne. Her resources were a driving but well-disguised ambition and a wily femininity. She had presented herself to Julius Caesar in October 48 BC as a heart-stealer of undisguised carnal actuality, as a flattering and beguiling younger woman, and she was to do the same again, in due course, with Mark Antony.

The measure of her success may be judged from the fact that Julius Caesar's son Caesarion and Mark Antony's twins Alexander Helios ("Sun") and Cleopatra Selene ("Moon") were born barely nine months after Cleopatra's first encounters with their respective fathers. No other queen in the whole of the ancient orient had been so accommodating.

Cleopatra had one further resource. She was well aware that the cost of Roman instability and civil war was economically unsustainable; she also knew that the only funds that could lift the burden of Roman state debt were lying in the treasure hoards and wealth of

Egypt. Secure in the possession and control of these, she was content in November 43 BC to play the long game, and wait.

The Second Triumvirate: The First Five Years (43–38 BC)

Cleopatra's analysis of the economy of Rome at that moment coincided with an unnerving exactitude with that of Lepidus, Mark Antony and Octavian. Their earliest measures as a Triumvirate were to proscribe, murder and make off with the estates of large numbers of leading men and families in Rome. On 7th December 43 BC, only ten days after their appointment and commission to "restore the Republic," Cicero, the foremost theoretician and advocate of the Roman Republic and its restoration, was one of the earliest to be proscribed and murdered, and his estate plundered.

The year 42 BC was likewise spent by the Triumvirate gathering forces and money by extension of the same merciless proscriptions. Towards the end of the year, Antony and Octavian crossed to Greece, and in October at two battles at Philippi crushed the remnant of the republican spirit and eliminated Brutus, the old Republic's final figurehead and the foremost among the assassins of Caesar. Following the attainment of these objectives, the Triumvirs were ready, unimpeded, to set about their constitutional mandate of "restoring the Republic" !

Their first move was to divide the Roman realm three ways between themselves. Did the Triumvirs realise how exactly their allocations matched their own personalities? The unpromising Lepidus accepted the unpromising North Africa. The world-weary and luxury-loving Antony received the venerable, wealthy and luxurious estates of the east. The west, Italy, Rome and Spain, bristling with social and economic difficulties, some of it newly or barely conquered territory, went to Octavian, bristling, with Agrippa and Maecenas, with pugnacious eagerness and business-like energy.

The only anomaly of the allocation was the grant to Antony of, in addition to the east, the province of Gaul. This was corrected in 40 BC with the timely death of the governor, Fufius Calenus, an ally of Antony, and the opportunist transfer of all its legions into the hands of Octavian.

As the 30s progressed, Antony was now to age from 40 to 50 and to feel inclined only to retire into the arms of Cleopatra; Octavian, Agrippa and Maecenas were to mature from 20 to 30, young terriers increasingly hungry for new experience and a new empire. Octavian himself, upon whom Antony might have thought that he had successfully palmed off a poisoned chalice, in the course of these 30s BC was able not only to neutralise the poison but also to convert it into an elixir of vitality.

In 40 BC the Parthians invaded from the east. It was Antony's fief and responsibility, but sending Ventidius Bassus eastwards to repel them, Antony remained for two years in Athens – not with Cleopatra, whom, following their concourse in 42 BC, he had left with twins only a few months old, but with Octavia, whom Octavian had given him to wife as part of a settlement between the two men, made at Brundisium in 40 BC in the October.

To his credit, Antony emerged from Athens to his triumviral duties in 38 BC and spent the last year of the first quinquennium of the Second Triumvirate not inactively, but following up with political settlements the victories of Ventidius Bassus. In Alexandria, Cleopatra continued to lie patiently in wait.

Meanwhile Octavian, Agrippa and Maecenas conducted Octavian's wing of the Triumvirate with pragmatic realism, businesslike vigour, and in accordance, it would seem, with an unfolding plan.

In 39 BC, while Antony on extended honeymoon with Octavia was operating through his commissary Ventidius Bassus, Octavian and Agrippa were consolidating Gaul and Italy militarily.

Maecenas was simultaneously at work contacting the poets Virgil and Horace and enlisting them in a subtle campaign of a literary nature, aimed at winning over the civil soul and loyalties of Italy.

The Second Triumvirate: The Second Five Years (38–33 BC)

In November 43 BC, the Senate had granted the Triumvirate a five-year tenure. In November 38 BC, the tenure was renewed for a second such period. Now the difference in sagacity and energy between Octavian (a. 25) and Antony (a. 45) became more obvious and divergent.

The second Quinquennium of the Second Triumvirate was transformed by Octavian into a period of stunning transition from the dead Republic into a new form of governance. Upthrust in morale, and, finally, the breath-taking originality of making every community swear a personal oath of loyalty to himself, swung the whole west solidly behind Octavian; and, from 32 BC onwards, the legal end of the Second Triumvirate, swept the whole Roman enterprise to the verge of a fresh world order and an entirely new and climactic phase of world history.

During this same second five-year period Antony's judgement slipped increasingly out of control. In 36 BC occurred his charade, the "Donations of Alexandria." At the climax of an exotic and gorgeous procession Antony solemnly conferred Egypt, Cyprus and Coile Syria upon Cleopatra (a. 33) and Caesarion (a. 11); Armenia, Media and Parthia upon Alexander Helios (a. 6); Libya and Cyrene upon Cleopatra Selene (a. 6); and Phoenicia, Syria and Cilicia upon Ptolemy Philadelphus (a. 2). For these ceremonies the children were all appropriately cutely clad, attired, no doubt, with a proud maternal hand.

If this event gave away the secret that Antony was now in thrall to the fantasies and grandiose delusions of the woman behind him, his action of 32 BC in divorcing his legal wife, Octavia, sister of Octavian, was the product of a mentality both insulting, insensitive and now entirely disengaged. While Antony had been thus languishing lack-lustre and day-dreaming in a historically stagnant east, Octavian had succeeded in realising a new vision, a new orientation, a pristine vigour and an unprecedented concentration of power in the west.

Following the Second Triumvirate

The insult to his sister in 32 BC provided Octavian with the opportunity and the excuse to strike. Taking the consulship in 31 BC he declared war, with sagacious and smart precision, not upon Antony, still a respected leading Roman fellow-citizen, but upon Cleopatra. Arriving in late summer 31 BC on Cleopatra's and Antony's favoured battle-ground in Greece, and campaigning with stunning speed, Octavian drew his naval forces face to face up against them at Actium on 2nd September. The battle of Actium was a signally inglorious defeat for Cleopatra and Antony. Cleopatra hoisted her canvas and simply sailed away. Antony followed.

The final climax and denouement of this unfinished confrontation occurred eleven months later in the first days of August 30 BC. Octavian, no longer consul, but vested this year with the influential popular office of "Tribune of the People," arrived in Alexandria on the first of the month.

Antony committed suicide. A face-to-face meeting was arranged between Octavian and Cleopatra. What was to happen as the doors closed upon this private interview?

With Julius Caesar and Mark Antony, Cleopatra had been able to play successfully the seductive part of the younger woman who is the fulfilment of every middle-aged male fantasy. For the younger Octavian (a.33), Cleopatra, (now a. 39), held all the attractive allure of an ageing tart.

How the dialogue between them went, nobody knows. For over a century afterwards, fanciful representations of the exchange were to be one of the favourite themes for training of the imagination in the schools of rhetoric in Rome. All we know is that when the dust settled on 10th August 30 BC, Gaius Julius Caesar Octavianus, a modest tribune of the Roman people, was discovered clasping the key to the treasure-house of Egypt; Cleopatra, to her bosom, the asp.

And whereas "Caesar and Cleopatra" and "Antony and Cleopatra" will for ever be suggestive of whirl-wind, earth-shaking romance, the title "Octavian and Cleopatra" is a non-starter and a contradiction in terms.

16

(c)

The First Decade of Augustus: The Restoration of the Republic (30–21 BC)

Octavian and Destiny

Octavian at the age of 33 had now reached the major turning-point of his career and life. It was a life that had already experienced more critical turning-points, and at younger ages, than any great personality in ancient history before him – Tuthmosis III, Agamemnon, David, Cyrus the Great, Alexander the Great, or even Julius Caesar.

Smoothed over by the passage of time, each stage of his life seems today to have rolled out successively in accordance with a premeditated programme. He had arrived in Rome in May 44 BC at the age of 18 as an unknown, but eighteen months later he was a consul and a Triumvir!

By the end of the first five-year period of the Second Triumvirate (43–38 BC), he had established a moral and a material ascendancy over Antony. By the end of the second five-year period (38–33 BC), Lepidus was nowhere to be seen and Octavian held Antony in a stranglehold.

To finish off Cleopatra and Antony in 30 BC, he had taken the post of a magistrate no senior than Tribune of the People – but the fact was that for statecraft, authority and seasoned experience, no other candidate in Rome could now approach or emulate him. His position as Tribune of the People was one of the most signal examples of Octavian's statecraft.

The Tribunate had been an office which had caused great turbulence in Rome in the opening decades of the first century BC. Sulla had abolished it, Pompey and Crassus had reinstated it, and both with equal lack of success. Octavian took it up – even embraced it – but with the two differences that unlike previous political figures, he solved the associated problems by exercising the office himself; and unlike previous Tribunes of the People he held the status not for a single year, but for life. He thus neutralised this controversial power and within a short time was able to use it to achieve dominance over all Roman home policy.

In the winter of 30-29 BC Octavian did what he had probably done at all previous crucial turning-points of his public career. He went into conference with Agrippa, Maecenas, and perhaps with his sister Octavia, to map out the projects and priorities for the future. The agenda this time was portentous and large.

Within Rome the mutually destructive senatorial rivalries which had brought the Republic to its knees were not yet extinguished; its hundreds of thousands of population needed feeding; there were issues of matrimony and citizenship to be resolved; the city itself was architecturally undistinguished. Other difficulties threatened the Italian peninsula. The swollen armies of the Civil War period and after needed to be reduced by demobilisation; men needed to be paid off and veterans settled; money and lands needed to be found.

Abroad, the boundaries of Roman rule were indistinct and needed to be fixed; peoples encroaching upon the eastern lands and provinces needed to be accommodated; within the boundaries, potentially unruly tribes and forces needed to be controlled.

Here were at least eleven formidable, overwhelming issues. Whoever was to tackle them would need to have much public favour; a firm grip upon home policy; upon foreign policy; upon state finances; and an effective propaganda machine. Yet of these five requirements, Octavian perceived himself to be in possession already of four.

There was immense war-weariness throughout the old Republic, and universal desire for a peace which only he himself was in a position to secure.

Holding for life the power of a Tribune of the People ("Tribunicia Potestas"), he would always be the senior partner in the determination of home policy.

Having acquired through his worsting of Cleopatra the wealth of Egypt, he took steps to be sure that no individual of senatorial rank should ever set foot in the province again.

As in the twentieth and twenty-first centuries AD, every revolutionary movement headed first for the broadcasting stations, so through Maecenas Octavian had already signed up all the poets, historians and writers. It only remained therefore to consolidate a hold upon foreign policy.

This was the social, economic and political situation facing Octavian on 11th August 30 BC at his emergence upon the unchallenged summit of moral authority. In the winter of 30 BC and the spring of 29 BC he must have considered with his closest confidants both distant solutions to all the problems that the immediate situation presented, and routes towards these solutions. For example, a conquest of Spain would solve four problems at once. It would subjugate the province; it would occupy the energies of military men; it would provide land for their veterans to settle; it would also bring into possession of Rome the wealth of the gold, silver and mineral mines of that peninsula, to supplement the coffers of Egypt.

Thus in this winter of 30–29 BC seed decisions would have been made about the boundaries of the future empire and the techniques of its control. Octavian was to spend the rest of his life pursuing the policy decisions of these crucial months resolutely to their conclusion.

For the decade 30–21 BC, the First Decade of Augustus, (for such was the name conferred upon Octavian by senatorial decree on 16th January 27 BC), it now becomes informative to focus attention upon the honours given to Augustus; the journeys taken by Augustus and his location year by year; and the illnesses suffered by Augustus.

It is noteworthy that no other single decade in human history before had ever concentrated so fixedly upon one individual, his decisions and his destiny.

There now culminated in the person of Augustus not only the hopes of the dying Roman Republic, but also all the social, geographical, imperial and historical dynamics of the ancient world. When, over four decades later, he was finally released from the burden of these responsibilities, Augustus by his work, his endurance and his decisions had laid some of the deepest foundations of the modern world.

The Honours of Augustus

Fourteen honours were conferred upon Octavian on his return to Rome in August 29 BC, of which the most meaningful to us might be his three triumphs on consecutive days: on 11th August for Dalmatia; on 12th August for Actium; and on 13th August for Egypt. At these triumphs the consuls and existing magistrates of Rome, abandoning the custom of preceding the chariot of the victorious commander at his triumph, meekly followed behind it.

Ten honours followed in the years 28–27 BC, including the name "Augustus" and – the first lasting impingement of Augustus upon the modern world – the alteration of the name of the month "Sextilis" to "Augustus."

Seven more honours were conferred in the rest of the decade, including the right to move the first formal motion at any meeting of the Senate and, at last, in 23 BC, the "Imperium Proconsulare Maius" ("Overarching Proconsular Authority") for life. For reasons buried deep in the constitutional practice of the old Republic, this authority placed in his hands the one missing lever of control – a firm grip, formally ratified, over Roman foreign policy.

The Movements and the Health of Augustus

It is important for this transitional phase of Republic to Empire (which to the Senate and people was publicly disguised and represented as the "Restoration of the Republic"), to observe where Augustus was throughout this decade, and what was the state of his health.

Between 30 and much of 29 BC he was in the east, where he remained until August 29 BC, when he returned home for his triumphs. He remained in Rome for the whole of 28 BC, in a year when, for the first time in twenty-two years, both consuls (he and Agrippa) were in Rome together for their whole year of office. In this year, he and Agrippa in concert carried out a review of the Senate and reduced its membership from 1,000 to 800.

Common sense now dictated that in addition to the revenue stream of the Egypt of the late Cleopatra, some other rich source of natural wealth should be available to the rulers in Rome. In 27 BC therefore, having been granted a province and Proconsular Authority ("Imperium Proconsulare"), Augustus set out in the month of August for Spain. He arrived in January 26 BC, and remained in Spain throughout the year.

In 25 BC he marked the conquest of Spain with the foundation of the city of Augusta Emerita (Merida), whose walls to this day – the second lasting impingement of Augustus upon the modern world – declare a mighty asseveration of his imperial intentions. Only late in 25 BC did Augustus return to Rome.

He remained in Rome throughout 24–23 BC In 22 BC, having refused the posts of dictator and consul-for-life, but having settled famine in Rome, he departed again, this time to the east. He did not return until 12th October 19 BC. All the achievements of Augustus throughout this decade of transition from Republic to Empire, were attained in defiance of chronic problems with his health. On his arrival at the port of Brundisium from the east in 29 BC, he was sickly, not for the first time, and before he could travel to Rome for his three triumphs, he had to rest and recuperate. On this occasion, famously, the poet Virgil read to Octavian his newly composed "Georgics."

From late in his consulship in 28 BC (from September) Augustus was ill until May 27 BC. On arrival in Spain (26 BC) he was taken ill again and may have continued so throughout 25 and into 24 BC. He was ill throughout 23 BC, being so bad at the climax that he did not expect to survive. After 23 BC he seems to have improved, and for the rest of his life (he died in AD 14) Augustus seems to have had only one serious further deterioration, in 6 BC. What was the nature of Augustus's ailments? Although lacking the historical perspective of us, his modern observers, Augustus must have been aware, from his very name and status, that he stood on a dizzy eminence of power, responsibility and loneliness which had been experienced by no other ruler of Rome, perhaps by no other ruler of men, before him. The Angst of his situation may had produced its psychological reactions within him. Physical symptoms were present, but one may suspect that the underlying condition was what a modern physician might diagnose as some category of "depression."

Summary of the Decade

By the end of the decade Augustus and Agrippa had revised and purged the Senate in 28 BC and in two successive steps in 27 BC and 23 BC, abolishing the Triumvirate and all memory of its works, had "restored the Republic" to the Senate and people of Rome.

In other words, by engineering the grants of "Tribunicia Potestas" and "Imperium Proconsulare" they had together installed Augustus as controller of home and foreign policy, head of the Senate and Imperator ("emperor"). The building policy of Augustus and Agrippa was at the same time transforming the material and architectural aspects of the city of Rome.

What further remained for their attention? In foreign policy, the eastern infiltrators, and the settlement of the northern boundaries to the empire; and in domestic policy, the moral front.

Unforeseen, there were also circumstantial pressures which were shortly to bring the younger members of Augustus's family to the fore. In parallel with the transition from Republic to Empire, circumstances were also to transform what had begun as Octavian's Republican (and nuclear) family into Augustus's Imperial (and extended) dynasty.

17
(D)

The Second Decade of Augustus: The Ascendancy of Augustus (20–11 BC)

The Family of Augustus

In 23 BC Augustus at the climax of his worst bout of illness, nearly died. Augustus, furthermore, had no son. These two reminders of the perils and the tragedy of mortality rivetted the attention of Augustus, as they have of posterity ever since, upon his family – his wife, his daughter, his step-sons, his most prominent niece, and his grandsons.

As Augustus himself in his first decade (30–21 BC) had been transformed from Octavian the Tribune into Augustus the Emperor, so now, as the members of the younger generation grew older, they were in his second decade (20–11 BC) inducted and integrated into imperial duties, and were also shuffled about in attempts to procreate a dynasty.

Livia Drusilla was the wife of Augustus. She was, in fact, his second wife. In 40 BC he had married Scribonia and by her had had, in 39 BC, one daughter, Julia. In 38 BC, he divorced Scribonia, and with eyebrow-raising haste married in January the also divorced Livia. Livia came to Octavian with one son, Tiberius, born in 42 BC, and fathered by her first husband, Tiberius Claudius Nero. Shortly after their marriage she also bore Drusus (b. 38 BC), who was accepted as the genuine son of Tiberius Claudius Nero and blood-brother of Tiberius. Livia remained a faithful wife and behind-the-scenes confidant to Augustus throughout his principate.

She had no further children, and she died fifteen years after Augustus in AD 29.

Julia (b. 39 BC) was the daughter and only child of Augustus. Her mother had been the discarded Scribonia. In 25 BC at the age of 14 she was married to Marcellus (a. 18), nephew of Augustus and son of his sister Octavia. Julia and Marcellus were therefore cousins. In the year of Augustus's most severe illness (23 BC), it had been in fact the far younger Marcellus who had died leaving Julia a 16-year old widow. In 21 BC, Julia was obliged to marry Augustus's lieutentant Agrippa (who was required to divorce Marcella, his wife and Julia's sister-in-law, for the privilege).

By Agrippa, Julia had three sons and two daughters in a period of nine years. On the death of Agrippa in 12 BC, Julia was then obliged in the next year to marry her step-brother Tiberius. By immoral behaviour she incurred banishment in 2 BC, disillusioned, no doubt, by her father's meddlings. She died in AD 14.

Tiberius (b. 42 BC) was the elder son of Livia and her first husband Tiberius Claudius Nero, and was the step-son of Augustus. He married Vipsania, daughter of Agrippa, but was required by Augustus in 11 BC to divorce her in order to marry Augustus's own twice-widowed daughter Julia (above). Augustus began to introduce Tiberius to public duties by taking him with him on his tour of the east (22–19 BC). Tiberius was never Augustus's favourite as a potential successor. Nevertheless, longevity decreed that in the year when that necessity arose (AD 14), Tiberius was the only feasible and credible survivor. He became therefore the second Roman Emperor, and he died in March, AD 37.

Drusus (b. 38 BC) was the blood-brother of Tiberius and the younger son of Livia and Tiberius Claudius Nero, but he was brought up entirely in the household of Augustus. He married the younger Antonia (b. 36 BC), the daughter of Mark Antony and Augustus's sister Octavia, and therefore Augustus's niece. By Antonia, Drusus had two sons and a daughter. The elder son, Germanicus, became father of the emperor Caligula (AD 37–41). The younger son, Claudius, became himself the fourth Roman emperor (AD 41–54) in succession to Caligula, his nephew.

Drusus himself died on the river Elbe in 9 BC. The younger Antonia, (b. 36 BC, and wife of Drusus (above)), was the daughter of Mark Antony and Octavia and was Augustus's most prominent niece. It was her destiny to be niece to the first emperor, sister-in-law to the second, grand-mother of the third and mother of the fourth.

Antonia the Younger: The View from her Boudoir

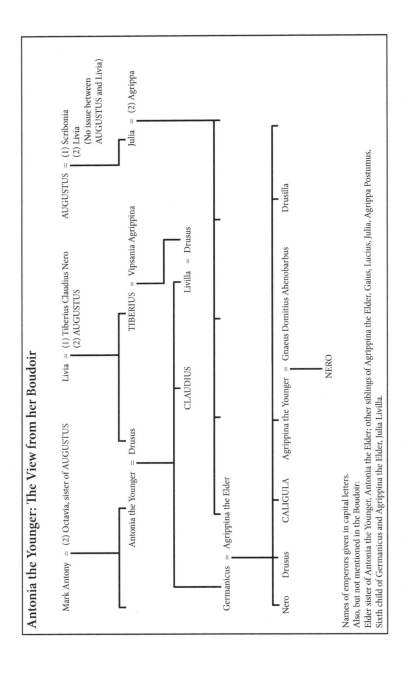

Names of emperors given in capital letters.
Also, but not mentioned in the Boudoir:
Elder sister of Antonia the Younger, Antonia the Elder; other siblings of Agrippina the Elder, Gaius, Lucius, Julia, Agrippa Postumus,
Sixth child of Germanicus and Agrippina the Elder, Julia Livilla.

Following the death of her husband in 9 BC, she enjoyed from the age of 27 a comfortable and indeed charmed widowhood, unaffected by any of Augustus's dynastic aspirations or interferences. She died six weeks after her brother-in-law Tiberius in April AD 37.

Gaius (b. 20 BC) and Lucius (b. 17 BC) were the first two sons of Augustus's daughter Julia following her marriage to Agrippa in 21 BC They were the first two grandsons of Augustus and his premier delight, and were adopted by him as his own sons in 17 BC. As such, they held precedence over Tiberius and Drusus, and there was no doubt about the intentions that Augustus entertained for them. Unfortunately, Lucius died at Marseilles in AD 2 at the age of only 19, and Gaius, (a. 24) in AD 4 in the east.

One sign of the contracting exclusiveness of Augustus and his dynasty ran conspicuously through this decade. Lucius Cornelius Balbus enjoyed a triumph for his victories in Africa in March 19 BC. Never again thereafter was such a triumph granted to any non-member of the imperial family.

The Family Legislation of Augustus

These brief notices do not complete the catalogue of the valorous, or the sexually eccentric, performances of the members of the house of Augustus. In spite of the latter, in 18 BC Augustus, solemnly invested with four different appropriate civic and legal offices, began to initiate the social measures which had probably been for a long time part of his purpose.

First, as they had done exactly ten years before, he and Agrippa again carried out a review of the composition of the Senate. Augustus then inaugurated detailed and significant social legislation.

All the so-called "Julian Laws" ("Leges Juliae") on elections, law-courts, public morality and above all against adultery and in promotion of marriage, were then carried out also in 18 BC. In 17 BC was also passed a law (the "Lex Junia") on the status of freedmen (formally liberated slaves) and of other slaves set free in an informal manner. This raft of social legislation was further emphasised and celebrated by holding for ten days, from 31st May 17 BC, the "Secular Games" ("Ludi Saeculares").

The "Secular Games" which were intended to mark the intro-duction of a new era ("saeculum"), had been held regularly in the Roman Republican past at intervals of 100 or 110 years. They had been established, and their ritual prescribed, in the ancient books of the oracles of the Sibyl of Cumae; and they were due for celebration again, so the public were told, in the year we designate as 17 BC. Augustus had a great penchant for communicating with the population of Rome through games, spectacles, processions, publicity and celebrations; and the revolution of the long, slow cycle of years back to a new start was an ideal symbol with which to underline social legislation, to bring together in participation the whole corporate population of Rome, and to engrave in the popular mind the notion of a purified new beginning to the whole state and empire.

Augustus Abroad

In foreign policy it had been the intention of Augustus and Agrippa, probably from as long before as 30 BC, to define and regularise the eastern and northern boundaries of Roman rule. The Second Decade of Augustus at last supplied the opportunity to attend to these imperatives. Indeed, Augustus began his second decade in the east.

Thirty-three years before, in a humiliating disaster at Carrhae, the consul Crassus had been killed and the Roman legionary standards had been carried away into enemy Parthian possession.

Augustus now, in 20 BC, successfully negotiated with Phraates IV, king of Parthia, for the return to Rome of these and other standards, and the symbolic cancelling out, therefore, of the disgrace of their original capture.

Tiberius meanwhile, under Augustus, worked on the establishment of Augustus's chosen candidate, Tigranes, as king of Armenia. Agrippa, independently, was quelling disturbances in Gaul, in Germany along the Rhine and, in 19 BC, in north-west Spain.

For the social legislation and the Secular Games of 18–17 BC, all three returned to Rome.

The Games over, the senior leaders fanned out again, exchanging their directions. In 16 BC Agrippa began a three-year tour of the east, and Augustus a three-year tour of the west. Tiberius (a.26) and Augustus's younger step-son Drusus (a. 22) were elected respectively praetor and quaestor (two lesser Roman magistracies) and remained in Rome.

Agrippa's tour of the east was largely supervisory, although he was offered on his return to Rome (and refused) a triumph for his success in settling the Bosporan kingdom. In 15 BC in Jerusalem he was generously entertained by a self-serving Roman client king who went by the name of Herod the Great. Later, in the year of his return home (13 BC) Agrippa was deployed to Pannonia. In 12 BC he took a period of convalescence in Campania and there, abruptly, in March, he died!

In the west, the establishment by Augustus at Lugdunum (Lyon) of a mint in 16 BC and an altar of the three Gauls to "Rome and Augustus" (the latter in 12 BC under the auspices of Drusus), indicated together the pacification of Gaul. Between 15 and 12 BC Tiberius and Drusus, having come out from Rome when the year of their office (16 BC) was over, were on regular raids and expeditions both into Bavaria and beyond the Rhine. In 13 BC Drusus was confirmed as "Legate of the Three Gauls." Following the death of Agrippa in 12 BC, Tiberius was transferred to the Pannonian frontier.

In 17 BC the Secular Games had commemorated the completion of a programme of social legislation. A significant achievement in the more untidy military arrangements was highlighted by a senatorial decree of 4th July 13 BC for the erection of an "Altar of Peace." (Carved panels of the "Altar of Peace" or "Ara Pacis" decreed July 13 BC, dedicated 30th January 9 BC, survive to this day as a vivid source for the history and art of Augustan Rome.) Gaul and Spain were now reduced to quiescence. It remained to turn to the northern frontier, and in 13 BC fifteen legions were brought up to mass there.

Summary of the Decade

By the end of his second decade, Augustus had sadly lost both his sister Octavia and his lieutenant Agrippa. At the age of 50 plus, he was not disposed to undertake lengthy provincial tours once again, but having advanced his family to dynastic status, he was now able to work through the younger generation, and principally through his step-sons.

While in many ways during this decade the smoke concealing the transition from Republic to Empire had drifted and the mirrors had been discreetly moved away, there had been an emphasis throughout these years on solid government. For half the time Augustus and Agrippa may have been away from home on foreign missions, but the social legislation needed for the majority of the citizenry of Rome and Italy, and for the status of their citizenship, had not been neglected.

The ascendancy of Augustus and his dynasty however, was not without its unforeseen cost in wider public life. There began to appear within the former governing classes the symptoms of a complacency, an unhealthy apathy and a lack of ambition in the face of this ascendancy.

In 17 BC Augustus had to increase fines for non-attendance at the Senate. In 11 BC the quorum for passing a valid motion in the Senate had to be reduced. Above all, there was in 12 BC such a shortage of qualified candidates for the Tribunate – that former storm-centre of Republican vendetta – that candidates of the lower, equestrian, order had to be forced into the posts!

18

(E)

The Third Decade of Augustus: The Splendid Isolation of Augustus (10–1 BC)

A Generation Hands on the Torch

For twenty years, from 30 BC onwards, Augustus, Agrippa, Maecenas, Octavia, perhaps a small group of associate advisers, had had two objectives for the Roman Republic.

The first had been to hand the Republic back to the Senate and People and maintain it in social tranquillity. The achievement of this target was signified and celebrated by the Secular Games of 17 BC. The second objective had been to pacify the peoples under the Republic's sway. With respect to Spain and Gaul, this was counted as attained by the decree of the "Altar of Peace" in 13 BC, the Altar itself (the "Ara Pacis") being completed and inaugurated in 9 BC. All that remained was to consolidate the Rhine/Danube frontier along the northern boundary, and to maintain agreement with the Parthians in the east.

In achieving so much in his first two decades, Augustus had done almost too well. His sister Octavia and his senior adviser Agrippa had died towards the end of the period. Maecenas had fallen out of favour and was to die in 8 BC. Augustus had no son and heir of his own body. He was obliged artificially to piece together out of grandsons and step-sons the best dynasty that he could.

The very formation of that dynasty was evidence that in another way Augustus had done too well. He had been sole ruler – although the constitutional reality was thinly disguised – for twenty years, yet he remained both popular and, with little exception, virtually unchallenged. Under his ascendancy the other members of the former ruling class had begun to become dependent. Leaving political control to Augustus and his family, they had been content to allow governmental ambition to subside.

Augustus in his third decade, his Decade of Splendid Isolation, must sometimes have begun to feel that he had overstayed his welcome. Yet the Empire (which was the former Republic) still needed to bed down; Augustus was needed both as a figure-head and active executive. He lived on and on. His journeys were fewer. The honours he received were fewer – he already had nearly all of them. His health settled down and continued for the main part to remain good; but no longer did he have contemporaries as his collaborators. From his fifties onwards, Augustus had to work with the younger generations.

The Scene in Rome

Historical sources are more threadbare about the decade 10–1 BC than about the two previous decades of Augustus.

The "Altar of Peace" inititated in 13 BC was dedicated on 30th January 9 BC. In 8 BC Augustus's "Overarching Proconsular Authority" ("Imperium Proconsulare Maius") was renewed for another ten years, and he took up again, as in 28 and 18 BC, the role of censor (reviser of the roll of the Senate) – but this time, being without the deceased Agrippa, in splendid isolation. This isolation was shortly to redouble.

In 6 BC the "Tribunician Authority" ("Tribunicia Potestas"), the organ of control over home affairs, was conferred upon the only possible candidate, Augustus's step-son Tiberius, for a period of five years. Yet immediately Tiberius travelled to the Aegean, and there in Rhodes announced his retirement from public life!

From 5 BC onwards, instead of appointing two consuls a year as the titular governors of Rome, Augustus began to reduce their year-long tenure and appoint after their premature retirement additional "suffect" consuls to take over their office. This device, over a period of years, enlarged the pool of men of consular experience available for provincial governorships and other duties of empire.

Also in 5 BC Augustus began to introduce his grandson Gaius (b. 20 BC) into public life, conferring upon him a seat in his Crown Council in 4 BC. The only honour left for Augustus himself was the title "Father of the Fatherland" ("Pater Patriae"). This was conferred upon him on 5ᵗʰ February 2 BC. The honorific address at the ceremony was spoken by the orator Marcus Valerius Messalla Corvinus, an ageing contemporary of Augustus. At Philippi forty years before he had been a general on the opposing side. The whole proceeding must have seemed faintly like an invitation to retire!

Also in 2 BC there was opened up to Lucius (b. 17 BC), grandson and adopted son of Augustus, a course of induction similar to that in 5 BC of his elder brother Gaius (above). On 12ᵗʰ May 2 BC Gaius and Lucius together presided over the dedication of the Temple of Mars the Avenger ("Mars Ultor"). It had been under construction, since it was decreed in 20 BC, to house the standards recovered by Augustus from the Parthians, and it was now at last completed.

The Empire in the West

The Romans had been interested in Spain since the third century BC. They had settled the southern coast of Gaul almost like an extension of Italy, by the end of the second century BC. It was Julius Caesar in the 50s BC who had thrust into inland Gaul and paid a reconnaisance visit to Britain. Now under Augustus Roman might began to consolidate the whole of Gaul and to press up to and beyond the Rhine and the Danube.

Augustus identified expansion on the northern frontier (Germany and the Balkans, the Rhine and the Danube) as the first foreign policy priority of his third decade. Now however, with Agrippa deceased, he had to rely upon his step-sons Tiberius and Drusus, who were, at respectively 32 and 28, no older than he had been himself during the tumultuous years of the Second Triumvirate (43–33 BC). Drusus had been allocated to Gaul in 13 BC and Tiberius posted to Pannonia in succession to Agrippa in 12 BC. In 11 BC Augustus travelled to Gaul to view the sphere of influence of his younger step-son, Drusus, and at the beginning of his third decade was found to be in Lugdunum (Lyon), inspecting the "Altar to Rome and Augustus" erected by sixty tribes of the three Gauls. No doubt he rejoiced on this visit, with Drusus and Antonia, on the birth of their younger son, Claudius. Little did he know that in welcoming this child, Augustus was also hailing his third successor as Roman emperor. He returned home in the same year.

In place of the "triumph" accorded in Republican times to a victorious general, Augustus devised instead the lower decoration "ornamenta triumphalia," which conferred upon the holder the right to possess certain of the insignia of a triumph, for life. In 12 BC these "ornamenta" were bestowed upon Tiberius for his achievements in Pannonia; in 11 BC Drusus received them for his capture of lands from the Sugambri and the Chatti. In 9 BC Tiberius pacified Illyicum and Drusus fought triumphantly to the banks of the river Elbe – but there, he died.

Whom now had Augustus to rely upon but Tiberius, Gaius (a. 11) and Lucius (a. 8)?

Tiberius was moved to the Rhine command. To the Danube and the Balkans Augustus posted his own contemporary, the veteran Sextus Appuleius, consul of 29 BC and commander in Spain and winner of a triumph as long ago as 27 BC. In 7 BC Tiberius operated against the Sugambri and was this time permitted a triumph. He received the "Tribunicia Potestas" (above) from 6 BC, but immediately went into retirement in Rhodes. The crisis precipitated by the retirement of Tiberius from public life brought on again the last bout of illness seriously suffered by Augustus. Yet searching his family, he found just one commander capable of taking over from Tiberius.

At the Conference of Brundisium in 40 BC, he had given his widowed sister Octavia in marriage to Mark Antony. As well as the prominent Antonia the Younger (b. 36 BC), the wife of Drusus, this union had previously produced, on 2nd October 39 BC, another daughter of the same name, Antonia the Elder, who in the course of time had married Lucius Domitius Ahenobarbus.

It was now to this nephew by marriage (b. 39 BC, consul 16 BC) that Augustus turned to take over command of the Rhine frontier and the offensive into Germany.

In 5 BC, Ahenobarbus constructed the "Pontes Longi" ("Long Bridges") between the rivers Rhine and Ems. In 1 BC he crossed the Elbe, reduced the Cherusci, and initiated treaties of friendship with sundry other German tribes. The Balkans meanwhile were rapidly over-run by Tiberius and his successor Sextus Appuleius, earlier in the decade. Their easily achieved quiescence was not to explode until the fourth decade of Augustus.

The Empire in the East

Good relations were maintained in the east. In 10 BC Phraates IV of Parthia sent his four sons, Vonones, Seraspadanes, Rhodapes and Phraates to live and be educated in Rome. In 8 BC Archelaus, Antipas and Philip, all sons of Herod the Great of Judaea by three different wives, were sent to Rome also to complete their education.

The death of Tigranes of Armenia in 7 BC opened disturbance again on the Parthian frontier, Augustus and Phraates IV supporting, respectively, different rivals as candidates. The succession was still unresolved when in 2 BC, Phraates IV was murdered and succeeded by Phraataces or Phraates V.

In 1 BC Gaius was empowered with the "Imperium Proconsulare Maius," the authority possessed otherwise only by Augustus himself, and was sent to expel Phraates V from Armenia and to conquer Parthia. However, Augustus remained in diplomatic correspondence with Phraates, and even while Gaius was on his journey, rapprochement was achieved before it came to blows.

It was however Herod the Great of Judaea, royal host in 15 BC of the late Agrippa, who was to become Augustus's most famed, or notorious, protegé. In 7 BC Herod ordered the execution of two of his sons, Alexander and Aristobulus, in a fit of paranoid jealousy for the protection and retention of his throne. The death of his own sons was a matter of no consequence to that senile old control freak. In 4 BC he further executed another son, Antipater, only a few days before his own death. Herod's kingdom thus fell to the first of his Roman educated sons, Archelaus (above).

So unpopular was Archelaus that in AD 6 Augustus and his inner council decided to depose him. They instituted direct rule by Rome itself. The province within which Judaea was situated was the province of Syria, and Augustus accordingly instructed the governor, Quirinius, to do for Judaea what the Romans did for every territory over which they assumed direct control – hold a census.

Perhaps near the beginning of the twelve-year period 6 BC–AD 6 the geriatric rages of Herod the Great suffered a further provocation. He sent out – no problem for a father who had recently commanded the death of three of his sons – an edict for the execution of all baby boys born or living in the town of Bethlehem, under the age of two.

From the maelstrom of this massacre there emerged just one escapee and survivor.

19

(F)

Augustus and Providence
(63 BC–AD 14)

Three Ripples and a Lucky Escape

Providence had endowed Augustus (or "Octavian" as he was called initially from virtually his first public appearance) with a supreme political ingenuity, outstripping all the manoeuvrings of his contemporaries. Privileged in his birth, and exceptionally favoured in his social and financial support, he was also able to make his opponents appear a party of incompetents. The era of the late first century in Rome needed the service of such a genius as his. Octavian alone had not only the vision, but also the practical effectiveness, to transform the expiring Roman Republic into a new-born force of empire.

He "expanded" upon the Roman scene in the second half of the first century BC in three ever-widening, rippling circles, and one lucky escape.

In the first circle, from May 44 BC to 1st January 42 BC he burst in twenty months from being a complete unknown to claimant to the title "son of god."

In the second circle from October 42 BC to August 30 BC he exploded in twelve years from the obscurity of being almost eclipsed to Saviour of the State.

In the third circle from August 30 BC to December 23 BC in seven years he both "restored" the Roman Republic and ensconced himself as emperor and esssential engine of the whole Roman empire.

The lucky escape occurred on the way, in late August 36 BC, when for a few hours after the disastrous defeat of the sea battle of Messana, Octavian in his lowest depths of despair, begged the only survivor who had escaped with him to put him to death. When morning came, his spirits lifted, and by the beginning of September his colleague Agrippa had swept the enemy, Sextus Pompeius, from the seas.

At the beginning of each of the first two circles, the impetus of Octavian was accelerated by events which only providence can contrive – four convenient deaths.

In the first circle (May 44 BC–January 42 BC) they were the deaths of his grandmother Julia (52 BC) which first brought him to the notice of his great-uncle and adoptive father, Julius Caesar; the death of Caesar himself (March 44 BC), leaving Octavian as his nominated heir; and then the deaths in April 43 BC at the battle of Mutina of both consuls for the year, Hirtius and Pansa, leaving in Rome the necessity of electing successors.

At the beginning of the second circle (October 42 BC–August 30 BC), the four convenient deaths were those of Cassius who, but for his suicide after the battle of Philippi (October 42 BC), might have been a formidable opponent in politics; of Fufius Calenus in the summer of 40 BC, which facilitated the transfer of eleven legions in Gaul into the hands of Octvian from those of Mark Antony; of Fulvia, the wife of Mark Antony; and of Marcellus, his brother-in-law, the husband of his sister Octavia.

These two timely family deaths enabled Octavian, at the Conference and Treaty of Brundisium in September 40 BC, to bestow his sister in marriage to the recently widowed Mark Antony. When Antony repudiated and later divorced Octavia, the propaganda value for Octavian was immeasurable.

These first two circles also see, in fact, the younger man comprehensively outwitting the older Mark Antony, time and again.

At their first interview in Rome in May 44 BC, Antony was abrupt and scornful towards the deferential 18-year old who presented himself as Caesar's heir and would-be avenger. Octavian played the part of a submissive, but observant, junior, and went on his way after the meeting knowing all that he wanted to know about his man – but concealing his knowledge!

Following this meeting, in two rounds Octavian worked his way from unknown heir of Julius Caesar to sole survivor and only authority in the bankrupt Roman state.

He did it by political acuteness in many diverse theatres and circumstances; by diplomacy; by ingratiation; by ruthlessness; by enigmatic self-concealment; by propaganda; by counsel of intimate friends; by decisive action; by long vision; by tenacity; by sponsor-ship; by Italian (as opposed to Roman) breadth of sympathy; by excluding Mark Antony from Italy; by support of close confidants and wider circles; by energy; by hunger for empire; by exploitation of the Roman susceptibility to superstition; by the weariness of his opponents; by the blessing of an outwitting intelligence which made his foes appear to be leaden-footed.

By such faculties and fortunes as these Octavian survived and conquered, just as, from then on, for the third circle of his expansion (30–23 BC) he was to continue to survive and, this time, to reign.

So Octavian amply filled the gaping vacuum in the poverty-stricken politics of Rome. In his first Eclogue of 38 BC Virgil wrote, "A god has made us this respite." When Octavian returned to Rome in the autumn of 29 BC Virgil was among those who met him. As he began to read to him his second composition, his "Georgics," it must have occurred to the poet that Octavian, his gifts, his arrival in the world, his deployment of his powers, his ultimate victory and his situation in 30 BC could all be nothing other than the work of providence!

The Third Ripple, August 30 BC–December 23 BC

So far, until August 30 BC, Octavian had been able to propel himself to the fore through the providential coinciding of his own superla-tive gifts with a time of depressed mediocrity within the Senate. Following the death of Cleopatra in that critical month and the emergence of himself as supreme citizen of the Roman world, he now had access to a range of pre-existing assets which he could add to his uncontestable resources.

His unparalleled human advantage was the possession of his friends, lieutenants and supporters, Agrippa and Maecenas. With them, during the winter months of 30–29 BC, he went into council and began to prepare for government. Together the three partners identified the problems of empire and tried to work out how to manage and resolve them.

Within the weakened Senate there remained still the potential of a revival of ancient political rivalries; there were swollen armies to be reduced by demobilisation; there were veterans to be paid off and resettled; there were hundreds of thousands of people within the city of Rome needing to be fed; there were problems of citizenship and matrimony within Roman society; the adornment of the capital city with architecture of suitable dignity was still far from finished; there were boundaries to be fixed to the empire; neighbours outside the eastern boundaries to be accommodated; unruly forces and tribes within the western and northern frontiers to be controlled.

The one element entirely in Augustus's favour was a universal war-weariness throughout the empire, an immense readiness to surrender into his victorious hands the mighty responsibility of lasting civil peace.

Further elements of which the colleagues were acutely aware were the two most influential constitutional powers evolved and bequeathed by the centuries of the earlier Roman Republic.

The "tribunicia potestas," or "tribunician power," had belonged since the fifth century BC to those who were elected by the common people to be their representatives at the seat and heart of government. A description of how its potentially obstructive force had arisen from the inoffensive to the uncontrollable has already been sketched out (chapters 12 and 16). Centuries before, providence had posted this ambiguous form of authority within the Roman constitution. It was there for the asking and the manipulation, and the fact that Octavian had already in 32 BC received from the Senate this "tribunician power" for life, indicates that he was aware of its flexible opportunities.

The "proconsular command" ("imperium proconsulare") was of later origin, beginning from the era when Roman power began to spread beyond the peninsula of Italy. With overseas colonies to govern, Roman consuls, following their year of office, would be deployed with quasi-consular authority to provinces which were in need of a firm and watchful hand. The legal instrument which gave a provincially governing ex-consul his authority abroad was this "imperium proconsulare." It was the exact overseas complement to the authoritatively controlling "tribunicia potestas" within Rome. It was a second form of authority, again previously installed by providence, waiting for Octavian, in his years as Augustus, to receive and wield as his own.

In 27 BC when he finally took the name "Augustus," and again in 23 BC, Augustus received from the Senate the "imperium proconsulare." In 23 BC he received it with the extended title of "maius" or "greater," indicating a seniority in the post above other proconsular or provincial governors. This authority was regularly renewed for the rest of his life.

Possessed of these two legal and legitimate entitlements, Augustus completed the third and most expansive circle (30–23 BC) of all three ripples of his enlarging influence. So abnormally long was his life for that era of primitive medicine, and so providentially was he spared, that from 23 BC onwards he still enjoyed another thirty-seven years of unassailed, benign presidency both over Roman history and over the future direction of the western world.

In 2 BC Augustus was present when his two grandsons, Gaius and Lucius, dedicated the Temple of Mars the Avenger. When forty years before he had set out to avenge the assassination of Julius Caesar, he had vowed to erect this temple. Within it he placed the despoiled Roman standards from the defeat at Carrhae (53 BC), which he had recovered by treaty from the Parthians in 20 BC. From AD 10 until the death of Augustus (AD 14), so universal was the omnipotence of the great and aged emperor that even history itself marked time, waiting for the curtain to close over his providential end.

Seven Inconvenient Deaths

Just as providence had established Augustus, in his early years, by, among other things, a series of convenient deaths, so it detained him until the age of 76 in a weary longevity by a series of inconvenient deaths – Marcellus, Octavia, Agrippa, Drusus, Maecenas, Lucius, Gaius.

He was weary because in the end he had no son of his own body to be his heir; weary because all his chosen nominees for the succession, even his grandsons, predeceased him; and weary because a complacent aristocracy was content to leave the burdens of government and empire upon his increasingly stooping and aged shoulders.

When finally in August AD 14 realisation dawned that providence was at last very shortly to release him from the bondage of his imperial governing office, there passed through both his body and his mind a shudder of grateful relief.

AUGUSTUS AND PROVIDENCE

Inheritance

From the fifth century BC	Tribunicia Potestas
From the third century BC	Imperium Proconsulare
From the first century BC	Extension of Roman citizenship to the Italian Peninsula

Early Years

63 BC, 23rd September	Birth into a well-connected Italian family Precocious intelligence with political bent
51 BC	Death of grandmother

Early Adulthood

44 BC, 15th March	Assassination of Julius Caesar Nomination as heir in Julius Caesar's will Companionship of Agrippa and Maecenas Support of older sister
44 BC, mid-July	Sponsorship for Ludi Victoriae Caesaris, Games in honour of Julius Caesar Appearance of a comet during period of these Games
44 BC, autumn	Sponsorship for purpose of bribing Mark Antony's legion
43 BC, January	Identified by Cicero as "a gift of Providence" Appointed third in command after the consuls Hirtius and Pansa
43 BC, April	Death in battle of the consuls Hirtius and Pansa
43 BC, August	Inauguration as consul; the appearance of vultures interpreted as auspicious.

Second Triumvirate

43 BC, November	Lassitude of Lepidus
42 BC, October	Suicide of Cassius
40 BC	Deaths of Fufius Calenus, Marcellus, Fulvia
38 BC	Literary support of Virgil, Horace, Livy
36 BC	"Donations of Alexandria" expose the folly of Mark Antony
36 BC, August	Survival at the sea battle of Messana

Octavian begins to make his own luck

32 BC	Desertion from Antony of Plancus and Titius, who reveal where the will of Antony is lodged
30 BC	Universal war-weariness
30 BC, August	Imperviousness to the charms of Cleopatra Acquisition of the wealth of Egypt
23 BC	Recovery from the most serious of all his illnesses, and thereafter longevity

Dates of Sundry Inconvenient Deaths

23 BC	Marcellus, son-in-law and nephew
12 BC	Agrippa, military and political adviser
11 BC	Octavia, sister
9 BC	Drusus, younger step-son
8 BC	Maecenas, literary adviser
AD 2	Lucius, younger grandson and adopted son
AD 4	Gaius, elder grandson and adopted son

Reputation and Place

Augustus has been called "one of the greatest servants of the human race."

World historians have noted, some with awe, how all Ancient History funnels down into the time and person of Augustus; and many of the influences of Modern History radiate out again, ultimately, from the same time and reign.

20

(G)

The Fourth Decade of Augustus: The Decade of the Disillusionment of Augustus (AD 1–10)

Augustus and Birth, Blood and Death

The consuls for 1 BC were Cossus Cornelius Lentulus and Lucius Calpurnius Piso. The consuls for AD 1 were Gaius Caesar, adopted son of the emperor, and Lucius Aemilius Paullus.

They served their years of office in direct continuity. Historians understand that there were no consuls for the year "O" because there was no year "O." Augustus had now passed 60 and had received every honour, authority, title, power and insignia with which the Roman people could decorate him. As long before as 28 BC he had designed plans for his Mausoleum. Now that he had seen almost every potential imperial successor die before him, he was even more aware of his mortality, and he was conscientious with extra anxiety about the succession. Should he die, he could see nobody appropriate to succeed him except for Gaius (a. 20), Lucius (a. 17) and the disaffected Tiberius (a. 42).

Neither did Augustus find that the bleak horizon was varied even by the interesting possibility of serious opposition from plotters and would-be usurpers. So far were the upper classes from being jealous of the custodianship of the Roman empire that they were content, if not willing, to leave it all to the emperor and his family. Indeed, providence itself seemed bent on allowing imperial responsibility to lie heavily upon Augustus's ageing shoulders.

In AD 2 his younger grandson and adopted son, Lucius, died. Still there remained Gaius who was steadily being introduced into the imperial order. For the purposes of negotiation with Parthia, Gaius had been invested in 1 BC with the "Imperium Proconsulare" for the provinces of the east. In AD 1, being still in the east, he entered upon his consulship, *in absentia*.

In AD 3 as the existing powers of Augustus were renewed by the Senate for another ten years, the fire departed even from the youngest successor of the pioneering generation. Of all people, Gaius wrote to Augustus presenting his resignation from public life, the 23-year old unloading the burden of empire onto the old-age pensioner! In AD 4, following wounds sustained while fighting in Armenia, Gaius died. Augustus and the Roman empire were now left with no qualified and potential successor but Tiberius, and he too for ten years had been in retirement.

Bereft even of Gaius, Augustus must have felt most acutely that the exhilaration of his early reconstruction years (44–23 BC) had by now become an ungrateful grind. Yet still he reapplied himself with grateful resolve to his duties, his city, his peninsula and his empire. Fortunately Tiberius was persuaded back into public office. As his first duty on resumption, he undertook a campaign in Germany along the river Weser.

There was no crown prince in the Roman empire. In early imperial times succession was designated by investiture with the most senior and potent pseudo-republican offices. Tiberius was marked out as the future emperor first by the "Tribunicia Potestas" for ten years, and then by adoption by Augustus as his own son – gifts conferred by Augustus in the same spirit in which they were received: *faute de mieux,* reluctantly, but for the public good.

In the same manner Augustus obliged Tiberius to adopt his nephew Germanicus, elder son of his deceased brother Drusus as his son and heir, in advance of Tiberius's own son, Drusus. The dynasty was therefore arranged as Augustus (a. 67); Tiberius (a. 46); Germanicus (a. 19).

Shortly, Germanicus was married to Agrippina, daughter of Julia and Agrippa and a direct grand-daughter of Augustus. The third and longest-lived son of Germanicus and Agrippina, the direct great-grandson of Augustus, born AD 12, assassinated AD 41, was to become the emperor Caligula.

Meanwhile Claudius, the younger brother of Germanicus, was created augur in AD 8 at the age of 18, and games were held in honour of both these brothers. In AD 10, at the age of only 23, Drusus, only son of Tiberius was advanced to the praetorship, and won the right to attend all Senate meetings. Triumphal insignia and praetorian rank were conferred upon Germanicus. The order of succession in the Roman empire was now the elderly Augustus; Tiberius, sole survivor of the next generation; Germanicus; and then the younger unknown quantities of the third generation.

By these unsatisfactory means Augustus contended, at the highest level, with the meagre and unyielding realities of blood, birth and death. Family misfortunes were not however the only cause of disillusionment of his last full decade. Other history concentrates on Rome; on home legislation for Rome and Italy; on negotiations in the east; and on war on the northern frontiers.

Augustus Slows

At home in Rome Augustus had to deal with his own advancing age and with the problems of shortage of manpower, both civilian and military.

He introduced a shortened period for the term of office of a consul, and the swearing in of "consules suffecti" or "consular substitutes," on a regular basis from AD 2 onwards. He found that people were unwilling to serve as aediles in AD 5, and he caused by means of the Lex Valeria Cornelia the formation of a committee of senators and equites ("knights"), to choose a select list, or list of "destinati," to put before the electoral assemblies of the people.

To counter shortage of military forces, the length of service of legionary troops was raised in AD 5 from sixteen to twenty years.

In this, his fourth decade, Augustus contrived to work, where he could, more through delegation to committees. His review of the Senate of AD 3 was by means of a triumvirate – "Tresviri legendi Senatus." Following a great fire in Rome in AD 6, a fire brigade, the "praefectura vigilum," was established. In the same way a military treasury ("aerarium militare"), a Corn Supply Board ("curatores frumenti") and a committee of three consular senators to regulate public expenditure, were set up in AD 6. In AD 7 followed another Board concerned with the food supply, "praefectura annonae," staffed from the equestrian order.

Problems in Armenia and Parthia continued to occupy Augustus until AD 6, but in AD 8 he established a consular committee to take over embassies.

Also in this decade Augustus's great programme of social legislation of 18 BC, twenty years before, was becoming in need of some readjustment. In AD 3 Augustus caused the Senate to pass the Lex Aelia Sentia; in AD 9 the Lex Papia Poppaea; and in AD 10 the Senatus Consultum Silanianum ("Lex" means "law").

The Lex Aelia Sentia of AD 3, by dramatically limiting the number of slaves that a master could set free during his lifetime, filled a loophole in the Lex Fufia Caninia of 2 BC, which had only curbed the number that a master could set free by his will at death.

The Lex Papia Poppaea of AD 9 adjusted the Lex Julia de Maritandis Ordinibus of 18 BC, which had been a failure in its intention to increase the birth-rate of the general population at large.

The new law offered increased incentives to marry, and held out reliefs and privileges to the mothers of three or more children.

The Senatus Consultum Silanianum of AD 10 dealt with the treatment of slaves of a master who had been murdered, but it was noteworthy primarily for its constitutional novelty. It was the first of such consular "Senatus Consulta," and seem to have come, significantly, when Augustus was featuring less and less in public life. This withdrawal of Augustus, appearing so much in his use of committees and other devices, is reflected also in his declining participation, during this decade, in negotiations with the east.

Negotiations in the East

In the east the greatest diplomatic activity concerned Parthia and Armenia. At the beginning of the decade, Augustus was heavily involved. While his grandson Gaius was negotiating in person with the Parthian Phraates V over the relationships of the Parthian and the Roman empires, Augustus was working effectively alongside him, although from Rome, by written diplomacy. In AD 4 Gaius died following fighting over the kingship of Armenia. In AD 6 Augustus supported the accession of Vonones to the throne of Parthia. Thereafter rulers of Parthia continued to succeed and replace one another without any interested participation from Augustus.

Even more in Armenia, following the death of Erato, widow of Tigranes III in AD 6, Augustus allowed an interregnum to follow until his death. The Bosporan kingdom likewise was left vacant from AD 7 until Aspergus took it over for himself in AD 10.

In Judaea Archelaus, son and successor of Herod the Great, became an embarrassment to Augustus. In AD 6 he was deposed and sent into exile and the Romans took over direct control of Judaea. They reduced it to the status of a secondary province under the governor of Syria, Quirinius and their first action, under the supervision of Quirinius, was to organise a census of Judaea.

The Military Disillusionment of Augustus

The great misfortune of Augustus, and perhaps of the whole empire, was his lack of a male heir. Kings of Parthia, or Herod the Great of Judaea, sent groups of sons to Rome to be educated at the heart of the empire. From Livia, Augustus sired nobody.

If in all other respects Augustus seems so far to have been the most fortunate of political leaders – survivor of illnesses; unthreatened by internal discontent or coup; never worsted diplomatically; never defeated militarily – one may suspect that his propaganda machine is still working effectively today. Nevertheless, part of the disillusionment of this, Augustus's fourth decade, was caused by his two first ever military reversals, the second of them a paralysing one.

In AD 6 the whole of Pannonia went into revolt. Tiberius, who was at that time campaigning successfully in Germany, was transferred back to the front which he knew (and where he was known) so well, and in three years of unremitting fighting he restored the province to order. The revolt however had had the effect of drawing Tiberius off from the north-western frontier.

It was here that occurred Augustus's greatest disaster. It seems to have been his aim to establish a line along the Elbe-Danube frontier in order to round out a coherent boundary. Marcus Vinicius opened the decade with a successful campaign and in AD 5 Tiberius advanced to the Elbe. In AD 9 however, with Tiberius diverted to Pannonia, there occurred the shattering catastrophe of the ambush and slaughter of no less than three whole legions under Quintilius Varus in the Teutoberg Forest.

In Rome the palace of Augustus was rent by his repeated cries, "Quintile Vare, legiones redde!" ("Give me back my legions!"). Thereafter Augustus took no further military initiatives.

Demoralised fatally by the loss of Varus and his legions, the old man seemed content to desist from any further expansion or adventurism. Following the dedication of the Temple of Concordia

Augusti in AD 10, it was as though he was calling it a day on his life's imperial ambitions.

The whole world too, at the same time, seemed as though it had gone into a grumbling political suspension, waiting for the 73-year old potentate to die.

21

(H)

The Decade in the Wake of Augustus (AD 11–20)

The Death of Augustus

The process of Roman transformation from Republic to Empire had at the same time transformed its principal agent, Augustus, from ruthless empire-builder and dynast to grateful and conscientious servant. Under providence his attitude and outlook had matured from youthful will-to-power to sense of national vocation. He saw himself, in his final years, as an instrument in the evolution of a coherent political organism which was both his vocation and his bride.

For Tiberius, the old-age devotion of Augustus to his empire was an obsession; the marvellous achievements of the senior generation, a burden. In the experience of Tiberius the uplift of creative leadership was cancelled out by the downdraught of disillusionment. He had opted out of the process in 6 BC, and had only been pressed back into it ten years later by necessity. Such was the unwilling partner that the infirm Augustus had to rely upon as, anticipating his approaching death, he continued to do his best to shore up the constitution, the empire and the capital city in their most vulnerable aspects.

The authority of the supreme emperor had, during his time, come to derive from a combination of two Republican constitutional offices, the "Tribunicia Potestas" and the "Imperium Proconsulare Maius." Only the emperor possessed both. In AD 13 Tiberius also was invested with both titles and offices, making him the equal of Augustus, and thus marking him, when Augustus should die, as the sole survivor, the constitutional successor and the new emperor.

Also in AD 13 Germanicus, adopted son of Tiberius, but in fact son of Tiberius's younger brother Drusus and his wife Antonia, was given a grant of "Imperium Proconsulare" and appointed supreme commander in Germany. Lucius Calpurnius Piso (consul of 1 BC) was appointed "Praefectus Urbi," senior officer with responsibility for the city of Rome.

On 11th May AD 14, Augustus performed the last great ceremony of his career and life, a "lustration" of the city of Rome. In Republican times, such a "lustration," a ritual purification of the bondaries of the city, had been performed in 70 BC. Augustus, while still Octavian, had performed it himself forty-two years later in 28 BC. By AD 14 the opportunist eye of Augustus on the calendar noticed that another forty-two years had passed.

Providence had spared him long enough to draw beneath his historic lifetime an emphatic line of conclusion. Symbolically embracing in this "lustration" not only the boundaries of the city of Rome but the boundaries of its empire, Augustus changed the ceremonial into a personal gesture of climax and farewell.

In the month of August of the same year he began to falter. He had time for a final interview with his successor Tiberius, and on 19th August AD 14 at Nola in Campania, early in the afternoon, the reins of empire passed by death into the hands of a less effervescent generation. The earliest decisions of that generation reflected at once the reality that the genius and authority of Augustus had been removed from the governing circle.

A Less Effervescent Generation

Ten years' voluntary seclusion (6 BC–AD 4) was plain indication that Tiberius (42 BC–AD 37) was to be a reluctant emperor. Upbringing in the household of Augustus had revealed to him well enough the trials and tragedies behind imperial triumphs. A hands-off administrator (though when he did intervene, heavy-handed), less of a judge of men and less of an ingenious improviser than Augustus, there rubbed off nevertheless upon Tiberius from his step-father, enough conscientiousness to try to present to the empire the best of his sclerotic mentality and limited enthusiasms.

Germanicus (15 BC–AD 19), who now stepped up to be his immediate heir, was, unlike Tiberius, innocent of any pre-imperial contrasts or Republican influences. The nephew of Tiberius through the marriage of Tiberius's deceased younger brother Drusus (39–9 BC) to Antonia the Younger (36 BC–AD 37), Germanicus came to birth when the transition from Republic to Empire was virtually accomplished. In his day, they had ceased to make them or to test them with the rigour of the previous generation.

He was the heir, but not the son, of Tiberius, who had been obliged by Augustus to adopt him over the head of his own son, also called Drusus (13 BC–AD 25). In the view of Tiberius, Germanicus did not match up to imperial standards of leadership and responsibility. His death in AD 19 was by poison.

Because of Augustus's preference for Germanicus, Tiberius's own son Drusus was destined to play a very insignificant part in the imperial scheme. His father made him a consul at his first opportunity, in AD 15, and again in AD 21. For six years, following the death of Germanicus in AD 19, Drusus enjoyed the status and prestige of emperor-in-waiting. In AD 19–20 he became, through his wife Livilla, sister of Germanicus (and therefore his own cousin), the father of twins, of whom only one, Tiberius Gemellus, survived. But by then Lucius Aelius Sejanus had already set upon the beautiful Livilla, eyes bulging with ambition and desire.

The name of this over-ambitious interloper should perhaps be appended to Tiberius, Germanicus and Drusus, the foregoing list of the three leading members of the post-Augustan imperial dynasty. Sejanus signalled a breach of etiquette and a flare of insolence which would never have occurred in Augustus's time; even more, his villainy and the horror-story of his career signified the emergence of something that had remained submerged under the Republican-coloured principate of Augustus – palace intrigue!

The emperor Augustus had always had an informal type of bodyguard without the need for formally constituted officers. One of the first acts of Tiberius in AD 14 was to put this association onto a more formal footing with the title of "Praetorian Guard." He appointed Sejanus to be, along with his father, the joint commanders of the Praetorian Guard; and later, Sejanus alone, following the departure of his father to a command in the east, to be the sole commander. Under Sejanus were to follow material improvements and advantages for the Praetorian Guard.

Meanwhile, the proximity which this post provided to the emperor and his court enabled Sejanus rapidly to observe that Livilla, the sister of Germanicus the heir, and the wife of Drusus the spare, would, if widowed, be an inestimable conquest for a thrusting and upwardly mobile adulterer. And indeed, while the unwitting Tiberius continued to place all innocent faith in Sejanus, Livilla, following the death of her brother Germanicus, accepted Sejanus into her bed.

The interplay of these four men, Tiberius, Germanicus, Drusus and the usurper Sejanus, gave the basic shape and colour to the reign, or principate, of the emperor Tiberius, the first successor of Augustus.

Augustus's Wake

Augustus was granted a public funeral early in September AD 14 and divine honours on 17th September. On 27th September occurred an eclipse of the sun, which the population deemed to be of divine significance.

At Rome, as the rule of Tiberius set out upon its way, Sejanus and his father were appointed to the posts of joint prefects of the Praetorian Guard; and on the military frontiers, Germanicus on the Rhine and Drusus in Pannonia were faced with revolts by their armies on the grounds of pay and conditions. Drusus dealt with the situation firmly and effectively.

Germanicus threw his forces across the Rhine in a diversionary tactic which was both unneccessary and ineffective. Making concessions then to the revolt of the legionaries, in AD 15 he reduced military service from twenty to fifteen years and then took his men back across the Rhine again in an invasion of the territory of the Chatti. The emperor Tiberius shortly showed his opinion of the young and reckless judgement of his heir-apparent. Military service was re-extended by him from fifteen to its former twenty years, and in AD 16 Germanicus was recalled home.

Germanicus was granted a triumph on 26th May AD 17 , and then sent by Tiberius on a mission to the east. He was accompanied by Gnaeus Calpurnius Piso and instructed to inspect and encourage Hierapolis, Sardis, Magnesia, Philadelphia and Cyme, cities which had been shattered by a recent earthquake. He was further commissioned to examine the provincial administration of Palmyra. He was forbidden, as all senators were forbidden, to enter Egypt.

Nevertheless, in AD 19 Germanicus did enter Egypt and make a cruise along the Nile.

Later in the year he returned to Syria and on 10th October at Antioch, aged 34, he died. Poison was suspected. Gnaeus Calpurnius Piso was tried and condemned, and in AD 20 committed suicide.

Tiberius was now free to bring home from Pannnonia his own son, Drusus (b. 13 BC), and designate him as his heir-apparent, and a triumph was granted to Drusus on 28th May AD 20.

About the same time the twins were born to Drusus and Livilla, but by then also the blossoming relationship between Livilla and Sejanus was also approaching a consummation.

Two Precocious Adolescents

Augustus/Octavian had been twelve years old when he had first impressed himself upon the public mind by his precocious funeral oration at the death of his grandmother, Julia. That had been in 51 BC. Now, in the dying days of Augustus, in a remote part of his empire and within a different culture, it was another twelve-year old, also destined to change the course of history in a dramatic manner, who created his first public impression.

Having escaped the Bethlehem massacre of new-born males by Herod the Great, Jesus of Nazareth had by AD 11, 12 or 13 reached that maturity which entitled him, or indeed obliged him, under Jewish law, to join the adult gathering which went up three times a year to Jerusalem to observe the three Great Feasts.

Following his first Jerusalem Passover, he was so enthralled by the whole experience that forgetting to return home, he stayed behind in Jerusalem to tax the Temple priesthood with precocious and penetrating questions about the meaning of the liturgy and the celebrations.

The material of the exchange between Jesus and the priesthood on that occasion is not recorded, but it is a safe guess that the experience of the Passover prompted a large proportion of the young man's questions.

Since after the Passover Supper, Psalm 118 was traditionally sung, it may be conjectured that the adolescent Jesus quizzed the

Temple staff, among other things, over the meaning of verse 22 of that Psalm: "The same stone which the builders refused: is become the head-stone in the corner."

Perhaps he even inquired about Psalm 118, verse 18: "The Lord hath chastened and corrected me: but he hath not given me over unto death."

22
(I)

The Decade of the Disillusionment of Tiberius (AD 21–30)

The Rise of Sejanus

Providence had given Augustus a charmed life and a charmed principate. Tiberius, his first successor – like almost all Augustus's successors – was to endure a much bumpier ride. Under Augustus, Rome was reformed constitutionally, morally, architecturally; provinces were formed and governed, foreign powers were curbed; advantageous public relations were sustained through commemorations and celebrations of national importance – the Secular Games of 17 BC, the lustrations of 28 BC and AD 14. Even the improvisations of the second, less fortunate, half of Augustus's reign (6 BC–AD 14) had by and large worked.

The reign of Tiberius by contrast falls into two distinct parts. First came the "civilised era" or "mitia tempora" ("gentle times") from AD 14 to AD 26. The followed the tyranny, AD 26–AD 37.

A semi-intermediate period, AD 26–AD 30, was characterised by the weariness of Tiberius and his attempts to retire; the complementary expansion in the ambition of Sejanus; the death of Augustus's daughter Julia in AD 28, and the death of Livia, widow of Augustus and mother of Tiberius in AD 29. Little did the general public (or, in the case of Sejanus, even Tiberius himself) know that during the "mitia tempora" life within the imperial palace was already seething. From AD 30 onwards came the dramatic change in tone and temperament which led to tyranny.

At the beginning of the decade Tiberius, either in spite of or because of the death of Germanicus in AD 19, was buoyant. He was 62, and if he should die soon, his son Drusus was the nominated and uncontested heir. His niece Livilla, wife of Drusus, had recently also borne him twin grandsons, and though one died in infancy, the other, his namesake Tiberius Gemellus ("The Twin") was enough for the old man to see two generations ahead. Of the liaison between Livilla and Sejanus, he had no inkling.

In AD 23 he was then smitten by the worst blow that ill fortune could contrive. At the age of only 36, his son Drusus predeceased him. In fact Drusus had been poisoned by Sejanus and Livilla, but at this stage, Tiberius was not aware of it. Nor was he aware of it two years later when in AD 25, after a respectable interval, Sejanus approached him and asked for the hand in marriage of the widowed Livilla.

Tiberius's refusal was not based on any awareness of the connivings of the couple, but probably upon ancient aristocratic prejudice. A woman of the Claudian house was born never to stoop to such as the Aelii.

Frustrated in his desire for Livilla, Sejanus nevertheless concealed his chagrin in the interest of longer term ambition. In AD 26 he even gained extra prestige for himself by being actively engaged in saving Tiberius's life. Heroically he threw himself on top of the emperor when, at a house in Tarracina, the roof fell in.

It was a timely rescue. Already Sejanus in his professional capacity had done much for the imperial body-guard, the Praetorian Guard, of which he was the commander. He had built up its number to nine cohorts and in AD 22 completed the building of the Castra Praetoria, the barracks, on a site of forty acres near the north-east of the city of Rome.

Now was exactly the time when the disenchanted Tiberius began to long to hand over his office, retire from his burden and retreat to Capri. His son was dead, but there was Sejanus, loyal captain of the Praetorian Guard, ready and waiting. His trustworthiness had recently been demonstrated by his risky life-saving enterprise at Tarracina. By way of reward, Sejanus found himself the most powerful individual in Rome, entrusted by Tiberius with full control and command of all affairs of the empire.

This period of partial transition brought to an end the "mitia tempora" or "more gentle times" of the first twelve or thirteen years of Tiberius. With increasing authority, Sejanus began also to increase in presumptuous cruelty.

Early on in the reign of Tiberius, a spate of trials had broken out on a new charge of "maiestas minuta" or "insulting the emperor

Tiberius." Guilt was not normally punished by the death penalty, but, as an early sign of the style of government of Sejanus, it was imposed firmly by him, for the first time, in AD 27. Continuing to advance in every form of authority and power under the sponsorship of Tiberius, Sejanus approached the year AD 31, and his consulship!

Antonia the Younger: The View from her Boudoir

For further insight into the bubblings deep down within the household of Tiberius during this decade, we may enter in imagination into the presence of the dowager and matriarch Antonia the Younger, niece of Augustus, sister-in-law of Tiberius, and widow of his deceased brother Drusus. Following the death of Tiberius in AD 37, she was endowed by the new emperor, her grandson Caligula, with all the privileges previously enjoyed by her late mother-in-law Livia (both widow of Augustus and great-grandmother of Caligula).

Antonia did not live long to enjoy these honours, for she survived her brother-in-law Tiberius for only six weeks. Nevertheless, during April AD 37, she might well have looked back over her life and the fortunes of her family. Were we privileged to be ushered into her boudoir during the closing weeks of her life and to ask for her memories of the decade AD 21–30, we might well have heard the elderly lady recall:

"When my uncle married Livia as long ago as the beginning of the consulship of Pulcher and Flaccus (38 BC), he had high hopes both for the families and for Rome. Within the family it never quite worked out as he expected.

"For a start, Livia gave him no children. Augustus already had his own daughter, my cousin Julia, but family advance was carried forwards by Livia's two boys, Tiberius and Drusus – in other words, by the Claudian side of the family, not the Julian!

"When we grew up, my uncle required me to marry his younger step-son, Drusus. It was an arranged marriage, but we were happy." She paused to hold back a tear. "I never wanted anyone else."

"My husband was only 30 when he died." Again, a pause as Antonia remembered the circumstances. She continued, without pursuing painful memories. "By then we had two sons, Germanicus and Claudius, and our daughter Livilla. Poor Claudius was lame and backward. He hid himself in his history books. Germanicus did well for himself, though. So did Livilla at first.

"Livilla married her cousin, Tiberius's son Drusus, and for six years was consort to the heir-apparent to the whole Roman empire. But Livilla was always easily led," said the mother, protective of her only daughter. "She fell into bad company. She was seduced by Sejanus, and together they poisoned Drusus! From then on she was always on the side of Sejanus. Eventually when Tiberius found her out, she killed herself.

"Uncle Augustus made Tiberius adopt my son, Germanicus. Following uncle's death, Germanicus was for five years heir to the whole Roman empire after my brother-in-law. But then Germanicus died when he was only 34. He left six children, though.

"His wife had been Agrippina – Agrippina the elder, that is, who was daughter to Agrippa and Augustus's daughter Julia. She was therefore Augustus's grand-daughter. Her poor children! They grew up just in time to run into all that trouble with Sejanus.

"Nero, the eldest of Germanicus's six, and his mother, were accused of plotting against Tiberius and were forced into exile. They never came back. Nero committed suicide seven years ago, and Agrippina died three years later. I believed that Sejanus had framed them, and as I became more suspicious of Sejanus, I secretly sent a tip to Tiberius.

"Drusus was their second boy. He definitely took Sejanus's side. When Tiberius found out, he kept him in the palace, but starved him to death. That was the year in which his mother Agrippina, my daughter-in-law, died.

"Caligula was the third son. He gave the address at my mother-in-law Livia's funeral. He was her great-grandson, you see. She was 86 years old when she died. It was only eight years ago.

"Everybody could see it was now dangerous to be a son of Germanicus and Agrippina. After Livia's funeral, I whisked Caligula away under my own protection. Later Tiberius calmed down and summoned him to Capri. He gave him the toga virilis and various favours and privileges.

"Of their three daughters, I worry least about Agrippina – Agrippina the younger that is – named after her mother. Does she know how to look after herself! She married Gnaeus Domitius Ahenobarbus. She's expecting a baby in the winter.

"Drusilla was always Caligula's favourite sister. Now that he's emperor, he's made her and his other two sisters all Vestal Virgins.

He's been very good to me, too. The equal of Livia! What would Augustus have said? I just worry about my son Claudius."

Perhaps such were the concerns and memories of Antonia the Younger in the last weeks of her life. She never knew that her son Claudius was destined within four years to become the fourth Roman emperor, following the assassination of Caligula; nor that the child Agrippina the Younger and Ahenobarbus were expecting was to be born the following 15th December, AD 37, that he was to be a boy and that his name would be Nero – the fifth emperor!

Outside the Royal Palace

The history of the decade of the disillusionment of Tiberius appears unusually lop-sided, dominated as it is neither by home policy nor by foreign policy, but by court intrigue! Hitherto the whole Roman world had been innocent of the tendency within great empires, to generate palace conspiracies. The situation was also a cause and a reflection of the psychological discomforts of Tiberius.

Nevertheless, certain events did occur elsewhere upon the three continents where the Roman empire was spread. In Africa a revolt had broken out in AD 17 in Numidia and Mauretania, but it was concluded in AD 24 with the defeat and death of its leader, Tacfarinas.

On the northern frontier there were the revolts of Florus and Sacrovir in Gaul in AD 21; there were rumblings in Thrace in AD 21 and AD 26; and there were revolts of the Frisii in Germany in AD 28. All were resolved.

In Judaea Pontius Pilate was appointed by Tiberius in AD 26 to the post of governor.

Almost two years later, the voice of John the Baptist, raised in the Jordan valley after a lengthy sojourn among the Essenes, began to herald a different, much more slow-burning, radical, but non-political revolution.

John the Baptist claimed to be an advance messenger preparing the way for an individual of exalted status who would shortly be following him. In comparison with the elaborate measures by which emperors in Rome were identified and enthroned, the procedure of John the Baptist appeared much more simple, streamlined and direct.

Round about AD 30 the distinguished rabbi Gamaliel was flour-ishing in Jerusalem. But John the Baptist did not identify Gamaliel as the one whose imminent arrival he had been predicting. Instead he proclaimed the one whose questions in about AD 12, following the Passover that year, had so memorably confounded the high priests of the Jerusalem Temple. He pointed at Jesus of Nazareth.

23

(J)

The Decade of Tiberius and Caligula (AD 31–40)

"Insulting the Emperor Tiberius"

As Tiberius reached his late sixties and began to falter, so Sejanus began to deploy his patiently maturing strategy. As he did so, he found waiting to hand a feature of the legal, political and social life of Rome which might have been custom-designed for his purpose. As he wielded it, it began to grow to disproportionate prominence and to discolour with terror both his own final ascendancy and the concluding tyrannical years of the emperor's reign. This weapon was the offence of "maiestas minuta," or "behaviour insulting to the emperor Tiberius."

By silent means and gathering custom, it had during the reign of Augustus become regular to think of the whole dignity, scope and embrace of the empire as concentrated in the person of the emperor himself. Any offence against the emperor, was an offence against the established order.

This assumption matured unrecognised. Its potential was barely observed by Augustus. Under Tiberius its outlines began to be more sensed in public and its sinister possibilities more adventurously exploited.

In AD 15 Granius Marcellus, governor of Bithynia, was charged in the Senate on two counts – one of extortion and the other that, by taking the head off a statue of Augustus and replacing it by the bust of Tiberius, he had been guilty of insulting behaviour towards the emperor Tiberius. Tiberius laughed off this "maiestas" charge, but made sure that in the matter of extortion, due justice was done.

During his "mitia tempora" (AD 14–26) Tiberius continued to treat allegations of "behaviour insulting to the emperor" in the same lenient way. In AD 17 he refused to proceed against Apuleia Varilla. True, the poet Clutorius Priscus was executed in AD 21 and in AD 25 the historian Cremutius Cordus committed suicide; but otherwise in AD 21 two Roman knights, and in AD 25 Firmius Catus, were actually punished for laying false accusations. However, the contours of what might become possible were now emerging.

For the charge of "insult" is subjective, flexible and indefinable, and therefore open to every form of self-seeking or malevolent abuse. It could become in Rome a pseudo-offence, handy in intrigue, blackmail and elimination of political opponents. Cunningly manipulated, it could satisfy the pride of an up-and-coming rhetorician; gain favour in the eyes of the emperor; and open the gates to a career generously rewarded with status and wealth – for if successful, an informer under the "maiestas" laws could walk away with one quarter of the defendant's property. The accusation of "maiestas" became an all-purpose tool (albeit a double-edged one) for carving out an ambitious and unscrupulous living.

As from AD 26 onwards Tiberius began to be increasingly absent from Rome, leaving Sejanus to wax prosperous and powerful as his spokesman, so the law of "maiestas" came to be used more frequently, and with more lethal intent.

The first death penalty imposed under Sejanus was in AD 27. Prior to the death of Livia, the widow of Augustus, in AD 29, "maiestas" already began to be used against the friends of Agrippina the Elder (widow of Germanicus) and her eldest son, Nero. After the death of Livia, it was turned against Agrippina and Nero themselves.

In AD 32 it was used, accompanied by the death penalty, against Gaius Asinius Pollio; in AD 33 against Asinius Gallus; in AD 35 against the poet Sextus Paconianus. But in this decade, the thirties AD, it was no longer in use by Sejanus, but by Tiberius, because of the events of AD 31!

The Last Years of Tiberius

Sejanus, as his ambition, his pride and his cruelty increased, did not go unobserved. Late in the year AD 30 a hint from his sister-in-law

Antonia revealed to the emperor Tiberius the true nature and intentions of his lieutenant.

First, for AD 31 Tiberius took for himself the consulship, in association with Sejanus. This gesture was intended to give the impression that Sejanus was being groomed as the first candidate for imperial succession. At the same time however, there was also an advancement for the young Caligula (b. AD 12), third and youngest son of Germanicus. He was summoned from the protection of his grandmother Antonia the Younger to Capri, and there invested with the "toga virilis," the augurate and a priesthood.

Early in October AD 31 Tiberius wrote from Capri to Sertorius Macro appointing him captain of the Praetorian Guard and entrusting to him a letter to be read out in open Senate. The 18th October AD 31 was the date when this letter was read out.

It was a long and involved letter, ostensibly in praise of Sejanus at first, but suddenly at its conclusion it veered round to an order to execute him. Sejanus was immediately put to death.

His eldest son was executed six days later and his divorced wife Apicata (having now at last disclosed to Tiberius that the death of his son Drusus in AD 23 had been engineered by Sejanus and Drusus's own adulterous wife, Livilla), committed suicide.

For six more years after the drama of Sejanus in AD 31, Tiberius reigned alone. Enduring a period of laborious isolation, parallel to, but far more negative than the splendid isolation of Augustus in 10–1 BC, Tiberius reigned with firmness and resolution, sometimes with cruelty and the terror of the "maiestas" law, always alone, but not without some conscientiousness and sometimes with charity.

When there was a financial crisis in AD 33 caused by the shortage of coined money, Tiberius alleviated it with a loan of a hundred million sesterces and by impounding, for the public good, the gold and copper mines of Sextus Marius in Spain. In AD 36 there was a great fire in Rome. Again Tiberius came to the succour of the crisis with a grant of another hundred million sesterces.

But Tiberius never enjoyed his imperial role. He drove with barren conscientiousness but without enthusiasm, the machine that was the creation of the genius of Augustus. When he died, his grandson Tiberius Gemellus was murdered by Sertorius Macro; the despised Claudius, younger brother of Germanicus, remained beneath contempt and so beneath observation!

There was only one survivor of the whole Julio-Claudian house, the youngest of the three sons of Germanicus, the 25-year old

Gaius. Gaius, also called Caligula, succeeded in March AD 37 to the titles and imperial insignia of Tiberius, and to a treasury solvent by 2,700 million sesterces.

A Deranged Emperor

Nero, the first-born son of Germanicus and eldest brother to Drusus and Caligula, had already been driven to suicide by Sejanus in AD 30. The deaths in AD 33 of Nero's mother, Agrippina the Elder, and younger brother Drusus, left the third brother, Caligula, the only male representative of his generation and the natural successor, in everybody's eyes, to Tiberius. His reign as emperor (AD 37–41) began as a fairy-tale.

He was everybody's favourite; he seemed to strive to please everybody. In October AD 37 he suffered a grave illness, almost serious enough to be fatal, and in consequence of which his demeanour seemed to alter. Following this illness and the death on 10th June AD 38 of Drusilla, both his favourite sister and a restraining influence upon him, Caligula began to express his principate in behaviour and manners increasingly arbitrary and bizarre.

In AD 39 Caligula exiled his two remaining sisters, Julia Livilla and Agrippina the Younger, the latter with her baby son, Nero. He ordered the execution of Marcus Aurelius Lepidus, the unfortunate widower of his deceased sister Drusilla; and of Gnaeus Cornelius Lentulus, commander of the army on the Rhine.

Interestingly from a future point of view, he appointed as commander of the Upper Rhine, Servius Sulpicius Galba (a. 41; consul AD 33). Another name that was, thirty years later, to become prominent after the death of Galba, was Titus Flavius Vespasianus, found in AD 39 prosecuting Agrippina the Younger.

Having instituted a purge of the Jews of Alexandria in AD 38, Caligula proposed also to erect a statue of himself in the Jewish Temple at Jerusalem. From this piece and deliberate and inflammatory aggravation he was only dissuaded in AD 40 by the friendship and diplomacy of Herod Agrippa.

Over AD 39–40 Caligula wintered at Lyon and, with his talent for angering populations, provoked revolt in Mauretania in AD 40 by summoning to him Ptolemy of Mauretania, successful victor in AD 24 over the rebel Tacfarinas, and there murdering him. Caligula then made a bizarre visit to the English Channel, but without crossing it, returned to Rome to accept on 31st August the honour of deification by the Senate.

Augustus had built the edifice of the empire with the assiduous devotion of one fulfilling a vocation. Tiberius, with a grim reluctance tempered only by a conscientiousness derived from his association with Augustus, had endured governing it. But Rome had no mechanism for dealing with an emperor who was young, headstrong, delinquent and unhinged. Barely had the principate of Caligula moved into the next decade, when an unconstitutional form of solution was applied.

An Alternative Transformation

From time to time the human race stumbles across, or is grateful to welcome, some Great Idea, which enhances the conditions of daily living or helps to explain its meaning.

Such Great Ideas take centuries to absorb, but the resources they provide are inexhaustible.

They include, inherited from prehistoric times, the mastery of fire, the development of language, the principles of cooking and the secrets of agriculture; from Mesopotamia the inheritance of writing; in more modern times they include Van Eyck's manipulation of oil as a medium for painting; Faraday's comprehension of electricity; Darwin's theory of evolution; Freud's hypothesis of the unconscious mind, and Lemaître's prediction of the expanding universe. Great Ideas descending from ancient times include the nation-state, from Egypt; the democratic freedoms of Greece; the codification of the law after the manner of Rome; and monotheism, or belief in one single Creator, derived from the Hebrew prophets.

From the unpromising background of the last years of the gloomy Tiberius and the first years of the eccentric Caligula emerges one other such Great Idea – the Idea of "Redeeming Incarnation." As Einstein's formula "$e=mc^2$" has an unexpected knock-on effect on the philosophy and physics of time, so "Redeeming Incarnation" surprises by an indirect transformation of the uncertainties behind the three basic questions posed by Gauguin, "Where do we come from?" "What are we?" "Where are we going?"

"Redeeming Incarnation" has seven phases: the birth of Jesus Christ early in the second half of the reign of Augustus; the announcement of John the Baptist in about AD 30; the ministry of

Jesus Christ, AD 30–33; his Last Supper, Crucifixion and Resurrection, spring AD 33; and the foundation and spread of the Christian Church and its Gospel or "Good News" (news, that is, of the "Redeeming Incarnation") from the early summer of AD 33.

The Great Idea of "Redeeming Incarnation" was neither discovered nor taught, but acted out in the early years of this decade (the Decade of Tiberius and Caligula) abruptly, painfully, directly, paradoxically. Thereafter the spread by the budding Church of the Good News of the Redeeming Incarnation was brisk, efficient, businesslike and expanding. The simultaneous mining and clarification of this Great Idea was deep, enterprising, hard-headed and thorough.

At the beginning of the decade AD 31–40, John the Baptist in Judaea looked back with a narrow focus to, and concentrated in his own person, all the traditions and significance, the Psalms, the worship, and above all the prophets of ancient Israel. By the end of the same decade, within a few years of the Last Supper, Crucifixion and Resurrection of Jesus Christ, the Jerusalem Church had sponsored beside itself a second branch in Antioch; and twelve hundred miles away from the metropolis in Rome, St. Paul's voice had been lifted in the provinces of Syria and Cilicia.

This Great Idea effected a transformation as dramatic and formative in human self-understanding as the transformation that Augustus had been able to achieve in secular politics; and it was achieved cleanly and promptly within the space of ten short years.

Proclaiming a message of "Redeeming Incarnation" acted out in Jesus Christ's birth, Crucifixion and Resurrection from the dead, and centring its life upon a regular sustaining meal of bread and wine commemorating the same creative death, the primitive Church established itself in a period of five years (AD 33–38) in Jerusalem and surrounding communities, attracting to itself both membership, controversy and persecution. By the end of the decade St. Paul was broadcasting the good news of Jesus Christ's "Redeeming Incarnation" not only within the narrowed bounds of the Jerusalem vision, but to the Mediterranean world, to the political arena and institution of the Roman empire, and to its dominant Graeco-Roman culture.

Four statements, which St. Paul was shortly to record in written form, represented the contours of the Great Idea of "Redeeming Incarnation."

"Christ has redeemed us from the curse of the law" (Galatians 3. 13, AD 52) "God made Christ, who knew no sin, to be sin for us; that we might be made the righteousness of God in him." (II Corinthians 5. 21, AD 55).

"For we conclude that a man is justified by faith in Jesus Christ, apart from the works of the law" (Romans 3. 28, AD 56).

"God forbid that I should boast, save in the Cross of our Lord Jesus Christ, by which the world is crucified unto me, and I unto the world" (Galatians 6. 14, AD 52).

The same Cross is the site of the achievement of "Redeeming Incarnation," and the location of the Ultimate Three Minutes in the story both of humanity and of the created cosmos.

24

(κ)

The Decade of Claudius and the Council of Jerusalem
(AD 41–50)

Caligula and Claudius

In contrast to the crucified and risen Christ, the emperor Caligula, having been declared a god on 31st August AD 40, survived his deification for only five months. On January 24th AD 41 he and his wife Milona Caesonia and their daughter Julia Drusilla were assassinated by Cassius Chaerea and other enraged officers of the Praetorian Guard – his own bodyguard!

It is useful to freeze the frame as the supercharged soldiers hunted through the palace, and to examine the situation with an objective, constitutional, eye. The emperor was dead. It was now some seventy years since the Senate had begun to feed out of Augustus's hand. Should the state now revert to Republican model and govern itself through the Senate led by two annually elected consuls? Or should it continue in imperial form? If the latter, should the emperor come from the Julio/Claudian house of Augustus? Should some other champion be appointed? If so, by what process?

These basic questions relating to the heart of the constitution did not go away. They continued to plague the Roman empire for many centuries; but in the immediate heat of the massacre and furore of 24th January AD 41, the rampaging praetorians answered the question instinctively for themselves. Careering hot-bloodedly through the royal palace, they just remained conscious that only two male survivors of Augustus's house remained – the infant grandson of Germanicus, (called Nero), and the idiot brother of the same popular and prematurely deceased idol.

Without any pause to consider constitutional options or nuances, they seized upon the latter. His name was Claudius.

A luxury-loving Roman woman, Valeria Messallina, had chosen cunningly when she had married in AD 39. By accepting the despised, ignored, studious, handicapped and under-estimated second son of Drusus and Antonia, Claudius (b. 10 BC), the uncle of the emperor Caligula, Messallina found herself on 25th January AD 41 empress of Rome and its dominions, and her husband the fourth emperor. On 12th February she gave birth to twins, Octavia and Britannicus.

Of ungainly appearance and carriage, the author of a history of the Etruscans and a scholarly authority on early Rome, without military background and having held no previous rank of any significance save the consulship of AD 37, Claudius was to surprise them all. Although erratic and sometimes cruel, he was an unexpectedly effective and conscientious emperor, of sound administrative judgement. His long vision was admirable; his short vision myopic, and his ultimate downfall. Yet of all the line of Drusus (the younger step-son of Augustus), Claudius turned out, against the odds, to be the most successful.

The Long Sight of Claudius

Picking up administration within a few days of his elevation, the new emperor settled with a letter the disturbances in Alexandria; recognised Mithridates as sovereign of the Bosporan kindgom; confirmed Polemo II in the Cilician kingdom; and augmented further the realm of Herod Agrippa by the gifts of Judaea, Samaria, Abilene and Lebanon. Practical, he also began the draining of the Fucine Lake and the construction of a new harbour as Ostia.

Such administration, coming to life after the paralysis of Tiberius, such common sense following the carousings of Caligula, were prominent features of the daily work and general principate of Claudius.

In particular, Claudius was obliged to deal with certain phenomena which had ballooned since the time of Augustus. In the era of Augustus, when the empire was still under disguise as a restored Republic, petitions from injured Roman citizens had been delegated to a number of varied patrons. Petitions from the provinces overseas had been dealt with by a skeleton administration of senators, governors and knights. Now all these appeals from at home and abroad had begun to accumulate in spate, and funnel down, upon the emperor and his imperial court.

The expert on ancient Rome was not so rigidly set as to lack administrative flexibility and ingenuity. To deal with empire-wide correspondence ("epistulae"), he appointed a freedman "ab epistulis" – Narcissus. To deal with day to day Roman petitions ("libelli"), he appointed a freedman "a libellis" – Callistus. The prudent balance left in the state treasury by Tiberius had been dissipated by Caligula. To deal with accounts ("rationes"), Claudius appointed a freedman "a rationibus" – Pallas.

Thus administration was restored by Claudius to an efficient working level. In AD 42 the province of Mauretania was divided into two. In AD 44 on the death of Herod Agrippa, Judaea was again restored to provincial status under the procurator Cuspius Fadus. Servius Sulpicius Galba was appointed governor of the senatorial province of Africa from AD 44–46, transferred from the post to which he had been appointed by Caligula in AD 39 as commander of the Upper Rhine.

In AD 47 Claudius and Lucius Vitellius took the post of censors until mid-48, and revised the roll of the Senate in preparation for some more "Ludi Saeculares" ("Secular Games"), those of AD 48, in celebration of the eight hundredth anniversary (dear to the heart of an antiquarian like Claudius) of the founding of Rome. In this celebration, when it came, Nero, the son of Claudius's niece Agrippina the Younger, was prominent alongside Claudius's own son Britannicus.

In AD 48 Claudius also began to contruct the Aqua Claudia and the Anio Novus, two new aqueducts improving the water supply of Rome, and the 330-mile Via Claudia Augusta, the road from Altinum to Donauworth on the Danube. In AD 49 he expelled all the Jews from Rome.

The Short-sightedness of Claudius

For the common mass of Rome, however, all this worthy administration was less eye-catching than the machinations of Claudius's wives.

In the time of Augustus and Tiberius, consorts and dowagers such as Livia and Antonia the Younger had kept a crushing control over any overweening aspirations on the part of junior female members of the household. The first Roman woman to show symptoms of discomforting ambition had been the eldest of Germanicus's daughters, Agrippina the Younger, the sister of Caligula. Agrippina the Younger was emphatically not Caligula's favourite sister, and in AD 39 he had banished her. For the greater part of this decade however, as the first consistent exponent of the politics of feminine court intrigue, Claudius's pleasure-loving wife Valeria Messallina propelled herself eagerly to the fore.

Once Claudius was proclaimed as emperor, Messallina worked through the early 40s AD to conserve her throne. In AD 41 she contrived the removal of Julia Livilla, third sister of Caligula. In AD 42 she removed another possible rival, Julia, the grand-daughter of Tiberius. In AD 46 Marcus Vinicius, formerly attached to the family of Tiberius, was also excluded by Messallina from the court. In AD 47 she moved successfully against the consul of AD 35, Valerius Asiaticus, and the consul of AD 27, Lucius Piso. Growing overconfident, and enamoured now of Gaius Silius, she was apprehended in AD 48 trying to remove Claudius himself, and was executed.

The equally ambitious and unscrupulous Agrippina the Younger, niece of Claudius, the sister whom Caligula had banished in AD 39, now saw and played her chance. A law was passed permitting the marriage of uncles and nieces. The colourful Agrippina, whose destiny was to be the daughter of an emperor-designate, and the sister, wife and mother of three successive emperors, married her uncle Claudius on 1st January AD 49, almost ten years after her original banishment.

Titus Flavius Vespasianus, who had prosecuted Agrippina so vigorously in AD 39, retired prudently into temporary obscurity.

By the end of AD 50 Agrippina had achieved for her son Nero the adoption by Claudius, as guardian to his son Britannicus, and for herself the title "Augusta." Nero was at that time 13, Britannicus, 9. Agrippina also secured from Claudius the return from exile of Seneca (banished AD 41), as tutor to her son Nero.

The Conquest of Britain

Claudius, although the younger brother of Germanicus, had no military background. The boundaries of the empire as inherited from Augustus were as complete as political prudence recommended. Nevertheless, it seemed to Claudius that it would neither harm nor overstretch the Roman state to annex the island of Britain. In AD 43 therefore, in order to win for himself his missing military reputation, he set about the conquest of Britain.

Aulus Plautius was the general chosen to lead the expedition. Claudius himself, the first Roman emperor to tread British soil, arrived in Britain for the final victory, and in AD 44 celebrated in Rome a victory "ex Britannia." To symbolise his enlargment of the territory of the Roman people through the conquest of Britain, he extended the "pomoerium" or boundary of the city of Rome.

Britain in the following years of the decade was steadily subdued by T. Flavius Vespasianus, who operated in the Isle of Wight, Dorchester and Exeter. Aulus Plautius was succeeded by Ostorius Scapula.

The Council of Jerusalem

Institutions are normally described and categorised on the basis of what their members believe or do, and not on the basis of what they abstain from doing. Therefore it has passed beneath the radar that in the case of Jesus of Nazareth, the religious movement founded upon his Crucifixion and Resurrection entertains total indifference towards a rite which is in other circles highly esteemed – the rite of circumcision. Others may surround circumcision with profound and solemn veneration, as a sacrificial jewel of health and hygiene or a proud and necessary badge of membership. Towards it, the Church, founded on the Resurrection of Jesus Christ, maintains neither favour nor disdain, but a complete and genuine indifference.

The root of this unselfconscious indifference goes back to the year AD 48 and to the Council of Jerusalem (Acts of the Apostles, chapter 15). The decision of this Council to dump circumcision is far more earth-shaking than it first appeared, or seems today. It strikes right down to the very heart or depths of the human collective unconscious.

In this unconscious, at foundation level, lurks among others the assumption that if by right rituals or conduct it is possible to "please" God or the gods, all will go well with those who know the rituals or observe the conduct. They will land up on the right, or favoured, side.

For purposes of shorthand, this whole deep current of human instinct may be known simply as the inclination towards "merit" or "works." It is the assumption that divine favour can be won by the proper ritual, formulae or conduct. It was under the ritual or "work" of circumcision that the Council of Jerusalem of AD 48 identified this human tendency and exemplified it. When therefore the Council was bold enough to jettison circumcision, it did so in favour of a truth higher than the notion of "merit" or "works" as the pathway to divine reward.

This higher truth, which may be given the title "repentance and faith," St. Paul was to explore in a short time, and more fully, in his Epistle to the Galatians of the last years of the emperor Claudius, and in his Epistle to the Romans in the earliest years of Claudius's successor, Nero.

Meanwhile, in the decade in which Caligula gave place to Claudius, a taste of what St. Paul and the earliest Church were beginning to learn appears in the first chapter of St.Paul's writing of the winter AD 48–49, his First Epistle to the Thessalonians.

"Grace," "peace," "faith," "hope," "love," "election," "Gospel," "Holy Spirit," "living and true God," "son from heaven," "raised from the dead," "delivered from the wrath to come" – what kind of community generated and gathered this assemblage of ideas? The first chapter of the First Epistle to the Thessalonians is a glimpse into a fiery crucible of debate and revelation in which the Great Idea of "Redeeming Incarnation" began to unfold itself, and in which the volcanic technical terms of its description were forged.

25

(L)

The Decade of the Rise and Fall of Agrippina the Younger (AD 51–60)

Palace and City under Agrippina and Nero

In all the years between the birth of Augustus in 63 BC and the death of Nero in AD 68, no woman of the imperial household was so driven by relentless ambition as the first daughter of Germanicus, named after her mother, Agrippina, and known as Agrippina the Younger.

She had been sister to the emperor Caligula, and through her grandmother Julia (the daughter of Augustus) and her second husband Agrippa, she was the direct great grand-daughter of Augustus himself. She had been banished from Rome by her brother Caligula, but by plotting and waiting patiently she came back to Rome in triumph on 1st January AD 49 as the wife of her uncle, Claudius and, in AD 50, "Augusta." It was she who controlled appointments and she who for seven or eight years governed by will and wiles both her husband Claudius and her son Nero.

If she was able to recall Seneca in AD 49 from exile, to be tutor to her son Nero, Agrippina was now able in AD 51 to secure for Seneca's brother, Lucius Junius Gallio, the post of governor of the imperial province of Achaea, and to place her nominee, Burrus, in position as Prefect of the Praetorian Guard.

Always jealous for the promotion of her son, whose promotion above Claudius's own son Britannicus, she had already achieved at the same time as, in AD 50, she secured for herself the title "Augusta," Agrippina also secured for Nero at the age of rising 14, in AD 51, the "toga virilis" or "maturity toga" and the title "princeps iuventutis," or "foremost of the younger generation." By AD 53 she saw Galba and Vespasian, men against whom she had a grudge, retire from life in Rome, Vespasian to succeed Galba as governor of Africa.

On 15th December AD 53, Nero became 16. At the age of 15 – earlier, therefore, than his birthday – he was married to Octavia (b. AD 41), daughter of Claudius and twin sister of Britannicus. In compensation, Octavia's fiancé, Decius Junius Silanus Torquatus, to whom Octavia, since the age of 2, had been betrothed by Claudius, was made consul for the year. The newly-wed Nero also made his first public appearance, speaking before the Senate in an appeal for the freedom of Rhodes, a freedom of which that island had been deprived in AD 44 for a series of public riots.

It was in AD 54 that Agrippina succeeded in an ambition where Messallina before her had failed. On 13th October, with a dish of poisoned mushrooms, she despatched the emperor Claudius.

Nero now became emperor, Seneca and Burrus chief ministers, and Agrippina dowager empress, emperor's mother, and patron of the most senior voices in the administration. She had made herself the most powerful and the most important empress in the history of the Augustan empire.

At some stage Agrippina contrived, among all other honours, to have her visage struck upon the Roman coinage. The high noonday of her power, however, was to last for barely a couple of years (AD 54–56). She had bequeathed her strength of will, her temperament and the subtlety of her scheming to Nero.

Together in AD 55 mother and son secured the removal of Britannicus, son of Claudius, only rival to the imperial throne, by further poisoning. In the same year Agrippina and Narcissus were able to remove Pallas from his office in the imperial treasury and replace him by one Phaon.

With Seneca, she secured favour for Seneca's nephew, Lucan, at court.

Thus by AD 56, under Agrippina's influence, imperial finance was centralised as securely in the hands of the emperor Nero as it had been under Augustus from 27–23 BC. But now Nero, when he reached his eighteenth birthday, was beginning to exert his own authority. Significantly, the image of Agrippina disappeared again from Roman coinage from AD 56 onwards.

For the adolescent Nero was no longer content with Octavia, the wife provided for him by imperial maternal scheming. As he began to approach the age of 18, at some time in AD 55 he found himself falling in love with Poppaea Sabina, wife of Otho, a future emperor of the year AD 69. A rising attraction towards Greek culture and expression in the adolescent emperor, combined with his wilful infatuation with Poppaea, signalled the beginning of the downfall of the emperor's mother.

In AD 57 Nero distributed a free gift of 200 sesterces per head to every citizen of Rome, and ordered that, to approximate public games more accurately to Greek ideals and precedents, Roman Senators and knights should participate in them.

In AD 58 he refused the perpetual consulship, but as his attachment to Poppaea Sabina intensified, he began to throw off Seneca, Burrus and Agrippina more and more, and also despatched Otho, husband of Poppaea, to be governor of Lusitania.

In AD 59 Nero secured the murder of his mother, Agrippina. On 15th December he attained his majority. In anticipation he threw the "Ludi Juvenales" ("Youth Games") in which a group of noble young men, formed as his bodyguard, the "Augustiarii," competed in Greek style. The spirit of irresponsibility was creeping into the driving seat of the Roman empire.

Thus the so-called "Quinquennium Neronis," the first five years of Nero's rule, which administratively was seen as the most tight and just period since the time of Augustus, came to an end. Administration was now in the hands of a single, headstrong young man who had been taught to brook no hindrance and to fall to any low device in order to satisfy his lusts, interests and will. In AD 60 he instituted the "Neronia," Greek style games in which Senators and equites ("Knights") were once again expected to take part. He expelled Rubellius Plautus, one potential rival to the throne, to Asia; on the strength of recent triumphs in Armenia, he apppointed Corbulo governor of Syria; to the governorship of the Spanish province of Hispania Tarraconensis, he appointed Servius Sulpicius Galba.

Empire and Provinces Under Claudius and Nero

A more fascinating variety of characters filled the sixth decade AD than any previous decade of imperial Rome: the ageing Claudius; the scheming Agrippina; the competent Seneca and Burrus; the adolescent Nero; behind them the personalities of Galba, Otho and Vespasian lingered in the shadows, waiting for their hour.

At the level of the imperial government of Rome and the provinces the responsible, almost vocational, conscientiousness of the Julio/Claudian house contined to express itself up until Nero had thrown off all restraint. In the provinces, irrespective of what was happening in the imperial household, it was a decade of tranquillity. Outside in the empire the "Quinquennium Neronis" was indeed a golden age.

While he was still alive, Claudius continued to improve the water supply to Rome. His Triumphal Arch of Claudius (AD 51) formed part of the Aqua Virgo, which he had started in AD 48. The Aqua Claudia, also begun in AD 48, reached completion in AD 52. In the same year Claudius expelled all magicians and astrologers from Rome.

Caractacus was defeated in Wales by Ostorius Scapula in AD 51. Also in AD 51 came about a change of rule in Parthia, when Gotarzes was succeeded, after an interval of disorder under Vonones, by Vologeses.

Vologeses attempted in AD 52 to invade Armenia, but then thought the better of it. Nevertheless, he reoccupied Armenia in AD 53, placing Tiridates on the throne.

An inscription in Delphi indicates that Lucius Junius Gallio, the brother of Seneca, ceased to be governor of Achaea by July AD 52. In the provinces, imperial procurators were given the right of jurisdiction.

In AD 55, one of the first delights of the newly elevated and crowned Nero was a statue in the temple of Mars Ultor, and an ovation following eastern successes by Corbulo in Armenia.

Following such success, Corbulo was confirmed in his command, alongside Ummidius Quadratus, against Armenia and Parthia.

In AD 58, AD 59 and AD 60, Corbulo attacked Armenia, destroyed Artaxata and Tigranocerta, placed Tiridates on the throne, and was rewarded at the end of the campaign in AD 60 with the governorship of Syria. In AD 57 Gaius Licinius Mucianus, a name to be remembered, was appointed governor of Lycia and Pamphilia.

Even more to be remembered was the name of a son born to the wife of a rising Roman official of Spanish origin, Marcus Ulpius Traianus. The child, born in AD 52, was given the identical name of his father.

The Roads to Rome

The connection between the female power behind the Roman throne, Agrippina the Younger, and the missionary St.Paul is an indirect and seldom appreciated corridor of history.

In was solely that in AD 51 Agrippina had arranged the appointment of Gallio, brother of Nero's tutor Seneca, to the post of governor of Achaea. It was before Gallio's court in Corinth that St. Paul appeared in the summer of either AD 51 or AD 52. Finding the detailed contretemps between St. Paul and the Jews too intricate for his understanding, Gallio summarily dismissed the case.

St. Paul had in fact arrived in Corinth in the winter of AD 48–49 and from thereabouts had written his Epistles to the Thessalonians. Following his abortive trial before Gallio, St. Paul remained in Corinth for a short but indeterminable time, and then returned south-eastwards to check in at Jerusalem and Antioch.

St. Paul was deeply affected by the way in which, in the four years since the Council of Jerusalem, he found that the balance of economic power had shifted away from Jerusalem in the direction of his own sponsoring congregation in Antioch. Setting out on his Third Missionary Journey without delay, probably late in the summer of AD 52, St. Paul began immediately to reinforce his message of Jesus Christ risen from the dead, with an appeal for funds on behalf of the poor Church in Jerusalem.

Settling from AD 53 onwards in Ephesus (after Rome, the second largest city of the Mediterranean world at the time), he wrote his short, epoch-making Epistle to the Galatians. It is a work of almost supernatural revelation, insight and maturity, worthy to stand in the front rank with any other product of world literature. It has, incidentally, also been described as the greatest blow for human liberty ever struck.

In this Epistle, pursuing back to its root the significance of the Council of Jerusalem's decision of AD 48 to renounce circumcision, St. Paul comes to identify one of the worst of human failings as being, not hypocrisy, nor self-deception, nor even murder – but boasting! Nevertheless, he asserts, there is one truth in which it is proper, wholesome and even wise to boast. "God forbid that I should glory, save in the cross of our Lord Jesus Christ, by which the world is crucified to me, and I unto the world" (Galatians 6. 14).

Similarly, writing to the Romans from Corinth in the winter of AD 55–56, St. Paul's words were "Where is boasting? It is excluded.

163

By what law? Of works? Nay, but by the law of faith. Therefore we conclude that a man is justified by faith, without the deeds of the law" (Romans 3. 27–28).

In AD 56 St. Paul completed his Third Missionary Journey with his arrival in Jerusalem and the handing in of his collection to the impoverished Church. Plotted against by the Jews of Jerusalem on account of his perceived renunciation of Jewish ritual and faith, St. Paul in AD 56, AD 57, or AD 58 was taken into protective custody by the Roman governor Felix, in Caesarea.

In AD 60 his case was heard by the new governor, Porcius Festus. St. Paul appealed to Caesar, and was transported to Rome. He was not alone. Retrospect suggests that during this decade, as Agrippina rose and fell and as Nero was waxing more dangerous and wanton, by one route or another, all the influential thinkers and personalities of the first generation of the Church, apart from St. John, were forsaking their haunts in the eastern Mediterranean and were converging upon Rome!

26

(M)

The Decade of Nero and the Year of the Four Emperors (AD 61–70)

Four Emperors?

The emperor Nero, even though no month is named after him, has left a far greater impression on the western mind and imagination than even the emperor Augustus. Nero's monstrosities form the earliest scar which introduction to the Roman empire inflicts on the tender psyche. Yet his cruelties and immoralities, foul and ingenious, deserve after due consideration to be reduced to their proper proportions.

Nero was no more than an immature and over-indulged juvenile delinquent whom, being a descendant of the family of Augustus, and the last of the Julio-Claudian line, the Roman empire was obliged to inherit, suffer and, for a time, to entertain.

For the Roman empire at large, the real problem came with the suicide of Nero in AD 68. What was then to happen to Augustus's empire? Eighteen war-torn months of eruptive militarism concluded the decade – not in indignation against Nero's excesses, but in an attempt to establish sovereignty on the vacant throne.

When at last a final secure victor emerged, it was clear that there was no going back to pre-Augustan Republican ways of governing. The Roman empire was a fixity, and by means of legal documentation, the Senate attempted to define and clarify the emperor's role.

The lusts and enormities of Nero occupied the first eight years of this decade. Though scandalous and repulsive they are, to the eye of history, merely of tabloid interest. Where an epic quality is found is in the marching and counter-marching of Roman armies in the last two years of this decade – the troops from the west, the

Praetorian Guard in Rome, the legionaries from the north and the disciplined soldiery from the east. Their grandeur, their grinding and their denouement settled the established system of Augustus for centuries to come.

Nero in Rome and Greece

Nero at the beginning of AD 61 was 23 years old, uncontrolled and uncontrollable. He had murdered his mother Agrippina two years before, and was unrestrained either by his two advisors Seneca and Burrus, by the Senate, whom he subjected to athletic indignities, or by his wife Octavia, for whom he had no affection.

AD 62 was a crucial year. Burrus died, Seneca fell and Octavia was divorced. Nero married instead his mistress and favourite, Poppaea Sabina, and in charge of the Praetorian Guard, in succession to Burrus, placed his most reckless and immoral cronies, Ofonius Tigellinus and Faenius Rufus. He executed Rubellius Plautus, and took all measures to eliminate challenge to his imperial powers and throne.

There were also four officials against whom he thought it necessary to take no precautions and whom he therefore overlooked – the governors of Lycia-Pamphilia, Hispania Tarraconensis, Lusitania and Africa. Their names were, respectively, Mucianus, Galba, Otho and Vespasian.

AD 63 was a quieter year, possibly because it saw the birth, death and deification of Claudia Augusta, daughter of Nero and Poppaea Sabina. Then on 18th July AD 64 a great fire broke out in Rome and lasted for nine days.

Accused of contriving the fire for his own purposes, Nero diverted the accusation to advantage by transferring the blame for the fire onto the Christians of Rome, many of whom he persecuted and executed. He set about the rebuilding of the Circus Maximus and the reconstruction of Rome, but since at the height of the fire he had tried, sensibly and scientifically, to combat the inferno with the introduction of fire-breaks, he was in fact accused of requisitioning and demolishing properties in order to build his own "Domus Aurea," the "Golden House" of Nero. Nero also reformed the currency in this year, but all these measures together could not hide the fact that the tide of public opinion was beginning to turn against him.

Provoked by the arbitrary and solipsist techniques of his governance, the first plot against the life of Nero was hatched in AD 65. It was led by Caius Calpurnius Piso, but was uncovered in April. Not only were Piso and his co-conspirators L. Junius Silanus and L. Antistius Vetus executed, but Seneca and his nephew Lucan, without protection at court since the death of Agrippina, were ordered to commit suicide.

The main reaction was to provoke a second conspiracy, the Vinician conspiracy of AD 66 with its headquarters at Beneventum. In spite of this, Nero felt it safe in September AD 66 to set out for a tour of Greece. He proclaimed the freedom of Greece, inaugurated the cutting of the Corinthian canal, and saw Halley's comet. More infamously, he began AD 67 by ordering the distinguished military commander, and governor of Syria, Corbulo, to commit suicide; and by commanding all four sets of successive annual Games in Greece to be concentrated into a single year. He then competed victoriously in all four.

The First of the Four Emperors – Galba

In the autumn of AD 67, the freedman Helius, whom Nero had left behind in Rome to govern the city and empire, came across to Greece to advise him to return to Rome. First, two sensible appointments were made in the east. Tiberius Julius Alexander was placed as governor of Egypt, and Vespasian moved across from Africa as imperial legate to pursue the escalating war against the disaffected Jews in Judaea.

Returning slowly and majestically, with the dignity that befitted an Olympic victor, Nero arrived in Italy in January AD 68, to be greeted in Naples with the news of a revolt in Gaul by Gaius Julius Vindex. Vindex was defeated at Vesontio by Virginius Rufus, but his uprising was a symptom that not merely Rome, but the whole empire, was restive. Vindex was in fact the agent provocateur of a more serious threat for Nero, which reached its head on 2nd April AD 68.

Nero's provincial governor of Hispania Tarraconensis, Galba, was now 70 years old. He had been born in Augustus's prime, and had been a protegé of Augustus's wife, Livia. He had been consul in AD 33, and had had long experience in provincial government. If not by blood, birth or adoption, he was by patronage a member of

Augustus's inner circle, and on the strength of this favour and experience alone, he was closer in spirit than Nero to the vision of Augustus. On 2nd April AD 68 the troops of Spain acclaimed Servius Sulpicius Galba, the governor of Hispania Tarraconensis, as emperor!

On 9th June AD 68 Nero committed suicide. Shortly afterwards his nominee as head of the Praetorian Guard, Nymphidius Sabinus, was murdered by Antonius Honoratus. The Senate and the Praetorian Guard accepted Galba as the emperor. Setting out from Spain, the new emperor arrived in Rome in the autumn of AD 68, ordered the execution of Cingonius Varro and Petronius Turpilianus, and placed Aulus Vitellius in the governorship of Lower Germany.

The Second and Third of the Four Emperors – Otho and Vitellius

The emperor Galba qualifies for what has come to be called the "Year of the Four Emperors" (AD 69), because he was indeed emperor during part of the year AD 69 – for its first fifteen days! A respected provincial governor, but blundering and vacillating in the highest office, Galba was usurped on 2nd January AD 69 by Vitellius in Lower Germany, who on that date was hailed as emperor by his own legionaries. On the spot in Rome, Marcus Salvius Otho and the Praetorian Guard had other ideas.

Turning against Galba, the Praetorian Guard murdered him on 15th January, and proclaimed Otho as emperor instead. But Vitellius was now on the march. Moving south from Germany with his legions he defeated Otho at Bedriacum on 14th April AD 69. On 16th April Otho committed suicide and on 19th April the Senate conferred imperial powers upon Vitellius.

But still it was not the end. The armies of the east resented the upstart declarations of the armies of the west, of the Praetorian Guard and of the armies on the Rhine, not least because they believed themselves to be commanded by a man of stature and calibre superior to all their colleagues' three candidates. They threw their loyalties behind the man who was steadily and effectively restoring order to the disaffected countryside of Galilee and Judaea.

The Fourth Emperor

Titus Flavius Vespasianus was proclaimed emperor on 1st July AD 69 by Tiberius Julius Alexander, governor of Egypt, in Alexandria; and on 2nd July by his own men in Judaea and Syria.

Within a few days the army on the Danube and the governor (appointed AD 66) of Syria, C. Licinius Mucianus, had also declared for Vespasian and sent two legions ahead into central Italy under his chosen representative, Antonius Primus. Mucianus and Vespasian followed behind.

On 24th and 25th October the forces favouring the third emperor, Vitellius, were defeated by Antonius Primus and the unfortunate city of Cremona was sacked. An attack by the Dacians on Moesia was repelled by Mucianus. On 21st December Vitellius committed suicide. The accession of Vespasian was immediate and unopposed.

Among all his other qualities, Vespasian also had two gifts which no emperor of the Julio-Claudian dynasty had ever possessed: two sons of adult age. The younger son, Domitian, was made urban praetor, but with the authority of a consul. The elder son, Titus, still filling his father's post in Judaea, and at the same time pursuing the siege of Jerusalem, was, with his father Vespasian, elected consul for the approaching year AD 70. A new dynasty and a firm administration thus took brisk, authoritative and complete control over the wobbling inheritance of Augustus.

Early in AD 70, with the arrival of Mucianus in Rome, the Senate confirmed the Lex de Imperio Vespasiani ("The Law of Vespasian's Accession"), laying the foundation of the principate of Vespasian and the legal authority of the new order. Vespasian himself arrived in Rome in the summer. In September his son Titus successfully entered and sacked Jerusalem.

Mucianus, who four years before had been governor in the provincial backwater of Lycia-Pamphilia, reflected ruminatively upon the tossing fortunes of a turbulent society. He had not only returned to his metropolitan city. Following Vespasian and Titus, he entered with Petilius Cerealis upon the suffect consulship.

Another Road to Rome

In AD 1514 Leonardo da Vinci, Michelangelo and Raphael were all living and working close to one another within a small acreage in the city of Rome. Vienna in AD 1787 saw the one and only meeting between Mozart and the young Beethoven.

But in Rome in the years AD 61–65 were concentrated St. Paul, St. Peter, St. Mark, St. Luke, St. Timothy, St. Titus, the author of the Epistle to the Hebrews, Linus (II Timothy 4. 21), who was the successor of St. Peter, and perhaps St. James.

From Rome in this decade were issued, in all likelihood, the Epistles to the Philippians, the Colossians and the Ephesians; and to Timothy, Titus and Philemon. The era of the long epistle was plainly passing. The Epistle to the Hebrews was the last of the genre to be admitted to the New Testament. Longer literature now concentrated on the life and figure of Jesus of Nazareth himself.

During the Neronian persecution of AD 64, or not long afterwards, there appeared in Rome the Gospel according to St. Mark.

With the fall of Jerusalem to Titus in AD 70, the leaders of the early Christian Church would have realised that it was by divine providence that, in spite of and in defiance of the persecutions by Nero, they had been moved to shift their headquarters from Jerusalem to the metropolis and capital city of the empire!

27
(N)

The Decade of Vespasian (AD 71–80)

Parallel Principates

Ninety-nine years before Vespasian, Augustus in 29 BC had sailed from Egypt and up the Ionian coast, had crossed Greece and arrived in Rome in the late summer. In the late summer of AD 70 Vespasian also arrived in Rome, having followed the same route. Other parallels between Augustus and Vespasian were to be less superficial.

The most pressing problem, for both emperors, was the state's finances. Augustus in his day had found them ruined following the Civil War, the collapse of the Republic and the end of the Triumvirate. Vespasian estimated that the empire would have to find 4,000 million sesterces to make good the profligacy of Nero. Augustus sometimes had to finance the empire out of his own Egyptian funds. Vespasian took initiatives in taxation, with confidence that the Senate would endorse them.

Equally, the problem in AD 71 of the settlement of military veterans was parallel to the problem experienced by Augustus in 29 BC. Vespasian followed Augustan policy and practice without alteration.

With respect to the Senate, Vespasian and his elder son Titus took the censorship in AD 72 and, like Augustus and Agrippa in 28 BC, revised the roll. Vespasian enjoyed however a more robust and co-operative relationship with his Senate than had Augustus.

The Senate of AD 72 was no longer the weary and degenerate remnant of republican families which Augustus had had to reform, nor was it the meek flock of timid politicians whom Tiberius had had to encourage. Fresh families, even from the provinces, and especially from Spain, had for a decade or more been sending promising candidates to trickle into it, stiffening it with a new earnestness and expectation. For this much more responsible and responsive Senate, a capable emperor, at last, was a great relief. The "Law of Vespasian's Accession" was a prime example of its new, businesslike, approach to senatorial functions.

Vespasian himself was of such a temperament that serious-minded senators and officers could easily work with him. Tiberius had had only the self-serving Sejanus. No conscientious public servant could have worked with Caligula or Nero. Claudius had had to use Greek freedmen.

Even the claims of Galba, Otho and Vitellius had been promoted primarily not by identifiable supporters, but by their collective armies.

Vespasian by contrast came to Rome proclaimed by Tiberius Julius Alexander, governor of Egypt and shortly to be Prefect of the Praetorian Guard, and by Mucianus, soldier and author, who defeated the Dacians on the march to Rome and eventually retired to literature. Tiberius Julius Alexander corresponds faintly to Augustus's Agrippa, Mucianus to Augustus's Maecenas.

Vespasian was able to reap the advantage not only of the post-Augustan Praetorian Guard, but also of the dynastic principle established by Augustus, and the civil service that had developed under Claudius.

Thus, the honours shown by the Senate to Domitian in AD 69–70 when his father and elder brother were still in the east, indicated that that body was now conditioned into and consenting to the dynastic principle; and the speed with which the administration – even before the new emperor arrived in Rome – snapped back into efficient operation, suggests that there was a strong and willing body of administrators, only waiting for a lead from an emperor of a similar mind.

There was a further respect in which the government of the empire improved under Vespasian and his sons. Following the death of Augustus the imperial women, Livilla, Drusilla, Messalina, Agrippina, Poppaea, had had their head. Under the Flavian dynasty (as Vespasian and his sons were named), any dangerous ambition among the womenfolk was held under greater control.

Governance of the Roman provinces, both east and west, continued in accordance with principles laid down, even before Augustus, in the later era of the Republic.

The peace that now, in the decade of Vespasian, settled upon imperial Rome and its provinces was not, as after the battle of

Actium (30 BC) the peace of exhaustion and war-weariness. It was the peace of relief and contentment that after turbulence the status quo had been restored.

The Establishment of the Emperor Titus

Vespasian was thus consolidated as emperor in the years AD 69–70. AD 71 was the year of consolidation of his son and heir.

In the spring of AD 71 Titus visited Egypt, accompanied by Tiberius Julius Alexander, the former governor, now advanced by Vespasian to be commander of the Praetorian Guard. In the early summer the two returned to Rome, where Titus was appointed co-commander, with Tiberius Julius Alexander, of the Praetorian Guard, and was granted "proconsulare imperium" and "tribunicia potestas" along with Vespasian. In June, Vespasian and Titus celebrated together a triumph "ex Judaea."

Vespasian was plainly designating his heir by endowing him, as Augustus had Tiberius, with the two supreme republican symbols of the "tribunician" (home) and "proconsular" (foreign) sovereign powers. With Domitian as the second son already acknowledged in public life, two years after the proclamation of Vespasian, the Flavian dynasty was firmly in possession of the reins of government of the Roman empire.

Thus, after the hiatus of AD 69, imperial government from Rome was resumed by the Flavians Vespasian and Titus under Julio-Claudian lines. As the decade advanced further, principles of administration and continuity going back to Augustus were maintained in the eastern provinces and in the west by this, the first imperial dynasty to have both a father and his own two sons in partnership. As a symbol of continuity with Rome's most solemn past, in AD 75 Vespasian rededicated and repaired the refurbished temple of Jupiter Optimus Maximus on the Capitol, part of which had burned down during the power struggle with Vitellius in the latter part of AD 69.

East and West

In the east it had always been the custom to govern territories through their native sovereigns, watched over by Roman provincial governors. It is a matter of interest only to specialists to piece together all the routine arrangements made as (for example) kings died in Commagene or Nabataea; Armenia Minor was united with Cappadocia; Cilicia Campestris detached from Syria and reunited with Lycaonia and Isauria; an imperial cult shrine was founded in Nicomedia; a gift of gates erected at Nicaea. Of greatest moment was the fall of Jerusalem to Titus in September AD 70.

Many of the inhabitants then fled to Antioch, but a hard core of Jewish resistance made their way to Masada. There in either AD 73 or 74 they staged their last stand before the new Roman governor, Sextus Lucilius Bassus, and the irresistible siege methods of the Roman army.

In AD 73 Caesennius Paetus, governor of the province of Syria, was succeeded by one bearing a distinguished name, M. Ulpius Traianus. This Trajan constructed the canal of the "country between the rivers" in AD 75, and by AD 76 had completed the energetic building of a road network in Galilee. He was accompanied, as military legate, by his son of the same name. M. Ulpius Traianus the son, picked up invaluable experience of the eastern provinces, to be kept in store against the day when he himself should become emperor.

In the west, Roman armies had always had more direct and proactive involvement with their provinces, than in the east. Britain especially was favoured during the decade of Vespasian, with a succession of strong and effective governors. Vespasian's first appointment was his son-in-law Petilius Cerealis, suffect consul of AD 70.

He defeated the Brigantes of Yorkshire and completed Roman conquest as far as the line of the later Hadrian's Wall. Vespasian replaced him in AD 73 with Sextus Julius Frontinus, a co-operator with Petilius Cerealis in AD 70 in the defeat of the revolt against Vespasian of Julius Civilis. Frontinus drove westwards, and by the time he handed the governorship of Britain over to his successor, Agricola, in AD 77, he had conquered the Silures of Wales. Agricola seems to have been briefed by the emperor (who had himself already had experience of service in Britain) to consolidate what Rome had so far achieved. In AD 79 he constructed a forum and a basilica in St. Alban's and established British tribal capitals in Cirencester (AD 79) and Exeter and Leicester (AD 80).

Vespasian also undertook sensible and probably financially prudent measures in Hispania Tarraconensis, Africa, Sardinia, and in the veteran colony of Orange, Gaul. He has left behind a conscientious, workmanlike reputation, striving for continuity with the best of his predecessors, with a dry sense of humour and, in finance, an inclination towards parsimony.

Covering the Costs of Empire

Parsimony he needed. The financial poverty at the beginning of Vespasian's reign was, like so many features of the reign of Augustus, remarkable for its parallel unhealthy condition. The state Augustus had entered upon had been bankrupted by the exactions of the Civil War and the Triumvirate, and by the supply and payment of unprecedented numbers of legions during the period of that Triumvirate. Vespasian also inherited an empire made bankrupt – through the follies of Nero!

Vespasian revived old taxes and invented new ones (most singularly a tax on urine, a specialist commodity in the tanning industry). He increased customs duties and, as the economy began to recover, put out sums of money judiciously on public works and the support of indigent senators. He dealt even-handedly with grant-receiving communities, allocating finance where appropriate, but where public lands and property had fallen into private hands, demanding back the state's due.

Financial recovery following Nero and the year of the Four Emperors was perhaps Vespasian's greatest, but unsung, achievement. Upon it the stability of his reign was based. He was praised by the historian Tacitus as the only emperor whose character was not made worse by his attainment of imperial office. The character of Agricola, appointed governor of Britain in AD 77, seems to reflect the modesty of lifestyle, the self-effacing industry and the conscientious embrace of the principle of the ruler as servant, that were all congenial to Vespasian himself.

There was a great fire in Rome in August AD 79, which destroyed the buildings on the Capitoline Hill, including Vespasian's own reconstituted temple of Jupiter Optimus Maximus. On 24th August AD 79 occurred the eruption of Vesuvius. Of the former ferocious fire and of the latter natural calamity and its consequences for Pompeii, Herculaneum and for Pliny the Elder, Vespasian knew nothing at all. Exactly two calendar months before the disastrous eruption of the volcano, on 24th June AD 79, with the self-depre-cating quip "I think I am becoming a god," he died.

Jerusalem and Antioch

On the fall of Jerusalem to Titus, while the remaining Jewish resis-tance movement fell back to Masada, the majority of refugees from the ruined city, whether Jews or Christians, fled to Antioch.

In Antioch the Jews rallied under Johanan ben Zakkai and remod-elled their religion so that it could express itself for ever after without its central place of worship, the Jerusalem Temple.

To the Christians of Antioch was brought in the normal course of commerce and inter-church communication, a document furtively put together in Neronian Rome, the Gospel of St. Mark. The enterprising Antioch church noted how shorn this treatise was of the incisive teaching of Jesus Christ. At the same time it felt itself surrounded by a heavy concentration of Jerusalem Jewish refugees; and it also sensed from the wider Roman empire something of the great relief stemming from the fair-minded authority, the grip and the governance of Vespasian.

The Antioch church enlarged St. Mark's Gospel with sermons of Jesus and by subtle touches adumbrating him as the second Moses; they added to the text quotations from the Jewish prophets and Psalms, and certain examples of Jewish-type *midrash;* they intro-duced the revised work with an impressive Jewish genealogy and they invested much of the continuity with the grateful contentment of the Vespasianic era. By these means the church of Antioch, some time in this decade, presented the world with their version of the Good News of Jesus Christ, the incarnate and crucified Redeemer, published under the name of St. Matthew.

28

(o)

The Decade of Titus and Domitian
(AD 81–90)

The Emperor Titus

Colleague with his father for almost ten years as consul, holder of the tribunician power and proconsular authority, censor; no emperor of first century AD Rome was so well prepared for his position, as Titus.

Possessing a powerful and justified military reputation, giantly overshadowing his younger brother Domitian, he succeeded without a hint of oppposition on the death of Vespasian on 24th June AD 79. Yet within two years, before, for all his previous preparation, promise and grooming, he could make a name for himself, Titus was dead. Poison by his younger brother and successor was suspected.

Titus had been brought up in the loose-living court society of Claudius and Nero, a fond suitor of his mistress, the Jewish queen Berenice. Nevertheless, he promised on becoming emperor to renounce everything that had been discreditable in his past.

His financial policies and his building programme of roads and aqueducts in Italy and the provinces continued seamlessly those of his father. Generous and abstemious as emperor, Titus promised from early after his succession that he would not be responsible, directly or indirectly, for the death of any citizen.

His short reign ensured that he had no time to blight his popular public reputation or to go back upon the clemency of his earliest promises. Posterity has therefore recorded him in the faultless light of his honeymoon period. Titus, and the memory of this short-lived emperor, remain radiant among Roman reputations.

In AD 80 he dedicated the Colosseum and began construction of the temple of Vespasian and the Baths of Titus. The Capitol and its temple of Jupiter Optimus Maximus, destroyed by fire in AD 69, rebuilt by Vespasian in AD 75, again destroyed by fire in AD 79, he set out devotedly and vigorously to reconstruct. Near to the Circus Maximus he began the Arch of Titus, which was later dedicated by his brother, the emperor Domitian.

At Pessinus a Stoa was dedicated to Titus; a stadium was completed at Laodicaea-ad-Lycum.

A colonnade was erected at Beirut by Berenice. However, on 13th September AD 81, Titus died, to be succeeded immediately by his younger brother Domitian.

The Emperor Domitian in the West

If Domitian did indeed poison his brother, one motive might well have been jealous enchantment with the vision of power. The reality was rather different. One may assume that Vespasian had intended his elder son to induct his brother into the ways of the principate, just as he himself had inducted Titus. Domitian however, under-exposed by Titus to the titles and exercise of office, lacking any military lustre or even experience, began to discover his personal shortcomings and inadequacies for the imperial task.

Domitian began by affirming continuity both with his Flavian predecessors and all previous emperors, but insecurity and fear seem to have been latent beneath the veil of his authority from the very start. There was a parallel between his own succession and that of his earlier predecessor, Nero, which was uncomfortably clear not just to the emperor but to the greater part of the population of Rome. The verdict of the poet Martial on Domitian's principate was that, hounded by this uncertainty, he almost undid all the good achieved by his father and his brother before him.

Nevertheless, outside Rome, the customary control of the provinces of the empire marched on.

In Britain Agricola advanced Roman influence into the highlands of Scotland. The shadowy battle of Mons Graupius may be dated to AD 83. However, the virtues which commended Agricola to Vespasian may have offended Vespasian's less competent son, and in the following year Agricola was recalled from this governorship. In about AD 88 the legionary camp at Inchtuthill was demolished, and Agricola's plans for the control of the Scottish highlands following his victory at Mons Graupius, were abandoned.

Domitian was acutely embarrassed that in comparison with his father and his brother he had to his credit no military achievements or reputation. During his first decade therefore, he went on campaign himself three times, to Germany in AD 83, to the Danube in AD 84–85, and to the Rhine and the Danube in AD 89.

In AD 82 Corellius Rufus was appointed governor of Germania Superior. A German war broke out, providing opportunity for Domitian to lead a war against the Chatti in AD 83, for which he took the title "Germanicus." Following this, it was deemed right in AD 85 to confirm the division of Germany into two provinces, Germania Superior governed from Mainz and Germania Inferior governed from Cologne.

Dacia, Moesia and the eastern Danube were stretches of territory that the Julio-Claudian emperors had failed to bring in as buffers within the Roman provincial system. In AD 85 Domitian tried to campaign along the Danube, meeting with military disaster and the death of Oppius Sabinus, and provoking the outbreak of a Dacian War. In AD 86 Domitian returned to Rome and claimed a victory over the Dacians.

While back in Rome, administratively Domitian divided Moesia also, like Germany, into two provinces of "Superior" and "Inferior." In spite of his alleged "victory" of AD 86 over the Dacians, Domitian did not in fact conclude the Dacian Wars until AD 88. In AD 89 he claimed at Rome a triumph over both the Dacians and the Germans.

The Emperor Domitian: the Other Provinces and Rome

In the provinces of the east there was very little movement. The Roman system of installing and co-operating with client kings, backed by strong provincial governors, maintained peace over those deeply Hellenised and long civilised lands. Interest was aroused in AD 88 by the revolt raised by an individual claiming to be the emperor Nero, returned from the dead. The only support rallied by this false Nero was from the Parthian enemy massed beyond the eastern frontier on the further side of the Euphrates.

Africa likewise was largely tranquil in the first decade of the emperor Domitian. In AD 85 there was a revolt of the tribe of the

Nasamones. The governor of Numidia, Suellius Flaccus, was defeated. The following year the revolt was only suppressed by genocide of the mutinous tribes. Yet the date and the restiveness are significant. Exacting taxes had been imposed upon the peoples of Africa in AD 85. These exactions may have followed upon the need of Domitian to find further sources of money in consequence of a landmark financial decision of AD 83.

In that year, Domitian made the boldest move of his early period. He increased pay throughout the armed forces by 33%, thereby placing heavy demands upon an exchequer which had only in the previous decade been brought back into stability by Vespasian.

It was a risk which many historians have since judged to have been the major fiscal error of Domitian's reign. In ancient times this was also the judgement delivered by the biographer Suetonius and the historian Dio. Coinage issued between April and September AD 85 seems to have been lightened in weight, suggesting that military payments were depleting the treasury. The revolt of the Nasamones in the same year may have been an indirect result of these measures.

The great fire in Titus's first months in AD 79, as well as his late father's policy of promoting public works, obliged Domitian to continue in Rome the programme of imperial building. The Capitoline temple of Jupiter Optimus Maximus, following its checkered career, was yet again rededicated on 7th December AD 82, only three years after it had been burned down.

Four years after the rededication, in imitation of the Greek Olympic span of four years, and in connection with the restoration after fire of the same temple and the whole Capitol, Domitian inaugurated the Capitoline Games.

In AD 88 he inaugurated a Secular Games, similar to those of Claudius of AD 48, intended to proclaim the start of a new and better era. In AD 90 he celebrated the Capitoline Games for the second time.

Domitian followed other imperial precedent in his concentration on the welfare of the city of Rome. In AD 85 he appointed the suffect consul Marcus Arrecinus Clemens as praefectus urbi, or "Governor of the City." In AD 89, following a previous edict of Vespasian, he reissued the same edict, banishing "astrologi" and "philosophi" from Rome.

However, he had in AD 83, at a time when the treasury of the Roman empire could not yet afford it, made to the army the grant of a pay rise of 33%! With this, he lost the balance of his budget and with it the equilibrium of his principate. Heavy expenditure and financial stress throughout the eighties had its effect on his personal judgement. Seven years after the pay rise, finance had to be found. There were wealthy Roman citizens to be plundered. In the nineties the emperor gave way. There broke out a reign of terror comparable to that of the Second Triumvirate of 43 BC, or Nero in the early and mid AD 60s.

In AD 93 was the trial of Baebius Massa and the executions of Arulenus Rusticus, Herennius Senecio and Helvidius Priscus. In AD 95 were the deaths of Acilius Glabrio and Titus Flavius Clemens, and the exile of the wife of Clemens, Flavia Domitilla.

Domitian did not fail to balance his budget. To that extent he was a conscientious emperor.

But in the end he balanced it in unjust, oppressive and unscrupulous ways. It was this reputation that incurred his assassination on 18th September AD 96 at the hands of a freedman of Flavia Domitilla. This is the reputation that has remained attached to the memory of the emperor Domitian ever since.

Would the death of Domitian, without successor, precipitate another outbreak of civil war, as on the death of Julius Caesar in 44 BC, or the suicide of Nero in AD 68? The Roman empire was now too firmly constitutionally established, and the Roman people too traumatised by civil war, for a third such catastrophe to arise. Nevertheless, tensions were high. The earliest events and actions of the reign of the next emperor reflect a final period of cautious awkwardness on the part of all those who were now conditioned, or resigned, to the imperial system.

The Emperors Nerva and Trajan

On 19th September AD 96, the day after the assassination of Domitian, Marcus Cocceius Nerva was recognised by the soldiery of Rome as the new emperor. Without delay, the Senate conferred upon him the next day, by decree, the two most fundamental offices of the Roman emperor – the "tribunicia potestas" ("tribunician power") and the "imperium proconsulare" ("proconsular authority") – and all other privileges and symbols of imperial authority. The return to orthodox Flavian exemplar was also effected immediately. The gold and silver statues of the emperor Domitian were within days pulled and melted down.

Nerva followed Titus in swearing that he would never put any senator to death. Citizens and senators who had received benefits from Domitian were protected by Nerva's clemency. Nerva worked to bring an end to senatorial vendettas. For his colleague in the consulship of AD 97 he chose the elderly confidant of Vespasian, Verginius Rufus.

In general the short reign of Nerva was characterised by caution. An old man, and perhaps feeling himself a caretaker, he surrounded himself with advisers of his own generation – that preceding the generation of Domitian. He aimed for conciliation in the Senate and in Rome, and for stability throughout the provinces. He continued the Flavian style of government from before, and without, the cruelty and rapacity of Domitian.

Nerva was childless, and accepted that he may not have long to live. Consulting with his body of sage and elderly councillors, specifically Frontinus and Ursinus, he agreed that the solution that would be best for the health of the whole empire, would be for him to adopt a strong candidate as his legal son and successor.

The consul of AD 91, Marcus Ulpius Traianus, of Spanish origin but of authoritative and glittering military career and of proven loyalty, stood out as easily the most advantageous candidate. He was adopted on 27th October AD 97. When Nerva died of a fever on 27th January AD 98, the wisdom of this constitutional device became apparent. So easily did the succession pass to Trajan that he did not even need to return to Rome until the autumn of AD 99!

The delight of the Roman people and of the empire in the character of Trajan himself and in the reality of his elevation to emperor, was concentrated by the Younger Pliny into his "Panegyric," his public address of the following year, AD 100. The title "Optimus" ("Best") coined by Pliny for Trajan in that loyal address of welcome remained with the office of emperor for ever. For consuls of that year, Trajan appointed the same Frontinus and Ursus who had been instrumental in his adoption by Nerva in October AD 97. The century ended with the constitution of the Roman empire more firmly cemented than at any time since the days of Augustus, and in the hands of an emperor who, for governing ability, was second only to Augustus.

The Late First Century AD and Today

In modern times, by Hadrian's Wall, an exciting archaeological discovery has taught the present generation details about military life on a distant Roman frontier with a vividness unknown before.

The Vindolanda tablets still had their writing and texture preserved when they were unearthed 1900 years later. Still in the process of restoration and translation, they contain miscellaneous letters and military orders dating from this decade, and throw light upon the daily life of the legions guarding the frontier where the Wall was shortly to be built.

John and John

The Christian Church suffered under the persecutions of Domitian in the last decade of the first century AD. It was emerging into sufficient international significance to attract the suspicion and animosity of the emperor. Flavia Domitilla herself is named in one of the catacombs of Rome.

Other Christian catacombs of the late first century AD have been found in Sicily at Agrigento and Syracuse. Archaeological remains demonstrate Christian presence in Syria, at Edessa and in Adiabene.

A glimpse of life under Domitianic persecution is revealed in the last book of the New Testament, the Book of Revelation. The plain passion of the author of Revelation is fuelled by anger at the tyrannous nature of the Roman empire and the number of martyrdoms the Christian body was obliged to suffer. A thread through the labyrinth of that lurid and mysterious work, emanating from the isle of Patmos, is the phrase "white garments," which is always an allusion to the sufferings, and the praises, of the martyrs.

The authorship of the Book of Revelation is attributed to "John the Divine." There is in the New Testament another John, the author of the Gospel of St. John and of three short Epistles. Although rough contemporaries, it is unlikely that the two writers were identical.

The latter St. John, Apostle and Evangelist, had a different destiny from the other members of the circle of Jesus. He was the longest lived of all the disciples. He was one of the few who did not die a violent death. Tradition separates him from all those who clustered around St. Peter and St. Paul in Rome, and locates him on the eastern coast of the Aegean, in the second largest city of the Roman empire, in Ephesus. Perhaps all three distinctive features are to be attributed to the unique custodianship of the mother of Jesus, entrusted to St. John by Jesus as he hung dying upon the Cross. In Ephesus John, and Mary the mother of Jesus, seem to have found refuge from the controversies and upheavals of contemporary Jerusalem.

In extreme old age, St. John also turned his mind and hand to writing in the Gospel genre.

He seems to have undertaken his task in consequence of long and deep meditation. His Gospel reflects a rising tide of Christian discipleship and self-confidence throughout the Roman world.

St. Luke, a decade before St. John, may have pitched the message of his Gospel for the Mediterranean. St. John was aware that he was interpreting the phenomenon of Jesus Christ to all the ages.

30
(Q)

"Where Can I Get A Drink?"
(AD 91–100)

The Feeding of the Five Thousand

Within the enlarging network of Church communities, all holding a common faith in Jesus Christ, common hospitality and common communications, there is little doubt that St. John in his lodgings in Ephesus was aware of the Gospel genre pioneered by St. Mark in Rome and developed by St. Matthew in Antioch and St. Luke. He appreciated the biographical programme by which their accounts of the ministry of Jesus led to a concluding climax in his crucifixion and resurrection.

However, when St. John came to supplement their work with his own contribution, his treatment of the genre was, like the rest of his destiny and background, entirely different.

St. John's Gospel was based upon six decades of recollection, meditation, observation and interpretation. The literature of St. Paul, composed in the late 40s, the 50s and the early 60s AD, had been passionate, energetic, unpolished, extravert; the measures of St. John, composed in the 90s AD and in his old age, were to be reflective, cogitated, ironical and intravert.

St. John began with a narrative (our "Chapter 1") introducing fifteen of the titles which, towards the end of the first century AD, had come to be applied to Jesus. He continued in later chapters with a series of "signs" performed by Jesus, each "sign" followed by an explanatory discourse. The Feeding of the Five Thousand in Chapter 6 of his Gospel was one in the sequence of these "signs"-and-discourses.

St. John himself made no division of his Gospel into chapters and verses. The system of chapter division still in use today (throughout the whole Bible) was drawn up, during his early career in the University of Paris, by Stephen Langton, Archbishop of Canterbury, who led the barons in forcing king John to sign the Magna Carta at Runymede in AD 1215. St. John begins his Chapter 6, according to the established (Langton) chapter notation, with the Feeding of the Five Thousand.

The Feeding of the Five Thousand is the only miracle (or "sign") of Jesus that is reported in all four Gospels. (The Feeding of the Four Thousand, described only in St. Mark and St. Matthew, is a parallel.) The natural question is, "Did this really happen?" "Did Jesus really feed a crowd of five thousand with the resources of only five loaves and two fishes?"

St. John follows the account of the Feeding of the Five Thousand with a note which supplies an indirect answer to this line of questioning. In the single verse 15 of chapter 6, he reports a brief episode which warns his readers not to use purely material criteria in their evaluation of Jesus.

Double Entendre

In the Gospel of St. John, many bystanders (commonly called "the Jews") are used as a shorthand allusion to all those who may be present at an event which has a double perspective, but upon whom it does not dawn that there may be an extended or interior meaning, a concealed reference or a "double entendre." Thus, the attempt to make Jesus a king (chapter 6, verse 15) is a materially-minded act, which grasps something of the majesty of Jesus, but fails to comprehend the nature of his realm or the inappropriateness of dignifying him with political office.

The same emphasis against a material interpretation of the Feeding of the Five Thousand is more unambiguously asserted by Jesus himself in the words, "Ye seek me, not because ye saw the miracles, but because ye did eat of the loaves and are filled," (chapter 6, verse 26) which he uses to open the discourse attached to and explaining the Feeding. The "double entendre" continues. From the beginning of his main discourse Jesus urges his hearers to be on the watch for the concealed reference. "Labour not for the meat that perisheth, but for that meat which endureth unto everlasting life, which the Son of Man shall give unto you" (chapter 6, verse 27).

Furthermore, the words "Labour not for the meat that perisheth" are a subtle reference to the Old Testament prophet Isaiah (chapter 55, verse 2). By three methods – the episode of the inappropriate kingship, by the echo of the Old Testament prophet, and by the nod given by Jesus himself towards the "double entendre" – St. John fends off the rationalist interpretations of those such as the nineteenth century scholar Strauss. It was the proposition of Strauss that the Feeding of the Five Thousand "worked" because the remainder of the crowd, prompted by the initiative of a young boy who had brought five barley loaves and two small fishes with him, all took out and shared together their previously prepared sandwiches and packed lunches!

Not directly, but by characteristic indirect and ironical allusion, St. John nudges his readers away from a mentality of crude or material literalism. When evaluating the Feeding of the Five Thousand we are to respond instead by listening to the interpretation and explanation of the miracle given by Jesus himself.

The discourse of Jesus that then follows (verses 28–59) selects from the Feeding of the Five Thousand the themes "feeding," and "satisfaction."

"Feeding" in the Feeding of the Five Thousand

St. John, and all who first read him towards the end of the first century AD, were well aware that there had been another occasion when Jesus had fed his disciples. By the time of the writing of the Gospel in the latter half of the decade of Domitian, Nerva and Trajan (the 90s AD) two or three generations of Christians had been feeding on this nourishment from Jesus for about sixty years.

At the Passover meal which became his "Last Supper," Jesus had commanded his disciples to eat broken bread (signifying his body, shortly to be crucified) and to drink wine (representing his blood, soon to be outpoured on the Cross). He had bidden them to eat and drink in this way in remembrance of him.

The two complex dimensions of "feeding" – the one material and literal, the other spiritual and sacramental – bind together the episode of the Feeding of the Five Thousand and Jesus' subsequent discourse and interpretation of it. They are the two members of the "double entendre" of St. John's Gospel, chapter 6 – the latter hiding behind the former.

"Satisfaction" in the Feeding of the Five Thousand

The consequence of the Feeding of the Five Thousand was that all five thousand participants in the picnic of bread and fish enjoyed the second theme of this sixth chapter of St. John – "satisfaction." They were "filled" (chapter 6, verse 12).

This is the same motif as that which is found in Isaiah chapter 55, verse 2, "Wherefore do ye spend money for that which is not bread? And your labour for that which *satisfieth* not? and in the late exilic Psalm 63, verse 6, "My soul shall be *satisfied,* even as it were with marrow and fatness: when my mouth praiseth thee with joyful lips."

Again, the identical word is used in St. Matthew, chapter 5, verse 6, "Blessed are they that hunger and thirst after righteousness: for they shall be *filled."* When Jesus is nearby or operating all are "filled" or "satisfied." This "Feeding of the Five Thousand" is therefore a complex meditation, involving scripture and "double entendre," upon the manner in which the presence of Jesus "satisfies." It points to Jesus as the only answer to the multi-layered existential question, "Where can I get a drink?"

Thus the "Feeding of the Five Thousand" is an event-and-interpretation combined, dealing with universal human questioning about "satisfaction." It is not only about the satisfaction of simple material hunger. It is also a demonstration of the much greater capability of Jesus to satisfy all the hungers, thirsts, deficiencies, longings, curtailments and inadequacies of our mortality. Between verses 16 and 24 of St. John chapter 6, there takes place a profound and mysteriously glowing transition from the "sign" of the Feeding of the Five Thousand to the full, barely interrupted discourse upon it. The interpretative discourse proper then follows from verse 35.

The "Double Entendre" Displayed

Like the transition from the "sign" to the explanation of it, the discourse which begins at St. John, chapter 6, verse 35, is woven throughout, sometimes to the point of repetitiveness. The repetitiveness serves to illuminate from a variety of angles the truths which St. John wants the discourse of Jesus to convey.

From his vantage point in the 90s AD, St. John knows that the destiny of Jesus is to die by crucifixion. He knows that on the Cross the body of Jesus is to be rent and pierced, and his blood shed. He knows that through this sacrificial suffering Jesus is to achieve the redemption of the world; and that this redemption embraces forgiveness of sin, the assuagement of every fear, the satisfaction of every human hunger and the gift of everlasting life.

St. John knows, finally, that Jesus used the occasion of the Jewish Passover to celebrate with his disciples that traditional Passover Supper which became in his hands his "Last Supper." He had seen that Last Supper become for ever after an institution at which, by means of bread and wine the human race could assert and adore Christ's redemption and make it, with certainty, individual by individual, their own. St. John understood that all those who partake of the Last Supper, however remote in time and space from its institution at Passover AD 33, will find the insufficiencies of their humanity "filled" or "satisfied."

Against this background the discourse of his sixth chapter winds over and over, asserting again and again in simplest language this redemptive process:

"I am the living bread which cometh down from heaven, that a man may eat thereof, and not die" (verses 50–51).

"Whoso eateth my flesh and drinketh my blood, hath eternal life; and I will raise him up at the last day." (verse 54) "As the living Father hath sent me, and I live by the Father; so he that eateth me, even he shall live by me." (verse 57) (All quotations from St. John's Gospel, chapter 6.)

The Ultimate Three Minutes

Throughout the discourse, as throughout the earlier phases of St. John's Gospel, there resounds from time to time the principle behind all existence in the abbreviated form "I am" – the same formula pronounced first to Moses, and received and passed on through Second Isaiah. Thus, the discourse of St. John, chapter 6, delivers in verse 35 the claim "I am the bread of life," and continues at verse 51, "I am the living bread which came down from heaven."

Whether Jesus actually spoke these words, or whether they are the insightful, cogitated, inspired composition of St. John, makes little difference. In these verses are pronounced in the ears of the whole human race, with the authority of the Creator himself, the promise of the cancellation of death and the reassurance of eternal life. St. John's Gospel chapter 6 is a passage universal for all mankind, especially in those gasping, unsatisfied, thirsty hours when any human being asks, on any level, "Where can I get a drink?"

31
(R)

The Decade of Trajan (AD 101–110)

Roman Spring

If a Roman Senator from one hundred years before the birth of Jesus Christ (100 BC), were to be revived a hundred years after the birth of Jesus Christ (AD 100), he would find that after two hundred years the city of Rome, its territories and empire, and its methods of governance, were unrecognisable.

In the Civil Wars of 49–42 BC, and the discomposures that began to be resolved only in 30 BC, Rome had suffered constitutional earthquake. The fortunate combination of genius and longevity in Augustus had secured a settled peace. There were aftershocks, slight in the case of Tiberius and Claudius, in the cases of Caligula, Nero and Domitian, severe.

Two hundred years after our notional Senator of 100 BC, as the first century Anno Domini (AD) drew to a close, there came to the imperial throne a governor whom history was to record as second only to Augustus for force of administration and for human understanding. Later emperors were to be saluted obsequiously as "Felicior Augusto, melior Traiano" ("Happier than Augustus; better than Trajan"). The title "Optimus" ("Best"), informally coined by Pliny for Trajan in his "Panegyric" of AD 100, became an official title of the emperor in the year AD 114.

Trajan was 45 years old when he became emperor in January AD 98. Like Augustus, he possessed the common touch. He behaved in Rome as a private citizen, submissive to the law. He was praised for his "civilitas" and for his "moderatio." Rejuvenation, or the return of spring to Rome, was therefore claimed to accompany his ascent to the imperial throne.

Blessed with firmer health than Augustus, Trajan did not, like Augustus, remain closer and closer to Rome as he grew older. On the contrary, he was frequently away from Rome, in the Dacian Wars of March AD 101 to December AD 102; and again of June AD 105 to AD 106; and in the Parthian Wars of his second decade. His death, in AD 116, at the age of 64, was out on a Parthian campaign.

The pace and manner of arrival of the new emperor in Rome set the tone for his forthcoming principate. On the death of Nerva he was holding the post of governor of Upper Germany, centred on Mainz. From there he visited the Danube, the troops in Pannonia, and then worked out a formal peace treaty with the Suebi. He returned to Rome late in AD 99, only in time for the consular elections of the year AD 100.

He entered Rome on foot, mingled and chatted with the crowd, benevolent and approachable to all; he greeted each individual in the manner befitting their social standing in the state. He did not, like Augustus, have to wade through slaughter to a throne; the system was there, waiting for the ideal man to operate. Trajan exercised a hands-off style of administration. He was consul only three times in his nineteen years; for over half of his reign he was out of Rome altogether.

The historical sources for the early second century AD are few, indicating a less controversial era than the decades that had gone before, attracting less comment from ancient contemporaries. We know little of Trajan's campaigns, administration and monuments, even less about his motives, policies or objectives.

War in Dacia

The first great enterprise of the second century AD was Trajan's Dacian campaign of March AD 101. It began as soon as the weather was warm enough for fighting, and it continued to the end of the following year. The second Dacian campaign was the eighteen months from June AD 105 to the end of AD 106. It concluded with the death of Decebalus, leader of the Dacians, and from then on Dacia became a Roman province. The monument to the conduct of these Dacian Wars was Trajan's Column, which was erected in Trajan's Forum in the following decade and which still stands today.

Why Trajan chose this part of the north-east corner of the empire to assert his authority; what was the course of the campaigns; why two were necessary; what were the motives and manoeuvres of Decebalus – all these essential elements in the progress of the campaigns are undiscoverable from the sources. Trajan's column, a mine of information about the social history of military life, is too ambiguous a source for the outline of the wars.

In AD 103, between the two Dacian campaigns, the Circus Maximus was completed in Rome. Other ambitious building projects were undertaken in the capital later in this decade. In AD 104 Nero's former "Golden House" was destroyed by fire. In AD 108 the Temple of the Vestal Virgins was pulled down and rebuilt, and the road called the "Via Nova Traiana" was laid. In AD 109 were put up Trajan's "Naumachia," the Aqua Traiana, and, on the site of Nero's former "Golden House," the Baths of Trajan.

From so much building, so soon after the Dacian campaigns, historians can only speculate that the campaigns were undertaken as much to gain and exploit mineral wealth, as to demonstrate Roman imperial power among potential barbarian insurgents.

Because Trajan was of a military temperament and made it his priority to campaign in vulnerable frontier provinces it is, following his Dacian Wars, of provincial government, rather than of administration in the city of Rome, that a greater body of evidence has come down to modern times.

Within Rome itself, Trajan continued to follow the initiative of Domitian in placing knights rather than freedmen in the most sensitive secretarial posts. Within Italy the emperor instituted very early in his reign an alimentary, or relief, scheme for poor families and orphan children. However, because the civilisation of Rome and Italy was relatively tranquil, all the more was Trajan able to indulge his preference for the camps of the armed forces in the provinces and on the frontiers.

Trajan and the Provinces

In Germany, Domitian's division of the territory into two provinces was endorsed and allowed to stand.In AD 106 Pannonia was also divided into two provinces, "Inferior" ("Lower") and "Superior" ("Upper"). The province of Dacia was created in AD 106 once Trajan had defeated the barbarians of the Dacian plains. The death in AD 106 of Rabbel II of Nabataea suggested the advisability of readjusting the whole general area of the Middle East.

Aulus Cornelius Palma Frontonianus, governor of Syria, temporarily annexed the kingdom of Rabbel II. Trajan then apppointed Gaius Claudius Severus as the first governor of the new, independent, province of Arabia. His first task was to found Bostra as the capital of Arabia Nabataea. Judaea also became a third, independent, province within this complex.

In AD 109–110 Pliny the Younger (author in AD 100 of the "Panegyricus") was commissioned by Trajan as governor of Bithynia/Pontus. His correspondence with Trajan during his governorship throws much light on provincial government under Trajan, life in the Greek east, and the mentality of Trajan himself.

Pliny notes that as a matter of policy Trajan drove the standard of provincial administration upwards by rewarding good provincial governors rather than by punishing the bad. Indirectly out of the correspondence is reflected the blunt common sense, the combination of humanity and efficiency which characterised and distinguished the reign of Trajan. Never since the third or early fourth decades of Augustus had the empire been governed by such instinctive humanitarian wisdom as under the emperor Trajan

Straws in the Wind

Under Trajan the Roman empire was at this point about to enter almost a century of tranquillity and peace, both constitutionally within the city and externally across the empire.

Following the foundations laid by Augustus and consolidated by Vespasian and Trajan, the Roman empire was due to introduce a period of placid contentment which was to remain a formative influence, and, for its blessedness, the envy, of all mankind. It would be inappropriate, at such an historic moment, to leap four centuries ahead and anticipate the fall of such an empire.

Nevertheless, very faintly under Trajan already, there began to assemble certain minimal forces which, ultimately taking four centuries to gather full momentum, were, with other associated influences, to bring the Roman empire in the west to a new phase of unrecognisable transformation.

These straws in the wind were three in number: the regularity of the absence from Rome of the emperor; the partiality of the emperor for the armed forces; and a barely discernible breeze of migratory population movement blowing from the north-east.

A Time of Consolidation

Early in the second century AD, within the shadows, and parallel to the empire of Trajan, a new institution was slowly forming. Within the Christian Church the period of great inspirational literature was over, as St. John, the last surviving Apostle who had known Jesus Christ, died. The Christian faith and the Roman empire had been born together in the early, breath-taking decades of the first century AD. In the early pedestrian decades of the second century AD, both together began to settle into a mood of steady institutionalism.

From this era the Epistle of Jude and its enlargement, the Second Epistle of St.Peter, were the only two complete works that in later times were finally accepted within the New Testament. The inauthentic ending of St. Mark (Mark, chapter 16, verses 8b to the end), breathes the second century AD with its glances back to St. Luke and the deterioration of its buoyancy into a hardening fundamentalism.

The inheritance left by the evangelists, by St. Paul, and by the other writers of what came to be known later as the "New Testament," took centuries to work out and digest. It was too rich for the fourth generation of the Christian Church, those who were sundered only by some seventy years from the death and resurrection of Jesus. They cherished what had been transmitted to them; they were nourished upon it and formed by it; but they were too close to it to appreciate even the half of its facets and the power of its message.

Divested of outstanding and prominent personalities, the Church at this stage was beginning to develop an internationalism, a spirit of coherence, a strength of administration, which were to knit it in the future into an efficiently regulated estate within the Roman empire. Its work in the second century AD was practical, foundation-laying, but unsung.

Possessing the solution to the thirsts and anguishes of mortality, but unrecognised, passing through tests of survival but teetering on the edge of world mission, it was at the same time both pathetic and heroic. Without many protagonists of genius, without any outstanding Biblical theologian or even method of finding an orientation in the rich heritage of its scriptures, by a process of dogged administrative consolidation, by world-wide contact and uniformity, and especially by the celebration of their Lord's Last Supper, the membership of the Church formed an identity, held a course, and developed an impetus.

For all that, one figure does stand out in the first decade of the second century AD – Ignatius of Antioch. Arrested during the outbreak of a certain persecution and transported to Rome to face martyrdom in AD 107, Ignatius as he journeyed wrote five letters to Asian churches, one to Polycarp and one to Rome itself.

The fact that Antioch itself had attained character and prominence within the fellowship of the early Church was a reflection of a catalogue of Christian centres that was unselfconsciously developing.

After Antioch, lesser sites in Syria by this time were Apamaea and Edessa. A circle of Church communities centred in Asia around Ephesus, as is indicated in the 90s AD by the Book of Revelation. The presence of the Church in Bithynia and Pontus is witnessed by the First Epistle of St. Peter and by Pliny's correspondence with Trajan. The main centre of Christianity in Greece was Corinth.

There is no solid evidence for Christianity in Gaul or Egypt at this time (although for Alexandria at least there is some in earlier decades), but it may be assumed that, as among the soldiery governing Britain, the faith was rooting itself in such less regarded provinces in informal ways.

32
(s)

The Decade of Trajan and Hadrian
(AD 111–120)

Trajan and Hadrian

The emperors Trajan (AD 98–117) and Hadrian (AD 117–138) have a fair claim to be after the founding emperor Augustus and the reforming emperor Vespasian, the greatest with whom the Roman empire was ever blessed.

Trajan by his Dacian and Parthian conquests enlarged the empire to its fullest ever extent, deep inwards to the north and east of its Mediterranean border heartlands. Hadrian possessed the most cultivated and investigative mind of any emperor that sat on the seat of government in Rome.

On the other hand, their elevations were fortunate in their timing. The constitutional mechanism put in place by Augustus took ten decades after his death to settle down. He combined all the social forces in a united flow, but it took time for the channel to wear smooth. Longest of all was the time taken to resolve the problem of the succession from one emperor to the next. Only when the system of adoption had been tried, tested and established, was it secure. Only in the cases of Trajan and Hadrian themselves was its operation, by designation, without serious contest.

For by the time of Trajan and Hadrian, the age of the fall of the Republic and the rise of the imperial system, the fear, the urgency, the rivalry, the drama, the daring, the blood, the fire, were over. For this reason the pace of interest of contemporary historians slackens. The "Annals" of Tacitus (AD 116 or 120) covers the Julio-Claudian empire (30 BC–AD 68). Suetonius's "Twelve Caesars" (AD 120) does not enter the second century AD There were some military adventures under Trajan, but the reigns of Trajan and Hadrian were mostly occupied with architecture and administration.

Arabia and Judaea

In AD 115 a revolt broke out among Jews dispersed in Cyrene and Alexandria, both colonies at loggerheads with their local populations. When in AD 117 it concluded, still the Jews in the homeland of Judaea itself showed themselves fractious. Lusius Quietus was appointed governor of Judaea and in AD 120, at a time when even in Dacia military cover was being reduced, an extra legion was drafted into Judaea.

The first concerns of Augustus in 30 BC had been to emerge as sole emperor/survivor and to stabilise the Roman state. The first concern of the decade AD 111–120, in which Trajan gave place to Hadrian, was to establish the province of Arabia. To this end Gaius Claudius Severus, the first governor, was given ten years from AD 106–116 to lay the foundations of provincial administration. The road from Bostra to Petra along which the administration ran was begun in AD 111 and completed in AD 115. In AD 119 the patrol of the recently conquered province of Dacia was reduced by Hadrian to a single legion, and the province itself downgraded from consular to praetorian status.

Building Policies

There was oportunity now, in this relatively contented context, to channel energies into confident and lasting architecture.

Early in the decade, on 1st January 112, the Forum Traiani and the Basilica Ulpiana were dedicated as monuments to the Dacian wars. In AD 113 Trajan's Column was added to the complex. Julius Caesar's temple of Venus Genetrix, having been rebuilt and completed, was dedicated, and a new harbour at Ostia also reached completion. In AD 118 Hadrian began reconstruction of Agrippa's Pantheon.

In 32 BC Augustus, with Agrippa and Maecenas had, in conflict with Cleopatra, had to strain every nerve to unite the west under loyalty to Augustus. Now the emperors were of western, Spanish, origin, and the building programme of Rome was extended to the

Italian peninsula. Trajan was so delighted with his new road from Beneventum to Brundisium that it appears on the coinage from AD 112 onwards. Trajan's Arch at Beneventum dates from AD 114. At Ancona in AD 115 improvements were made to the harbour, and finally crowned with another Arch of Trajan.

Outside in the provinces, earthquake victims were succoured – in northern Syria on 13th Deember AD 115 and in north-west Asia Minor in AD 120. Other monuments were erected: Trajan's Arch in Asseria, Dalmatia, in AD 112; a shrine of Trajan at Smyrna in AD 114; the monument of Philopappos in Athens in AD 116; the library in Ephesus; and, after his accession, a monumental gate and court to Hadrian at Perge in AD 117.

The Death of Trajan

Having enlarged in the previous decade the empire's boundaries along the eastern Danube by the conquest of Dacia, the restless Trajan set out on 27th October AD 113 on his Parthian Wars.

In a number of ways, his reign up until that time had marked an appropriate completion to the imperial movement given its earliest and fullest impulse by Augustus. No other emperor since Augustus had understood as well as Trajan how to channel the currents of Roman aspiration and idealism both in favour of his own advantage and the advantage of the whole Roman empire. As Augustus, an Italian rather than a Roman aristocrat, had been able to perceive and guide the travails of Rome from his own provincial but wider perspective, so Trajan, of Spanish rather than even of Italian origin, was able to perceive from a yet more international field of vision, the imperial task to which he had been called.

Thus under Trajan senators and soldiery of the eastern empire began to increase in number, so that their contribution to governance and control began to be equivalent to that of the west. The power of freedmen was reduced, and while the emperor gathered more and more decision-making to himself and into the circle of the peripatetic court which followed him round the empire, the dignity and respect due to the Senate, stationary in Rome, was never diminished, but rather enhanced.

Trajan understood how Augustus had at one and the same time both restored the Republic and yet taken into his own hands a firmer grip of the administration of the empire. He was able to repeat the

same formula, with the redoubled effectiveness of popular familiarity and appeal.

Having assembled such a bequest, in his campaign of AD 114
Trajan annexed to the empire Armenia, Mesopotamia and Assyria.
He received from the Senate the title "Optimus" ("The Best") and
wintered in Edessa. In AD 115 he captured Ctesiphon (Baghdad)
and returned to winter in Antioch. On 27th February AD 116 he was
given the title "Parthicus" by the Senate. He never returned to
Rome.

On 9th August AD 117 at Selinus in Cilicia, on his way home from
the Parthian Wars, he died, aged 64. He was succeeded two days
later by Hadrian. In AD 118 his eastern conquests, except for
Armenia, were abandoned. Hadrian was not prepared to extend
Roman forces and energies up to or beyond the Tigris and the
Euphrates.

Hadrian and the Spanish Connection

Trajan's death in AD 117 left the last three years of the second
decade of the second century AD under the command of the
emperor Hadrian (born AD 76, emperor AD 117–138).

Hadrian took the consulship in AD 118 and AD 119, his
colleagues being, respectively, Gnaeus Pedanius Fuscus in AD 118
and in AD 119 Publius Dasumius Rusticus. The consuls of AD 120
were Titus Aurelius Fulvus Antoninus and Catilius Severus, son-
in-law of Marcus Annius Severus, praefectus urbi ("Governor of
Rome") and himself consul, for the second time, in AD 121.

Background studies of these personalities reveals a strong
Spanish element in their appointments, in line with the Spanish
origins of Hadrian himself. Thus there was already dominant in
Rome that Spanish connection which was in AD 138 to provide the
aforementioned Titus Aurelius Fulvus Antoninus, as successor to
Hadrian.

"Most Happy and Prosperous"

Hadrian remained in Italy for the first three years of his reign, until
the spring of AD 121.

This was not to prove typical, for in retrospect, Hadrian seems to have spent almost as much time in the provinces and out of Rome as within it. He followed his first three years with a western, and then an eastern, emergency tour.

In the course of the western tour, in Britain in AD 122 he ordered the construction of Hadrian's Wall. By now however, the radical reforms of Augustus between 30 BC and AD 14 had been entrenched by a century's experience and had been consolidated by the firm and businesslike hand of Trajan. The great era of the founding of the Roman empire was now established, complete and irreversible. It remained for Hadrian and the second century AD to build upon the foundations and enjoy them before, with the end of the second century, there followed the first ripples of early erosion.

Before that process began, with Hadrian and the Roman people the whole era was in safe hands, secure politics and civil tranquillity. Hadrian has been described as "the most remarkable of all Roman emperors" and "the intellectual emperor." Ancient writers stressed his restless travelling, his insatiable inquisitiveness, his complex, many-sided personality. His military and frontier policy, his obsessive generosity to the Greeks and his ruthless treatment of the Jews were the three elements which had the greatest long-term impact.

The famous words of Edward Gibbon in his "Decline and Fall of the Roman Empire" (ch. 3) pronounce a verdict which appropriately belongs here, at the end of the "long" first century AD and at the passage into the era that begins with the emperor Hadrian: "If a man were called to fix the period in the history of the world during which the condition of the human race was most happy and prosperous, he would, without hesitation, name that which elapsed from the death of Domitian to the accession of Commodus. The vast extent of the Roman empire was governed by absolute power, under the guidance of virtue and wisdom. The armies were restrained by the firm but gentle hand of four successive emperors whose character and authority commanded involuntary respect. The forms of civil administration were carefully preserved." A creative, colourful and turbulent "long" century was over.

Growing Secretly

The Christian Church was not prominent in the early decades of the second century AD It was digesting its inheritance and cogitating upon its future mission. Its most prominent names were the martyrs Ignatius of Antioch and Polycarp of Smyrna. One of its bishops, Papias, retailed scraps of memory from St. Peter and the primitive Church.

By some, the "Shepherd of Hermas" is accredited to this decade; and the Rylands papyrus, a fragment of St. John's Gospel, an ancient piece of writing still in existence today, is believed to descend from these early second century AD times.

Otherwise the Church at this era has been likened to a small pilot-light, "the little flame, pale and flickering though it be, which trembled in the souls of the elect like a faint dawn."

33

The "Century" of the Two Watersheds
(50 BC–AD 120)

The "Long" First Century AD

63 BC	23rd September	Birth of Gaius Julius Octavius
49 BC	10th January	Julius Caesar crosses the Rubicon
45 BC	September	Caesar nominates Octavius as his adopted son, and heir
44 BC	15th March	Assassination of Julius Caesar
30 BC		"Tribunicia Potestas" for life conferred by the Senate on Octavian
30 BC	1st August	Suicide of Mark Antony
30–29 BC	Winter	Octavian, Agrippa, Maecenas and others plan the new politics of Rome
27 BC	16th January	Octavian takes title "Augustus" and office "Imperium Proconsulare"
17 BC	26th May–3rd June	"Ludi Saeculares" ("Secular Games")
9 BC	30th January	Dedication of "Ara Pacis" ("Altar of Peace")
6 BC (?)	Birth of Jesus Christ	
2 BC	5th February	Grant to Augustus of the title "Pater Patriae" ("Father of the Fatherland") and dedication of the temple of

		Mars Ultor ("Mars the Avenger") and the Forum of Augustus
AD 14	19th August	Death of Augustus; Tiberius emperor
AD 27		Pontius Pilate appointed by Tiberius as governor of Judaea
AD 28 (?)		Preaching of John the Baptist
AD 30		Beginning of the Ministry of Jesus Christ
AD 33	Passover	Crucifixion and Resurrection of Jesus Christ
AD 33	Pentecost	Foundation of the Church
AD 37	16th March	Death of Tiberius
AD 37	18th March	Caligula emperor
AD 38		St. Paul in Syria and Cilicia
AD 41	24th January	Assassination of Caligula
AD 42	25th January	Claudius emperor
AD 48		Council of Jerusalem
AD 52	18th September	Birth of Marcus Ulpius Traianus (Trajan)
AD 53		St. Paul, having passed through Asia, Macedonia, Achaea, Philippi and Thessalonica, arrives in Corinth
AD 54	13th October	Death of Claudius; Nero emperor
AD 62		Arrival of St. Paul in Rome
AD 65 (?)		St. Mark's Gospel
AD 68	9th June	Suicide of Nero; Galba emperor
AD 69		Year of the Four Emperors
	1st–15th January	Galba
	15th January to 16th April	Otho
	16th April to 21st December	Vitellius
	21st December	Vespasian
AD 70	Late summer	Arrival of Vespasian in Rome
AD 75 (?)		St. Matthew's Gospel
AD 79	24th June	Death of Vespasian; Titus emperor

AD 81	13ᵗʰ September	Death of Titus; Domitian emperor
AD 85 (?)		St. Luke's Gospel and Acts of the Apostles
AD 95 (?)		St. John's Gospel
AD 96	18ᵗʰ September	Death of Domitian; Nerva emperor
AD 98	27ᵗʰ January	Death of Nerva; Trajan emperor
AD 117	9ᵗʰ August	Death of Trajan
AD 117	11ᵗʰ August	Hadrian emperor

The First Watershed

It seems to stretch the humour of historians beyond a joke to call a period of 170 years a "long" century. Nevertheless, events which formed the fulcrum upon which the whole of human history turned prove to have extended beyond a single century, and in both directions. Since they also form a single unit, even at the cost of trespassing upon a comical convention, they have been gathered together, and are here summarised, as the components of a "long" century.

On 10ᵗʰ January 49 BC Julius Caesar finally made the desperate and momentous decision to embark on civil war. When by superior ruthlessness, military technique and will-power he had conquered and slaughtered his enemy, Pompey, and emerged victorious, he discovered that, like his predecessor Sulla earlier in the century, there was no other power in Rome equal to his own. He accepted the title, descended from the ancient Republic, that Sulla had also accepted, "Dictator," for a span of ten years. He also in 45 BC nominated Gaius Julius Octavius, the son of his niece Atia and grandson of his sister Julia, as his heir.

There still survived in Rome an indignant spirit of Republicanism to which the notion of a ten-year dictatorship was as abhorrent as the notion of a king. A knot of Republicans conspired together to assassinate Caesar on 15ᵗʰ March 44 BC, and thereby plunged Rome into fourteen years of further civil strife.

When this ended in 30 BC, Roman control, especially in the east, was still (remarkably) firmly grounded; and in the west Roman and Italian loyalties were concentrated with an unprecedented compactness. War weariness was everywhere, and with a possibility that intact Roman rule would survive, the opportunity at last presented itself to embark upon a lasting peace. Would the final survivor of almost twenty years of civil disruption, Julius Caesar's nominated heir Gaius Julius Octavius (now called "Octavian") show himself capable of exploiting the situation?

Octavian's measure in 32 BC in gathering together the whole west in a personal oath of allegiance to himself, showed that he was already thinking ahead beyond the conclusion of the civil disorders of the Triumvirate. He could therefore grasp the opportunities of the situation imaginatively and authoritatively.

Octavian was more observant than Julius Caesar. It had not been a mistake to go back to the ancient Roman Republic to borrow a title to express his uncontested one-man rule – but it had been a mistake to borrow the title "Dictator." For himself, Octavian chose in 30 BC the ancient but less obtrusive title and powers of a tribune of the people, which he accepted from the Senate for life.

This was a supreme, but disguised, power over the formation of all *home* policy.

Three years later in 27 BC, in taking for himself the title by which he has been known universally every since, "Augustus," he also accepted from the Senate the grant of proconsular authority. This was another Republican power, giving him a supreme, but disguised, grasp upon the formation of all *foreign* policy. Augustus was thus more firmly established as "Dictator" in Rome than ever the insecure Julius Caesar – but the titles under which he concealed his dictatorship and the affability of his demeanour made it possible for him to persuade the Senate and people of Rome that he had restored to them their Republic!

It must have been in the autumn and winter of 30–29 BC that Octavian, Agrippa, Maecenas, perhaps Octavian's sister Octavia, and a few others, planned the scheme of new politics which was to transform the fortunes of Rome and, by conferring internal civil peace, to endure for centuries. At home it was needed to reform society, especially the Senate; to settle the veterans of armies dangerously swollen by civil war; to restore morality and matrimony; to curb the numbers of freedmen; to feed the population and to water it; to stiffen general morale; to beautify the capital city; to irradiate every proceeding with poetical propaganda. Abroad it was necessary to round out the boundaries of the empire and maintain the peoples within it in peace and contentment.

The celebration of the Secular Games in 17 BC became the signal that the tribune-for-life of 30 BC had, with the support of his circle and the good will of the civilised world, achieved his objectives in *home* policy.

The dedication of the "Ara Pacis" ("Altar of Peace") on 30th January 9 BC was the assertion that the perpetually renewed proconsul of 27 BC and onward had, with appropriate assistance, achieved his objectives in *foreign* policy.

On 5th February 2 BC the grant of the title "Pater Patriae" ("Father of the Fatherland") and the dedication of the temple of Mars Ultor ("Mars the Avenger"), symbolised together that Augustus's life's work was accomplished. Nevertheless, it was the will of Providence to spare Augustus for another whole sixteen years so that later adjustments could be made and firmer legislation for his home and foreign policies be framed – but above all so that the number of living Romans who could remember late Republican times before Augustus, could dwindle significantly away.

Granted that every human individual is unique, Augustus was an individual more unique than others. His personality could not be assessed alongside other stereotypes, and his achievements in politics could not be, and never have been, equalled! While the restored "Republic" – the ever less disguised empire – endured, the personalities who succeeded Augustus in the post of emperor were more types of the common human clay, stock personalities, almost from the sketchbooks of the comic playwright Plautus – or from P.G. Wodehouse!

In the "long" first century AD, which now stretched out to AD 120, Augustus was followed by the severe Great Uncle (Tiberius, AD 14–37); the Wastrel Nephew (Caligula, AD 37–41); "Somehow He Gets It Right" (Claudius, AD 41–54); the Racy Profligate (Nero, AD 54–68); the Great Crash (The Year of the Four Emperors, AD 69); the Stern Soldier (Vespasian, AD 69–79); the Soldier's Son (Titus, AD 79–81); the Choleric Inadequate (Domitian, AD 81–96); the Capable Stop-Gap (Nerva, AD 96–98); the Imperturbable Maestro (Trajan, AD 98–117); and the Investigative Maestro (Hadrian, AD 117–138).

With Trajan, the empire found an emperor born in imperial times (AD 53), of provincial stock (Spanish), instinctively sympathetic to the common man, administratively competent, militarily firm, knowing his own mind. With him the empire reached its furthest geographical extent. Under him it embarked upon almost a century of radiating contentment, order, prosperity and peace. The successor of Augustus who most intuitively understood Augustus laid the final coping-stone on the monument of the imperial achievement of Augustus.

From the reign of Trajan begins that period which Gibbon has marked as that in the history of the world during which "the condition of the human race was most happy and prosperous."

From a wider perspective, all the currents of ancient history, from Mesopotamia and Egypt, from Assyria and Babylonia, from Media, Persia and western Asia, from Israel, the Aegean and from Greece, had flowed together and concentrated down into the period and reign of Augustus.

Not only that, but all the currents of modern history, the boundaries of European nations, the languages, laws, culture, mentality, religion, dynamism of subsequent centuries fan out from the era of Augustus.

"The empire of Augustus has been compared to 'a great reservoir into which the currents of ancient history flowed, and out of which arose all the streams of later history in the western world'" (Dame Veronica Wedgwood).

By the workings of an incalculable providence, Gaius Julius Octavius, born 23rd September 63 BC, died 14th August AD 14, more commonly known as "Augustus," came to be set at the watershed of all human history. And yet there was more!

The Second Watershed

Some time shortly before AD 30, when Pontius Pilate, having been appointed by the emperor Tiberius as governor of Judaea in AD 27, was exercising his nervous but conscientious authority, one John the Baptist appeared in the deserts of the same province, proclaiming a cosmic and climactic message that there was yet another watershed at hand!

Introduced by John the Baptist in such terms – which were not exaggerated – Jesus of Nazareth entered Galilee on foot and embarked on a three-year period of teaching, healing and travelling which brought him ultimately to Jerusalem.

Put to death by contrivance of the authorities by crucifixion, at Passover time in AD 33, Jesus of Nazareth three days later rose again from the dead, undisputed victor over it, and thereby discloser to human vision of otherwise unimaginable vistas of possibility and hope. These extreme events, it should be principally noted, were preceded by the celebration by Jesus of Nazareth of his Last Supper.

By AD 38, within a year of the death of Tiberius, St. Paul was trumpeting the resurrection of Jesus Christ about the Roman provinces of Syria and Cilicia. Within fifteen years he had gone through Roman Asia, Macedonia, Achaea, and the towns of Philippi, Thessalonica and Corinth. By AD 62 he was proclaiming the risen Christ in Nero's Rome.

Other unsung apostles and evangelists were working in the eastern Roman empire. Within a generation of the Last Supper, Crucifixion and Resurrection of Jesus Christ, a shadow universal Church was in efficient formation.

Linked by correspondence in the first generation (AD 33–63), the Church began to cohere and draw inspiration during the second generation (AD 63–93) from compiled accounts of the birth, life, passion, suffering, death and resurrection of Jesus Christ. These were published successively by St. Mark for the persecuted Christians of Rome (about AD 65); by St. Matthew for the growing church of Antioch (about AD 75); and by St. Luke for the Graeco-Roman world (about AD 85).

In the third generation of the existence of the Church (AD 93–123), the compilation of St. John (about AD 95) equipped it to go out to face all the ages with the unique message of Jesus Christ's Redeeming Incarnation.

All these consequences were unforeseen by Julius Caesar when, on 10th January 49 BC, he gave command to his troops, warriors and legionaries to force the crossing of the river Rubicon.

34

The Century of the Climax of the Ancient World
(AD 101–200)

The Second Century AD

More than a Golden Age

The first century AD, with its historic watersheds, whether "short" or "long," was heavy with destiny, individualism and colour, much of it lurid. By contrast the second century AD was monochrome – yet the colour was gold!

It was so declared by the historian Dio in the third century AD; by Gibbon (by implication) in the eighteenth century AD; by Mommsen in the nineteenth century; and by Helmut Galsterer in the twentieth century. This age of gold however came to an end with the death in AD 180 of Marcus Aurelius; under his son Commodus, emperor AD 180 to the 31st December AD 192, there emerged a colourful individualism once again.

If however the first eighty years of the second century AD were an age of gold, at least it was 24-carat "gold." There were none of the violent contrasts, there was nothing of the adventurism, the cliff-hanging drama of the first century. The second century AD was not the volatile ferment and did not suffer the shifts of fortune of its preceding century. Its characteristics were solid, its mood earnest and worthy. Sober, ponderous, safe, its leaders and its institutions acted as though conscious of, and building upon and conserving, a hard-won and treasured heritage.

The Roman empire of the second century AD may be likened to an edifice of cathedral dimensions which, in the last decades of the second century was beginning to prove a building too monumental for its inhabitants. Not through their own incompetence or neglect, but through the magnificence of its own overwhelming proportions, the Roman empire was in these later years to begin to dwarf its residents and then to suffer the earliest tremors of its erosion.

The favourable historical judgements delivered upon the greater part of the second century AD rest upon two enterprises: the steady, unopposed Romanisation of all territories within the Roman empire; and the "consensus of Nerva" (AD 96–180), the self-effacing responsibleness of the individual members of the governing classes.

The "Consensus of Nerva"

From Nerva and Trajan onwards, until Commodus, emperors, as former senators, worked with and understood the Senate in a partnership that was advantageous to all. Thinking men had come to see that serious and benevolent government of a wide, secure and powerful empire could no longer be guaranteed, as it had been under Augustus, by one man alone. Around the emperor had to circulate a like-minded team of subordinate administrators, all of them willing to accept his place in a hierarchy and to work reliably within it in the interests of just government for all.

Examples of such administrators had been Agricola in the 80s, Pliny the Younger at the turn of the century, and Trajan himself.

On his death in 117 Trajan was succeeded by the heir he had already designated by adoption – by Hadrian, the restless emperor, the imaginative emperor, the lover of Greece, the architect emperor, the dilettante, poet, traveller and romantic. His building of Hadrian's Wall (AD 122) was the first symptom of the far- and long-distant erosion which was to begin to undermine the Roman empire. It indicated the earliest limitation and revised deployment of the army which was to characterise Hadrian's reign.

No longer was the army to stand on the frontiers ready, as in Trajan's time, to dash to invade and colonise new territories beyond; it was placed now on the frontiers with a defensive mentality, no longer to enlarge them but to contain them, to defend against invaders and, when there was no enemy in view, to prepare by strenuous military exercise and training to repel boarders. The emperor Hadrian realised that now the Roman ambition for conquest had reached its furthest feasible extent.

Trajan (AD 98–118) and Hadrian (AD 117–138), the former conquering and the latter organising the empire, spent more time away from Rome than remaining within it. Hadrian originally adopted as his heir Lucius Ceionius Commodus, but this nominee predeceased him. On his death-bed Hadrian then hastily adopted Titus Aurelius Fulvus Antoninus, also known as Antoninus Pius (AD 138–161). His family had, since the late first century, been slowly pushing upwards and forwards through the senatorial ranks. So successful had Trajan and Hadrian been in securing the frontiers and composing the populations within that Antoninus, their opposite, for twenty-three years never even felt obliged to leave Rome. Remaining at the centre, he governed the empire by correspondence and decree.

In AD 147 Antoninus Pius granted tribunician power ("tribunicia potestas") and pro-consular authority ("proconsulare imperium") – the ancient powers which together signified heirdom to the emperor – to Marcus Aurelius. He continued then to reign for another fourteen years, and was due on his death to be succeeded by Marcus Aurelius.

Marcus Aurelius however had other ideas. He insisted at the death of Antoninus that both he and Lucius Verus should be adopted as co-heirs. Verus was adopted as brother to Marcus Aurelius and endowed with the necessary constitutional powers. He performed imperial duties as a faithful equal to his adopted brother and co-emperor, and beat back a Parthian invasion of Syria to beyond the Euphrates again, but he died in AD 169. Marcus Aurelius was left to reign and soldier on alone until his death in AD 180.

He was followed on the imperial throne by another individualist. The "consensus of Nerva" was wrecked. The time of amplitude praised by Mommsen and of prosperity and peace lauded by Gibbon came to a close. The comment of Dio was that the age of gold had deteriorated to an age of iron and rust!

Just as instability reappeared in the family and mind of Commodus (emperor AD 180–192), so it reappeared in the state. In the mind of Commodus it took the form of delusions of grandeur, under which he began in the earlier part of AD 192 to believe that he was Hercules. In that state, in a throw-back to the first century, the emperor was assassinated on New Year's Eve, 31st December 192, and the imperial throne was taken by the Prefect of the Praetorian Guard, Pertinax.

Pertinax was emperor for three months. There followed four years of civil war. The ruling elite and the consensus that had endured for over eighty years were fatally wounded. The accession and restoration of civil order by Septimius Severus belong more appropriately to the third century AD.

The Romanisation of the Imperial World

The tranquillity and order prevailing in Rome throughout the reigns of Trajan, Hadrian, Antoninus Pius, Lucius Verus and his longer-lived colleague Marcus Aurelius, favoured powerfully the second great influence which shaped and coloured the second century AD – the settlement and Romanisation of the provinces.

Provincial government, especially where the army was concentrated and influential, assimilation, citizenship and cities developed in equal pace with one another to ensure and continue a peaceful and prosperous empire. Agriculture flourished in Gaul, the west and Africa, arboriculture in Germany. Trade prospered. The distinction between "home" and "foreign" policy became blurred as all policy became both provincial and imperial together.

There was a discernible westward shift of population, to which only the army ran counter.

Moving to the east and north, in opposite direction to the civilian drift, the army came to be concentrated in greater numbers on the Danube. During this century, the army, bearing civilising and Romanising influences, rose to its greatest effectiveness in all Roman history.

Striking now a defensive posture on the Danube and the Euphrates, the army became indirectly an instrument of imperial colonisation and Romanisation. Its presence taught Latin language, Roman ways, town-planning, law and civilisation, and encouraged trade.

It fostered also within all cities the development of a familiarity with common urban institutions: Roman forum, basilica, temples, baths, theatres and circuses. As the century progressed circumstances within such cities favoured increasingly generous grants of Roman citizenship to provincial inhabitants. Yet hardly had this golden Rome matured into a presiding metropolis, a "late antique" city, than its superannuation was to follow.

A Landscape Reconfigured

Ever since he chronicled a span from the second century AD to the fifteenth, with power and gripping authority, the historian Edward Gibbon, with his title "The Decline and Fall of the Roman Empire" has held the European imagination locked within his own assumption. In the twentieth century later historians have begun to wriggle sufficiently free from Gibbon's presupposition to consider whether, instead, these centuries might be read, less dramatically, as a simple organic development.

Another way to evaluate the second century AD and the four that followed may be expressed in a fourth, and final, metaphor from geology. Putting aside talk of watersheds, historical currents and reservoirs, it is possible to speak, alternatively, of flowing and ebbing spring tides.

The natural basin enclosed within the forests of Germany to the north, the Sahara to the south, the Euphrates to the east and the Atlantic to the west was, from the time of Augustus to Hadrian, filled up with the incoming high tide of Romanisation (not without strong undercurrents from Greece and Israel and lesser rivulets from Mesopotamia and Egypt). There the tide stood and rested for a century, performing its irresistible Romanising scouring. Then the tide began to ebb again, leaving behind a landscape thereafter permanently reconfigured. What are the signs, signals and symptoms of this alleged turning of the tide?

The earliest are the building of Hadrian's Wall and the forsaking of conquest beyond the Euphrates, as though Hadrian recognised that in Britain north of the Wall, and that east of Mesopotamia, his predecessor Trajan had entertained ambitions beyond an unwritten natural limit; automatically with this followed a changed philosophy of the army, straining at its given frontiers no longer as an advancing or attacking, but as a defending, conserving force. A third symptom was the gesture of Marcus Aurelius in taking an equal partner as co-emperor.

There were other, lesser symptoms of the melancholy withdrawal of the ebbing tide: man-power problems; poverty of new ideas; decline of real political activity of the Senate; economic difficulties; external and civil wars; problems, following the assassination of Commodus, of succession and instability at the centre.

All these were the earliest signs that the inward flood of Romanisation was now lapping along its high watermark, but progressing no further. The tide was on the turn and preparing to ebb.

In later centuries all these indications were to develop momentum and to become powerful centrifugal forces, destined ultimately to depose the Senate from the seat of government, and even Rome itself from the seat of empire!

A New Beacon

The Christian Church meanwhile fitted itself discreetly into the imperial administrative background of the second century AD. It was content to show itself as tight in efficient administration as was the empire; and indeed, through early development of the episcopal system, to unveil the most administratively competent and unified institution of the whole empire.

Its heroes were Ignatius of Antioch, Polycarp of Smyrna, Irenaeus, Justin (Apologist and Martyr) and Tertullian.

In AD 190 the works of the liturgiologist Hippolytus revealed that in the preceding decades the Church had also ruminated over, and produced, its earliest statement of belief, the Apostles' Creed. This was a handy, easily memorable formula, encapsulating and passing on the centre and heart of the Christian belief and hope.

In its uncompromising and laconic assertions of one God, the Creator; and of Jesus Christ and his redeeming death, the Apostles' Creed summed up the way in which Christian believers, in the light of ancient Israelite literature and the more recent four Gospels, interpreted the phenomenon of Jesus Christ, his birth, his teaching, his death, his resurrection and, preceding both these latter, his Last Supper.

In its stark claim that there were three "Persons" – God the Father, Jesus Christ the Incarnate Word, and the Holy Spirit – in the one God of the Israelite Psalms, Prophets and Scriptures, the Apostles' Creed threw out challenges for the future which were equally uncompromising!

35

The Century of the Superannuation of Rome (AD 201–300)
The Third Century AD

Shocks and Dislocations

As the forlorn image of the ebbing tide carries the imagination forward into the third century AD, it continues to uncover within the Roman empire scenes of increasing disorder and chaos. At the heart of the travails of the third century AD was the one gift that Providence and nature had denied Augustus, dynastic succession. This innate flaw in the Roman imperial constitution had been masked from AD 97–180 by the "Consensus of Nerva." With the assassination of Commodus on 31ˢᵗ December AD 192, it was back to war once again for the principate and the throne.

But since the last civil war – that following the suicide of Nero in AD 68 – much else, apart from the "Consensus of Nerva" had changed. It was no longer simply enough for contenders for imperial office to march on Rome, as Galba, Vitellius and Vespasian had done in AD 69.

Things were happening on the frontiers that could not be neglected.

Septimius Severus, the final victor in this outburst of civil disorder, found it necessary and expedient, immediately after his final march on Rome (June AD 193), to march out again on military campaigns in the eastern empire (AD 194–196), in the west (Lugdunum (Lyon) in AD 197) and on the eastern frontier (AD 198–199). He did not return to Rome again until his tenth year, AD 202.

Military obligation and the frequency and patterns of it began publicly under Septimius Severus (AD 193–211) to draw the emperor away from the capital city and the Senate and toward the sphere of the army. The centre of imperial power began to shift out of Rome to wherever the emperor happened to be on his travels. What had begun under the emperor Trajan (AD 98–117) as a barely observed distortion began to take the form of a regular trend. It was the diametric opposite to the practice of Antoninus Pius (AD 138–161); but this was the shape of administration of the Roman empire, and the rest of its complexion, increasingly throughout the third century AD. The third century AD however was suffering also from the dictates of geopolitical laws much older than the childlessness of Augustus or the peregrinations of Septimius Severus. Since the fall of Old Kingdom Egypt, a rapid turnover of leadership had been a symptom within many a political organism that it was in trouble. And since prehistoric times, convergence upon Mediterranean and Aegean lands had been from the east and the north.

It was by steady emergence of such age-old echoes, by the shocks and confusion of both internal disorder and external pressure, that the tranquil second century AD partnership of Senate and emperor was prevented from ever being reconnected; that the number of years emperors were able to survive proceeded to shorten; and that the roll-call of emperors and the dislocations between them proceeded to enlarge.

The Emperors

Internal disorder disposed of, among other emperors, Philip the Arab (AD 245–249); Gallus (AD 251); Aemilian (AD 253); Gallienus (AD 253–268); and Aurelian (AD 270–275).

Efforts to relieve pressure on the northern and eastern frontiers accounted for other emperors: Gordian III (AD 238–244); Decius (AD 249–251); Claudius II (AD 260–270 – one of the few emperors to die of natural causes); Valerian (AD 258); and Carus (AD 283).

Short were the reigns of Gordian I and Gordian II (AD 238); of Pupienus and Balbinus (June to August AD 238); and of Quintillus (AD 270); of Tacitus (AD 275–276); Florian (AD 276) and the sons of Carus (AD 283–285). It was only with the accession of Diocletian (AD 285) and his radical reorganisation of administration, with an emperor and a deputy-emperor both east and west, that firm government and stable order returned to the whole empire.

Yet though many emperors were short-surviving, and though few of them could settle for more than a short time in Rome, still the emperor was the emperor, and the centre of all power began to concentrate literally and geographically upon the person of the emperor, whoever he might be.

The emperor was, for example, the fountain-head of law. That his pronouncements and decrees should be the more watertight and secure, there travelled along with his permanent body of other court professionals, trained lawyers, who could couch his decisions in the least ambiguous language, and assert by their very presence and services that Roman law found its origins and proper interpretation only in the emperor.

This was but one example of the increasing centralisation of all sovereign power in the empire – but centralisation around an itinerant emperor and his attendant retinue. Above all, because of the military nature of the times, even more than civilian interest, the army began to ascend into the position of senior constitutional partner alongside the emperor. It proved to be an uncomfortable partner.

The Army and the Senate

In a century, the Roman army doubled in size. Septimius Severus at the beginning led a force of thirty-three legions, of which twelve were disposed along the Rhine/Danube frontier, and eleven on the eastern frontier from Cappadocia to Egypt. By the end of the century Diocletian controlled sixty-seven legions and was fencing the northern and eastern frontiers with a band of steel.

The army also represented the heaviest item of expenditure in the whole of the finances of the Roman empire of the third century AD. The emperor alone had to assemble the wherewithal to fund all elements within it – recruitment, provision, pay and, where necessary bribery – bribery either to elevate himself to office in the first place, or, once enthroned, to maintain loyalty.

The army therefore began to exert influences in political and economic realms far from the immediate military sphere. It could make emperors (Macrinus, AD 217; Maximinus Thrax, AD 234; Decius, AD 249; Aemilian, AD 253; Valerian, AD 253 etc. etc.), and could unmake them (Macrinus, AD 218; Gordian I and Gordian II, AD 238; Aemilian, AD 253; Florian, AD 276, etc., etc.).

Through such growing influences the Roman army obliged the emperors to institute empire-wide taxation to cover all its finances, and centralised into the emperor's hands all coinage and the minting of money.

The army stimulated the building of roads for more rapid communication for the emperor's administrative orders or military instructions; for the emperor's own personal passage; and, where necessary, for the passage of goods and the passage of the army itself from one part to another of the empire.

The emperors chose to cease appointing senators to military commands, and appointed instead equites ("knights"). Constitutionally therefore, in these and other ways the army drove a major wedge between the emperor and the Senate.

A further indirect result of all these necessities was the formation of a single "economic space" of the whole Roman empire, the envelopment of the totality of it in a common homogeneity and culture. Everybody had to pay the same taxes; everybody came to use the same coinage; the old exemptions of Rome and of the province of Egypt could no longer be constitutionally or economically sustained, and were in AD 285 abolished.

Everybody moved along the same network of roads. By a feat of specifically third-century engineering this network was filled in, with towns along the roads, from Carlisle in Britain to Hierosykaminos in Egypt and from Gades (Cadiz) in Spain to the eastern reaches of the Fertile Crescent. The roads carried the same administrators, decrees, commercial enterprise, tax regulations, customs, dreams, aspirations and governing assumptions. All roads led, however, no longer to Rome, but to the emperor.

If governmental power was flowing from the Senate and People of Rome into the hands of the itinerant emperor, correspondingly the city of Rome itself was beginning slowly to decline in status and prestige. Military commanders, rather than senators, controlled, and tweaked, the emperor's ear. The minting of coinage was withdrawn from Roman hands and spread around to crucial centres in different parts of the empire.

In AD 285 Rome and Italy, in losing exemption from taxation and all other privileges, found themselves on equal understanding with all other provinces of the empire, without exception or special recognition.

Artistic movements no longer flocked to Rome for patronage, or emanated out from Rome, but, by-passing Rome, would leap from province to province.

The description "late antique" begins to creep into the vocabulary of modern historians, as they begin to eye the Middle Ages and set out to describe the sunset city and its diminishing hold upon empire.

Tectonic Movements

Rome was now not so much in decline as in superannuation. The gathering on the northern frontiers of "pre-states" or incipient political units; the appearance in AD 253 of a Celtic group called the Franks; the invention of the water-mill in the Var region of southern France; trade-patterns in north-eastern Gaul and in the river Po that have a flourishing future ahead of them; a road system linking Roman towns across and beyond the whole continent of Europe; religions not directed towards a plurality of deities, but springing out of a single creed and coalescing each around its own single system – the signs are all there of the ebbing of the tides of Ancient History and of the uncovering, as the tides recede, of barely laid outlines, the indistinctly discerned foundations of the future medieval world order.

This was no mere period of transition. Tectonic plates were on the move. The luxury trade formed its own sub-culture in Roman Denmark; the declining gods of Greek and Roman mythology fled to a final refuge on the Moselle; in Germany Mediterranean agri-culture began to mingle with northern European practices and crops; in consequence of a domino effect resulting from the throwing back of impatient nomadic tribes from the Great Wall of China, Alamans and Goths were found pressing on the northern frontiers of the Roman empire. Within these mighty shifts the fate of the Christian Church can no longer be treated as a mere footnote or sprouting social phenomenon within the history of the Roman empire. It begins to be a force of its own to be reckoned with, a "third nation" beside the Roman or Latin west and the Greek east – for although itself dividing eastwards and westwards, it nevertheless embraced the faithful, whether their speech or inheritance were Greek or Latin, in a common set of over-arching and earth-transcending beliefs concentrated around Jesus Christ's work of human Redemption.

The Christian Church

As the Church began to drift out of the mists and backwaters and into prominence as a social force within the main stream, its first experience was a clash with Rome over questions and principles of worship. Believing in, and worshipping, the one true God and Creator known to the world in Jesus Christ, it could not accept worship of the emperor, or acts of sacrifice to the emperor (however nominal, minimal or perfunctory) as other than a degrading and unfaithful idolatry. The persecutions by Decius (late AD 249– March AD 251) centred around this controversy.

The tolerance of Gallienus (AD 260) brought in forty years of relief to the Church from persecution, as acceptance of its reality as an institution within the Roman empire consolidated. The worst persecutions, those of Diocletian, belong early in the fourth century.

The prominent names of the century are Cyprian, Arnobius, Lactantius and Origen; the major trends, the movement towards formation of the canon of Scripture, and the opening of two centuries of rumination and revelation concerning the Holy Trinity and concerning Jesus Christ's Incarnation.

36

The Century of Kaleidoscopic Mutation (AD 301–400)
The Fourth Century AD

Constantine and his Legacy

The emperor Diocletian (AD 285–305) possessed a clear understanding of the dynamics of the Roman empire of his day, and astutely analysed its problems. They were: geographical coverage, far beyond the communications technology of the times; external pressure on the eastern and, increasingly, on the northern frontiers; and internal competition for the imperial throne.

These three problems did not foil or deter Diocletian himself, for he acted effectively to counter them; but remorselessly they undermined his successors, and in the long term drained their energies away.

For the Roman empire, the fourth century AD opened as Diocletian had stabilised it in AD 285. On the vulnerable frontiers there were concentrated more defence forces than ever before.

To contend with the twin problems of disaffection and distance, he had divided the empire into its two natural halves, the east and the west. The government of the east he had entrusted to a co-emperor or fellow "Augustus," Maximian, and a junior colleague or "Caesar," the emperor Galerius. Likewise in the west, which he governed himself as "Augustus," he had taken as his co-emperor but junior partner or "Caesar" one Constantius Chlorus.

On 1st May AD 305 the two "Augusti" retired and the two "Caesares" took their place as co-"Augusti" or senior emperors, each appointing his own fresh colleague or "Caesar" as new junior and second-in-command. Unluckily for the constitution of

Diocletian, early death and military intervention broke the chain of the system.

In the west, as early as AD 306, Constantius Chlorus died at York. His soldiers immediately acclaimed the son of Constantius, Constantine, as their new senior emperor or "Augustus." Constantine himself then appointed no "Caesar" as his co-adjutor. He could, potentially, have been designated a usurper against his own father's chosen deputy and successor, Severus, the most recent western "Caesar;" but the death of Severus in AD 307 meant that from then on there was no opposition to the rise and rise of Constantine I.

Three emperors became two emperors when Constantine defeated the eastern "Augustus," Maxentius, at the battle of the Milvian Bridge (AD 312). It was a battle whose course and result persuaded Constantine to throw in his lot with the Christians. Two emperors became one when the emperor Licinius fell to Constantine in AD 324.

Constantine then reverted to the dynastic system or principle of Augustus, Vespasian, the "Consensus of Nerva" and Septimius Severus. At his death in AD 337 he left the Roman empire in the hands of his three sons, Constans, Constantine II and Constantius. Apart from the emergency surrounding Jovian (AD 363), the dynastic principle continued to prevail throughout the fourth century AD. By AD 350 Constantius was the sole survivor of the three sons of Constantine, eventually to be succeeded in AD 361 by the last of that house, Julian the Apostate. When the emperor Julian died, rashly campaigning on the eastern frontier only two years later, there was no system for appointing the new emperor save the ancient alternative of military acclamation.

This lottery threw up the emperor Jovian, who, having made peace with the Persian enemy, pursued an ignominious escape route with his army back to Constantinople, but died in camp on the final stage of the journey. Again the army officers made an emergency appointment, and the new emperor, Valentinian I (AD 364–375), entered Constantinople on February AD 364.

The dynasty of Valentinian I, who after achieving a military reputation comparable to that of Trajan died in AD 375 fighting on the northern frontier, consisted of his brother Valens, (co-emperor with him from AD 364, but in the east), until his death in AD 368; his elder son Gratian (AD 367–383) and his younger son Valentinian II (AD 375–392). The dynasty established itself with difficulty against usurpers, and the younger generation both died young, Gratian aged 24 and Valentinian II only 22.

At Adrianople in AD 378, at a battle after which his body was never found, Valens led the Roman army into conflict with over 10,000 Goths, where the Roman name suffered its worst defeat since Cannae (216 BC) – almost six hundred years before!

Following the disaster of Adrianople, the Roman empire was left with an imperial family consisting of Gratian, then aged 19, and his eight-year-old brother Valentinian II. As their co-emperor, Gratian elevated to the throne Flavius Theodosius, known to history as Theodosius I.

When Theodosius I died in AD 395, he left as co-emperor his sons Arcadius, 17, (emperor alone since AD 383), emperor of the east; and Honorius, 10, (emperor since AD 393), emperor of the west.

When the fourth century came to its close, the barbarian Stilicho was guardian to Honorius; Arcadius was under firm control of his wife, the empress Eudoxia.

The fourth century had been a century dazzling and momentous not only for its imperial rulers, but also for its profound changes in culture, mentality and assumptions. By hidden but sweeping processes the empire founded by Augustus began to be transformed into the society of the early Middle Ages. Every element of continuity within the Roman empire began in this century to undergo processes of subtle but irreversible mutation.

Continuity and Mutation

In the fourth century AD, beneath the overt tale of events, the historical foundations of the whole complex of the Roman empire, already fissured and split in the third century AD, began to shiver, granulate and dissolve. The kaleidoscope of the Roman empire shook and astoundingly rearranged itself. Various forces that had caused the ancient foundations to crumble away, reassembled themselves into a new whole and a new order.

Superficially the empire appeared to congeal into a single unit. The same taxes, currencies, traditions, education, law, commerce, town planning, literary and artistic aspirations prevailed across the whole land mass and the seas. There was a common culture, mentality and set of assumptions. There were only two languages, and they akin to each other. The pattern of roads that ran from continent to continent belonged to the same imperial authority. The appearance was of monolithic solidarity. But the reality was a kaleidoscope of seething change.

Change was discernible, most ominously, in the composition of the army. From some 350,000 men in the third century AD the army had now reached a figure of some 500,000.

Mercenary soldiers – barbarians, Germans, Sarmatians, Alans, Armenians, Arabs, even Huns – were recruited into the army on an unprecedented scale. By the end of the century on the continent of Europe such mercenaries formed the most effective battle-field battalions in the defensive force.

Less menacing, but numerically equally significant, was the growth of fourth century AD bureaucracy. Taxation was now needed to pay for this swelling army, the largest item in the imperial budget. Bureaucrats, of whom only 180 named persons can be traced in AD 259, rose to something like 6,000 in the premier tier only, in the course of the fourth century AD. Yet in spite of such enlargements, the Roman empire in the fourth century AD was beginning to contract. Areas of eastern Britain, formerly occupied by Roman militia, were found flat and vacant by pioneering migrations of Saxon peoples exploring westwards from Federsen Wierde on the Weser estuary. In many other ways, the mentality of the early European Middle Ages began to sketch itself in.

A common feature of that mentality came to be a retreat from ancient polytheistic solutions to the mystery of existence, creation, life, fortune and death. In their place rose up belief systems focused upon one God, or at most two competing gods. Specifically the paganism of ancient Greece and Rome began to wilt and crumble before faith in Jesus Christ and his Resurrection. The sequence and cycle of Christian festivals began to dispossess the observance of ancient pagan rites.

In the third century AD Rome, formerly centre of the empire, came to be displaced in status by the temporary locations of the emperors themselves, wherever they might happen to be.

Early in the fourth century AD this drifting centre came to be better established and stabilised by the emperor Constantine I – but not in Rome. It stood instead in Constantinople. It represents to hindsight a virtual institutionalisation of the widening gulf within the empire between the wealthier Greek-speaking east and the poorer, Latin-speaking west.

The imperial bureaucracy, admirably efficient in many ways, could not penetrate everywhere. Defensive walls began to be built around certain towns in North Africa, Spain and Gaul.

Sometimes associated with these newly-walled communities, sometimes separated, individual strong men broke loose from imperial control and gathered their own private armies and bands of clients. Such "warlordism" was not yet feualism, or even pre-feudalism, but it was a foreshadowing of a feature which medieval society was later to wear.

Equally faint and incipient, not even lurking, but forming further back in deeper shadow, was a slow crystallisation out, of Germanic states and of the Byzantine state.

Typology in the interpretation of the scriptures; in art a swerve away from naturalism and a tendency towards allegory; assaults by literature on astrology and fate; in literature and theology, further allegory – these were all fourth century intellectual features shortly to reappear as profoundly influential within the medieval mind.

The coming of monasticism and of asceticism all reflected a new view of the self, which was a breach with the Graeco-Roman world and a harbinger of the medieval.

Under the influence of the Gospel of Jesus Christ, and now administered by the bishops through the Church, there grew up a new style of charitable giving. Institutions unheard of before – almshouses, orphanages, hospitals – began to be established. Rich donors, now persuaded not to let their left hand know what their right hand was doing, began to give anonymously. The recipients of their gifts were, without restriction, or test of citizenship, the most desperately poor.

Cathedrals, feast days of local saints, the aristocratic status of bishops, all began to advance to a profile and a prominence that reached its culmination in the walled cities of the Middle Ages.

Some historians date the last day of the Ancient World to 31st December AD 406, and the first day of the Middle Ages to 1st January AD 407.

The Splendour of the Eternal Trinity

The Hubble telescope, named after a great astronomer of the twentieth century and launched in 1990 into nearer space, has sent back to the world majestic photographs of towering splendours in the

Eagle Nebula, and spectacles of awesome beauty in distant corners of the universe.

In the same way, in the fourth century AD the Christian Church had its specialist observers who, looking through and behind the New Testament scriptures, pieced together new, unseen and unforeseen truths in the far distance. They were, above all, St. Athanasius (AD 298–373) and St. Augustine (AD 354–430) in the Latin-speaking west; and Basil of Caesarea (d. AD 379), Gregory Nazianzen (d. AD 390) and Gregory of Nyssa (d. AD 394), known collectively as the Cappadocian Fathers, in the Greek-speaking east.

In the light of Jesus Christ, his origins, his identity and his Incarnation, they penetrated behind the New Testament narrative to the essential nature of the Creator, and discerned, reaching out from realms beyond the human intellect, God the Holy Trinity, three Persons in One God, Father, Son and Holy Spirit. In modern terms, they discerned the work of God in creation to be not just a "one-layer" activity, a "Big Bang" or explosion at the dawn of time, but a "three-layer" process in which the moral or spiritual components of "Redemption" and "Sanctification" are essentially and contemporaneously combined.

In the Holy Trinity, the Father, the Son and the Holy Spirit, three Persons in one God, reside such answers as can best satisfy the human mind, to such questions as "Where do we come from?" "What are we?" "Where are we going?" Here are to be found the final solutions to every human quest, the final satisfactions of every human hunger.

37

The Century of Diverging Destinies (A) The East   (AD 401–500)

The Fifth Century AD

Two Types of Consolidation

Ever since Rome, in the second century before Christ, had come to dominate the whole Mediterranean, different characteristics between the western and the eastern sections of that informal empire had been plain. These differences were finally acknowledged and publicly institutionalised by the emperor Constantine I in his foundation of Constantinople (dedicated 11th May AD 330), and transfer of the seat of government from Rome to Constantinople.

Later in the fourth century AD, Theodosius I (AD 378–395) was the last emperor to hold single rule over both eastern and western empires. In the fifth century AD the two segments of empire were now to drift finally apart upon currents carrying them to entirely separate destinies.

When Theodosius I died in AD 395 leaving his elder son Arcadius (b. 378) as emperor of the eastern Roman empire, based upon Constantinople, and his younger son Honorius (b. 383) based in Milan as emperor of the west, he had in fact signalled that at last the two halves of the empire were on the point of parting company. With the opening of the fifth century AD the eastern empire was to continue along a voyage of singular statehood. The western empire was to become a chess board.

Thus in the east the long reign of Theodosius II (AD 408–450), the cliff-hanging of the Isaurians (AD 457–491) and the sagacity of the elderly Anastasius (AD 491–508) protected the empire from such incursions as it suffered from Goths, Huns and Persians, and maintained and consolidated the fabric of a firm and often largely peaceable civilisation.

In the west the first quarter of the fifth century AD was to see Roman authority trampled by Goths, Alans, Sueves, Vandals, Burgundians and Franks.

In the half century that followed, Roman imperial control in the west slowly declined until, in the year AD 476, the new peoples who had entered the porous boundaries of the former empire suddenly awoke to realise that it had all evaporated away!

In the last quarter of the fifth century AD the new entities of early medieval Europe began indvidually to discover, define and establish themselves.

This century was to reveal therefore, in the east the consolidation of the established; in the west the consolidation of the new.

Theodosius II and the East

Women and eunuchs played powerful parts behind the thrones of Arcadius (AD 395–408) and his son Theodosius II (b. AD 401; emperor AD 402–450) in the east. Intrigue and ambition were woven with the same complexity as in any powerful and luxurious court. Yet the instabilities of internal court politics produced in the empire some surprisingly stable results. The prefect Anthemius (AD 405–414) held the eastern empire on a level course throughout the death of Arcadius in AD 408 and the following uncertain period of the minority of the child emperor Theodosius II. The defensive and financial measures of Anthemius were sound enough to leave the whole eastern empire solvent and buoyant from AD 414 onwards.

Theodosius II, raised to imperial status in AD 402, dying 48 years later in a hunting accident and at the end of a reign of remarkable and merciful stability, was the longest-serving emperor in all the annals of the Roman empire. Through the services of his sisters, educators, appointees, officers and bureaucrats, he was able to maintain the eastern empire in an enviable condition of security and tranquillity.

The reign of Theodosius II was also supported by an ingrained oriental respect for Roman imperial inheritance, traditions and continuity; and by a solicitude, common for the emperors of the eastern empire, for the unity of the Christian Church. Theodosius called the Council of Ephesus in AD 431. His successor Marcian (AD 450–457) called the historic Council of Chalcedon in AD 451.

The Survival of the Roman Empire in the East

When Theodosius II died in AD 450 without male heir, once again a problem of succession, old as Augustus, returned to haunt his empire. A month later, an unknown, Marcian, also of unknown sponsorship, became emperor with observable, but not insuperable, contest or opposition.

In home policy Marcian attempted by the Council of Chalcedon of AD 451 to reverse some of Theodosius II's Second Council of Ephesus of AD 449. In foreign policy he took against Attila, the leader of the Huns, a much firmer policy of resistance than Theodosius, and with the death of Attila in AD 453, both eastern empire and eastern emperor were relieved of a barbarian burden.

When a superior civilisation enchants and educates a more barbarous one in its advantages and attainments, it must expect that among the beneficiaries of its custodianship there will be a number who feel a right to recognition within that superior circle and even to office within it.

This happened to an overwhelming degree within the empire of the west, where the complexion of the whole army was transformed by cultural converts, and where Stilicho, the Vandal who became guardian to the emperor Honorius, was the supreme model.

With a much lower profile, and with a home-grown rather than an external infiltrating community, the same phenomenon occurred in the eastern empire.

The district of Isauria on the south coast of Asia Minor had nourished a rugged and barbarous people of independent nature and of little ambition outside general banditry, guarded as much by the rough terrain of their boundaries as by the general intransigence of their nature.

Nevertheless, recruits from this unpromising territory came forward to join the army of the east, just as the Burgundians, Huns, Alans, Sueves and others had been recruited to the army of the west.

Following the death of the emperor Marcian in AD 457, it was to these Isaurians that his successor Leo I (AD 457–474) then turned.

He increased their recruitment into the army and favoured one exceptionally gifted Isaurian general, Zeno, with the hand of his own daughter, Ariadne. When a son was born to this Isaurian and Ariadne, and also named Leo, Leo I installed the child a co-emperor with himself in AD 473, thereafter leaving him, upon his own death shortly afterwards in AD 474, child emperor at the age of seven, of the whole eastern empire.

The sole gift to the empire that this child Leo II was able to give, was the appointment of his father Zeno as his own co-emperor. Ten months after this elevation, the child Leo II died, leaving his father, the high-flying Isaurian ex-barbarian, as sole emperor of the east.

Zeno endured a turbulent reign, chiefly rendered insufferable by the jealousy and the revolts of his original patron's, Leo I's, relatives; and of Leontius and Illus, other Isaurian rivals envious of his advancements. He died in AD 491 leaving Ariadne his widow.

Following the death of Zeno, not quite the whole Byzantine Isaurian dynasty was therefore extinct. There remained the widow Ariadne, the daughter of Leo I and mother of Leo II, an Isaurian by marriage and an elder of unmatched experience. To Araiadne the senators of Constantinople now turned, and in a civilised gesture which rejected civil war, military coup or popular acclamation by soldiers, invited her to nominate the best candidate to serve as the next emperor. Her choice was a surprise, but a success.

Anastasius (AD 491–518), was already sixty years old. Yet he and his civil service, by unspectacular diligence and with the competent prudence of experience, succeeded in settling the eastern empire in greater sagacity and tranquillity than any previous emperor of the fifth century AD. Anastasius died in AD 518.

In the east in the fifth century AD, under Theodosius II and Marcian, under the Isaurians and Anastasius, the Roman state, although under peril from Huns, Ostrogoths and Persians sailed on in relative serenity. It was otherwise in the west.

The Church, East and West

Within the Roman empire the Christian Church had by now, by the fifth century AD, grown and advanced to the status of a parallel institution. In the two separate halves of the empire it reflected in its life and development the conditions of its political contexts and surroundings.

In the west, the theologians to whom it looked were St. Augustine (AD 354–430), St.Ambrose (AD 339–397) and Pope Leo I (AD

440–461). The Church in the west responded to the invasions by barbarians, the alarums and march of arms of the fifth century, by withdrawal into a spiritual reality above the transience of fast-changing political scenario and rapidly-moving military background. It developed in discipline and in monasticism a hold upon a superior spiritual truth. It coalesced into a unity acknowledging solidarity under a common leadership, and strengthening the powers and responsiblities of the Pope.

In the east the Church's theologians were Cyril of Alexandria (AD 412–444); from the third century Origen; and from the fourth century the Cappadocian Fathers, Basil of Caesarea, Gregory Nazianzen and Gregory of Nyssa. Under the eye of a sympathetic state, and relatively at peace, it was free to explore and indulge theological differences. The concern of Theodosius II summoned the Council of Ephesus of AD 431 and the inconclusive Second ("Robber") Council of Ephesus of AD 449. The interest of Marcian assembled the Council of Chalcedon of AD 451.

The Council of Chalcedon (8th October–1st November AD 451) did not resolve all the passionate issues of faith and unity to which its delegates aspired, but it did achieve such steps forward as to mark it as an event of major significance in the life and history of the Church.

On its third day, 10th October, it approved among other historic doctrines and formularies, the Nicene Creed of AD 325 and the letter of the late Cyril of Alexandria (d. 444) on the unity of the Church. A week later on 17th October it accepted with acclamation the Tome of Leo on the primacy of the Bishop of Rome.

In the second half of its proceedings, the Council of Chalcedon drafted on 22nd October 451, and agreed and signed on 25th October, the Chalcedonian Definition of the Christian Faith on the Person of Jesus Christ "in two natures."

During its sessions of the remainder of October AD 451, the Council established the patriarchate of Constantinople, effectively but controversially counter-weighting both the political aspirations of the late Cyril of Alexandria, and the ecclesiastical aspirations of Pope Leo I, concerning the see of Rome.

In spite of epoch-making gains, the Council of Chalcedon left behind certain anomalies and loose ends productive of disquiet, dissatisfaction and ultimate discontents.

The acceptance enjoyed by the Church in the east meant that it was not under the same pressure to unite as was the western Church.

Nevertheless, pastorally all component points of view played a full part in the social, charitable and religious life of the east.

Sometimes marred by schism and retaliation, always attempting to realise on earth concern for the poor, at least the Church continued, by celebrating and sharing the Eucharist, to sign-post unhesitatingly the way to the spiritual realm and to commend that self-denial intrinsic to the Gospel of the Incarnation, Crucifixion and Resurrection of the Lord Jesus Christ.

38

The Century of Diverging Destinies
(B) The West   (AD 401–500)

The Fifth Century AD

The Sack of Rome

The eastern half of the Roman empire thus presented an appearance of reasonably regulated unity. The west was by contrast a much more diverse and romantically crumbling scenario.

Within the shadow of creeping decay, multiple enterprises of potential and vigour were in fact beginning to sprout into new forms of life. Twenty-five years of barbarian incursion (AD 401–425) were followed by fifty years (AD 425–475) of dissolution and the regroupment of new heirs. In the final quarter of the century (AD 476–500), successor states, finding their place and their feet, were beginning to test and flex youthful muscles.

Invasions as early as AD 401 and AD 406–7 were the preliminaries to the great demoralising indignity of the sack of Rome in AD 410.

In AD 401 Alaric, leader since AD 390 of the Visigoths, moved from the Balkans for the first time into Italy. He was soundly defeated by the Romano-Vandal Stilicho, who had been appointed under the will of Theodosius I to be the guardian of the boy-emperor Honorius. In AD 375, Valentinian I had moved his centre of government from Rome to Milan. In consequence of the retreat of Alaric back across the Alps, Honorius and Stilicho now moved it yet again from Milan to Ravenna.

To defend Italy on the north-east, Stilicho recalled forces from Britain. They never returned to Britain again; nor were they adequate to guard the western provinces and the western boundaries of the empire. On the night of 31st December AD 406–1st January AD 407, Asding and Siling Vandals, Alans and Sueves crossed the frozen northern Rhine on foot and within a few months, conquering and looting as they went, had forced an irreversible invasion passageway to the Pyrenees!

During the same winter freeze, Burgundians and Alamanni, crossing the Rhine further to the south, disposed themselves in northern Gaul in immovable contingents and settlements inside Roman imperial territory.

Seventeen months later, on 1st May AD 408, Arcadius, the eastern emperor, died.

Tensions between the western emperor, Honorius, and his guardian Stilicho, could no longer be contained. On 22nd August AD 408 Honorius ordered the execution of his guardian, and Stilicho, as an obedient servant to the house of Theodosius I, submitted. There remained now no firm military resistance to the Visigoth Alaric. Late in the autumn of AD 408 he was actually besieging Rome, and could only be bought off with a bribe.

Frustrated in negotiation, and still militarily irresistible, Alaric again marched on Rome on 24th August AD 410. This time he took, sacked and looted it.

The Sack of Rome in AD 410, although viewed with sanguine political calculation by the regency of Anthemius in Constantinople, and even by Honorius in Ravenna, spread through the empire at large a panic and a demoralisation which were little assuaged by the death of Alaric later in the same year, and by the decampment of his successor, Ataulf, to Gaul. Such were the catastrophes of the west in the decade AD 401–410.

The "Fall" of the Roman Empire in the West

In other western quarters the Vandals, Alans and Sueves, those tribes who had made the midnight crossing of the frozen Rhine on New Year's Eve, AD 406–407, and reached the Pyrenees by AD 408, penetrated them by the autumn of AD 409. For a few years (AD 410-414) Alaric's Visigoths too, now under Ataulf, settled north of the Pyrenees.

Joining then in AD 414 with Roman forces, these Visigoths crossed the Pyrenees, and in a few campaigns further southward (AD 414–418), made short work of the Vandals and Alans, although many others, still heading south in retreat, occupied the southern tip of Spain and in AD 425 ventured to make a first crossing into

Africa. Meanwhile in AD 418 the victorious Visigoths again returned back north of the Pyrenees, accepting from Honorius grants of land in Aquitania.

The first quarter of the century was over, and the fires of barbarian irruption began to die down. Following the accommodation between the intruders and Honorius in AD 418 and onwards, a lengthy barbarian-Roman sunset blessed southern and Mediterranean Gaul, although the northern provinces became the unstable playground of Burgundians, Alamans, Franks and Romano-British refugees.

The political landscape was now, however, altered for ever. As the nascent states of the early Middle Ages began to jostle into their territories, a species of governmental organisation was maintained from Ravenna, until the death of Honorius in AD 423.

As in that year, from the east, Theodosius II began to survey the consequences of the turbulent last years of the reign of the late Honorius, if one thing was clear, it was that the days of one-man imperial authority across the whole Roman empire could never return.

Theodosius II surrendered his nephew Valentinian III (aged 6) to be proclaimed Augustus and emperor in the west on 23rd October 425, conscious that it was the poisoned chalice of a feeble and nominal authority. While therefore in the east Constantinople continued to consolidate, the Roman west under the child Valentinian III, for whom his mother, Gallia Placidia, sister of Honorius, stood regent, continued to crumble.

When the first quarter of the fifth century had elapsed therefore, the boy Valentinian III was on the throne of the Roman empire in the west; all European territories except Italy were in the hands of invaders, infiltrators and usurpers; for economic support and provision Italy depended upon the wealth and grain of north Africa; north Africa itself was falling under the shadow of Vandal occupation; behind the throne imperial officials and generals were competing for personal ascendancy; and one of them, named Aetius, held in his hands a trump card – an intimate acquaintance with the Huns!

Following this combination of situations, it is no surprise that within fifty years even the appearance of Roman government had been ground away to an ignominious stump. Yet from the standpoint of the history of the Middle Ages, this influx of new Germanic states, having been driven inside Roman boundaries by marauding Huns, had sunk deep roots. In the rich humus of Roman civilisation they were beginning to inherit the full dignity of mature, independent entities. The Roman empire in the west may have shrivelled away, but its place was taken by barbarian successors which had become adopted, recognisably Roman, children of the civilised tradition.

It was the general Aetius who finally in AD 433, when the young emperor was fourteen years old, emerged as master and penultimate presider over this transforming process.

For twenty-one years policy in the western Roman world was dominated by Aetius, the maturing Valentinian III, and a third party, Attila, leader of the Huns. There is plainly discernible a strange turn-about in Roman strategy, which began by using the Huns to control the other barbarian peoples, and then used the other barbarian peoples to expel the Huns. The key to these apparent contradictions is to be found in the varying attitudes and loyalties of Attila the Hun.

On achieving supreme influence at court, Aetius took advantage of various earlier dealings and relationships established with the Huns to use and deploy them principally against the Goths, Burgundians and bagaudae – that is, other sundry local insurgents representing one-issue grievances. This state of affairs lasted until AD 441, when Attila began to turn his forces to the invasion of Roman territory.

To resist Attila, Aetius made recourse to those Roman forces normally stationed in Africa to keep watch against the Vandals, but at that time temporarily located in Sicily. The consequent exposure of Africa and its fall to the Vandals, producing for Rome the loss of all the wealth, supplies and foodstuffs of that province, meant a heavy economic blow to the western empire, crippling it and impoverishing and starving its military arm.

Since Attila the Hun had now declared himself the enemy, Aetius, reversing his earlier pattern from AD 433 to AD 441, of alliance, and acting now in concert with the Germanic tribes, was able to defeat the Huns convincingly in AD 451 at the battle of the Catalaunian Plains. Within ten years, following the unexpected death of Attila the Hun in AD 453 and the collapse of his chieftainship and authority, even refugee Huns were seeking sanctuary within the borders of the remnant Roman empire in the west.

Attila, Aetius and Valentinian III had formed an unlikely triad. Following Attila, the demise of the other two members was even more bizarre. In AD 454 Valentinian slew Aetius, some say with his own hand. In March AD 455 two members of Aetius's bodyguard had his revenge, when they assassinated the emperor.

Some might think this a deplorable way to run a disintegrating empire, but by this stage, nothing mattered very much. The end came neither with a bang, nor even with a whimper, but as an unobserved evaporation.

In AD 460 first the Visigoths of Aquitania, then the Burgundians to the north, realised that they had been spontaneously cultivating Roman-style civilisation while Roman imperial control had been withering away. The deposition of the last emperor of the west, Romulus Augustulus, on 4th September AD 476, was without ceremony or memorial.

His father Orestes, leader of the army in Italy, proclaimed Romulus Augustulus emperor in the year AD 475. Within a year, Orestes's authority had collapsed. A junior officer, Odoacer, summarily murdered him, and allowing Romulus Augustulus to live, simply hung him out to dry.

Such a gesture was actually nothing beyond a mere informal constitutional acknowledgement that the successor states had now in fact no further bonds to break!

The Old Order Changeth

Once Augustus and Agrippa had fought in Spain; Tiberius and Drusus in Germany; the emperor Claudius had been born in Lyon; the second century emperors had sent out proconsuls from Rome to govern the quiet western provinces.

Now in the final quarter of the fifth century AD the Visigoths consolidated their grant and inheritance in Aquitania, and the Burgundians and Franks settled in northern Gaul. The Sueves and other Visigoths took uncontested possession of Spain, and the Vandals of north Africa. The Ostrogoths claimed Italy; the tribal states of Anglo-Saxons and Picts flourished in the British Isles.

The Roman empire had faded, but new young enterprises of green virility and promise were beginning to emerge in its place.

Further back, a hundred years before Augustus, Rome had conquered Greece miltarily, but had fallen prisoner to Greece's intellectual brilliance. Now, six hundred years later, Germanic arrivals had conquered and entered into Roman territory, but had in turn been taken into thrall by Rome's superior cultural inheritance.

39

The Northern Frontier
(10,000 BC–AD 500)

Points of the Compass

It is safe to say that in the four thousand years (3,500 BC–AD 500) of the foregoing survey, no adventurous seaborne footprint from the west was ever planted upon the beaches of the eastern Atlantic.

Likewise, virtually nothing from the south impinged upon the coasts of the Mediterranean, except for that which came up along the Nile.

Eastern encounters veered and varied wildly although always with a remorselessly western drift, finally settling down to an uneasy equilibrium.

At the time of the colonisation of Crete from the east (about 5,000 BC), the whole Mediterranean basin leaves an emptily echoing effect behind. When Hadrian (AD 117–138) came to abandon Roman eastern expansion beyond the Euphrates, mature political states were confronting each other face to face and toe to toe.

Between these two eras lie over five thousand years of rising enterprise and adventure, suppported by five millennia of another unseen and unmeasurable dynamic – population growth.

It was adventure, invasion, trade, but behind them the supporting phenomenon of population growth, which likewise account for events and incursions along the most penetrable and permeable of all four frontiers, the north.

Over the thousands of years (10,000–3,500 BC) that the peoples of the eastern quarters were developing their farming economy, painfully, slowly, the message was communicating itself to the scattered families and tribes along the northern steppes and forests, that they were the poor relations.

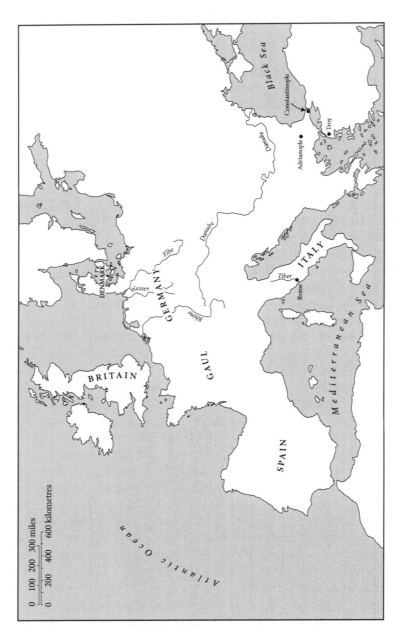

3 Western Europe from the Black Sea to the Atlantic Ocean

Down from the north-west coast of the Black Sea and across the Danube there trickled, over the millennia, various timorous practitioners of painted pottery, entering a sparsely populated, if not virgin, Aegean paradise. Their Hun and Gothic successors thousands of years later in the fifth century AD, were to arrive in fierce and fast-moving numbers and were to discover a populous and powerfully advanced civilisation. A long, long survey of the northern profile shows (just like the eastern profile), how the world over the millennia had been filling up.

The Indo-Europeans

The foundation in about 3,000 BC of a single city, Troy, signalled that northerly and easterly interests were converging with sufficient impetus to form a fixed institution. Established more likely by experienced and commercially-minded traders from the east than by infiltrators and speculators from the north, Troy's geographical position betrays its purpose and function as a dropping-off point for merchants from the east opening up fresh markets to the north.

For seven hundred years Troy was the only port, and even point, to represent such peaceful trade between east and north. Then a new phenomenon erupted.

Luwian invaders (about 2,330 BC) swept down upon Troy and on along the eastern coast of the Aegean, leaving behind unashamed traces of the most ruthless barbarism and cruel mishandlings of local people, ever yet known to mankind! The Indo-European peoples were discovering the softer climates of the south.

Much of the story of the northern boundary is the story of the Indo-Europeans. A few may have been agriculturalists, but the majority seem to have been nomadic raiders and warriors along the northern steppes and wastes with some sort of cradle in the Ukraine, in the Dnieper valley north of the Black Sea. Being nomads, except where, like the Hittites, they settled down, they left few traces behind them in the archaeology. Instead, the main testimony to the Indo-Europeans and their marches lies in the spoken word and the science of linguistics.

A common family of words for "metal," whether copper, bronze or iron, links all the dialects of the Indo-European languages from east to west, from the Old Indian "ayas" to the Latin "aes." Indo-European movements began therefore after the development in

Anatolia of metallurgy, somewhere between 4,000 and 3,500 BC Perhaps passing acquaintance with trade from the south, metals from the south, civilisation from the south, climate in the south and other rumours from the south tempted powerful Indo-European leaders to form groupings and sweep south in search of new life and lands, adventure and plunder. The Luwians sound like the first of such groupings.

Most forcibly between 2,100 and 1,800 BC further waves of the same Indo-European peoples – Hittites, Hurrians, Minyan ancestors of the Mycenaeans – thrust themselves into Anatolia and the Mediterranean basin. They were followed between 1,400 and 1,200 BC by the Phrygians and the Dorians. They came not by one, but by four, routes: between the Caspian Sea and the Black Sea; west of the Black Sea and across the Dardanelles; over the mountain obstacles of the Balkans; and by-passing or crossing the Alps.

The Indo-Europeans in their successive eras and generations were to invade in three separate phases: the downpour of the Indo-Europeans themselves during the Bronze Age (3,000 -1,050 BC); the frustrated tribal lappings by the Gauls and Celts during the "classical" age (800 BC–AD 200); and the preliminary seepage of AD 253 leading to the apocalyptic inundation (AD 378–476) by every tribe of ambitious steppe-dweller, which was to sweep in the Middle Ages.

If ever there were explorers and adventurers from the west or the south, for them the Atlantic and the Sahara were impassable. Some propulsion, most likely of all, population increase, rained cascades of human beings out of the steppes of Russia and the forests of Europe into the relatively untouched and inviting lands and climates of Anatolia, the Aegean, Greece and Italy. The most prominent and still living survival of the peak of the Indo-European migrations – the horse – was introduced into the Mediterranean world some time (perhaps 1,700–1,500 BC) during the later stages of the long period (2,300–1,050 BC) of these northern population movements.

The final curtain on this dark and spectacular era was brought down by the Peoples of the Sea (1,300–1,191 BC) who,mysterious as they are, seem to have originated in the north. The Indo-European migrations left behind, in the Mycenaeans and the Dorians and in their Greek successors, a long train of uninterrupted consequence which laid the foundations of all succeeding European history, intellect and culture.

The Gauls, Celts and Germans

In 237 BC Lutarius and Leonnorius led an invasion of Celts and Gauls which entered, spread across and occupied large territories in Anatolia. It was like a throw-back to the great Bronze Age migrations. It was probably one result of the break-up of the empire of Alexander the Great. The inheritance of an enormous distance from the east coast of the Aegean to northern India was often impossible for Seleucid kings to patrol.

Otherwise the days of the "Glory that was Greece" (800–146 BC) and the "Grandeur that was Rome" (753 BC–AD 200) amount roughly to a thousand years during which other invasions from the north were reduced in manpower and motivation, fewer in number, and for the most part vigorously repulsed.

For example, before the foundation of Rome the populations of Latins and Etruscans that became native to Italy seem to have been accumulated from a combination of migration from the east and natural reproduction as much as leakage from the north. The first really storming invasion from the north fell upon Rome some eight hundred years later than the most recent previous equivalent incursions (the Dorians of 1,200 BC) into the peninsula of Greece.

Just as the inhabitants of Rome were beginning to achieve some form of worthwhile communal identity after a century of poverty, they were demoralised and decimated by an invasion by the Gauls in July 387 or 386 BC, which defeated their army and sacked their city. Yet these Gauls, leaving only the Capitol undamaged by their attentions, turned again to the north.

The next northern assault upon Italy and Rome did not really count, for it was generated internally from Mediterranean politics. It was the passage of Hannibal across the Alps in 218 BC in the course of the Second Punic War. Although his manoeuvre was applauded as a marvel of daring and radical strategy, neither Hannibal nor his admiring observers were to know that he was "pioneering" a route and an orientation already followed many times before from ancients eras.

By the end of the second century BC, a hundred years after Hannibal, Rome was peacefully radiating civilised influence out via the north-west of Italy and all along the Mediterranean coast of Gaul. Drawing along the south of Narbonnese Gaul a pattern of civilisation indistinguishable from the Italian, this current of Romanisation seeped up in the contrary direction, not from north to south, but from south to north. It was about this frontier that the Roman general Marius met, between 104 and 101 BC, the first serious northern invaders of the Roman Republic.

In 114–113 BC Rome had begun to feel the first hostile contact with peoples from beyond the Rhine. The Germanic tribes of the Teutones and the Cimbri were beginning to intrude.

Growing more bold, they descended upon Orange and in 105 BC defeated a Roman army under Caepio and Mallius. It was then that the Romans appointed their most effective warrior, Marius, to the German command.

At Aix-en-Provence in 102 BC Marius defeated the Teutones. The most daring, and perhaps desperate, invasion of the Cimbri, came down upon Italy through the Alpine passes in 101 BC. It was firmly routed by Marius at Vercellae.

Defence of the Northern Frontier

These dangerous confrontations with formidable tribes from the north provoked in the Roman mind a reverse dynamic. The drive of the northern menace should be met proactively. In the long term, anticipation of peril from that point of the compass produced in the collective Roman mind a reverse south/north policy which was to prevail for almost another five hundred years.

Thus, when Julius Caesar (59 BC) was looking for new lands to conquer, it was natural for him to press out to the north. When his adopted son the emperor Augustus (30 BC–AD 14) had, by the conquest of Spain in 26–25 BC, pacified the western half of his empire, he turned his mind to the Rhine and to the north.

On account of this reverse current the Italian peninsula, instead of being the suffering victim of northern infiltrators and invaders, began as a conscious matter of defensive policy to send up from the south, from the opposite direction, enormous pressure of military and cultural forces.

Towards the middle of his principate (about 15–1 BC) Augustus sent his step-sons Tiberius and Drusus, supplemented later by Sextus Appuleius and Lucius Domitius Ahenobarbus, to conquer and round out the territory of the Roman empire as far as the Elbe. In his old age, the loss in AD 9 of the three legions of Quintilius Varus in the Teutoberg Forest reduced the ambitions of Augustus and confined his dwindling enthusiasm to the natural boundary of the Rhine.

Along the eastern Danube the emperor Trajan (AD 98–117), between the years AD 101–106, in an ambition parallel to that of Augustus, thrust the forces of the Roman empire upwards again from the south into Dacian lands north of the river; but this was the furthest extent of Roman imperial ambition to the north. Population pressures which were producing at about this time a stalemate between the Roman and Parthian empires in the east, were, in the north, on the point of causing a turn in the tide.

Septimius Severus (AD 193–211) was obliged to deploy twelve legions to hold his northern frontier along the Rhine and the Danube. In AD 253 a new Germanic tribe, the Franks, appeared on the banks of the Rhine. Twenty years later, in spite of resistance, they had crossed the Rhine and established themselves in Gaul. In the meantime, fighting in preservation of the Danube section of the northern frontier, two Roman emperors, Decius (AD 251) and Valerian (AD 258) had met their deaths.

For the rest of the third century AD barbarian assaults were regularly chipping, nibbling and gnawing at the northern frontiers. By the end of the century the emperor Diocletian was obliged to mass legions far more numerous than those of Septimius Severus along the northern boundary, resisting especially the menace of new tribes and new populations in increasing numbers along the Danube.

The emperor Constantine and his dynasty (AD 306–363) successfully held these potential invaders at bay. The catastrophic defeat of the Roman legions at the battle of Adrianople (AD 378) brought thousands of Goths across the Danube, not only within the boundaries of the Roman empire but also, as mercenaries, within the employment of the Roman army. This victory also opened the opportunity for Alaric and the Ostrogoths to lodge, a generation later, in Balkan territories.

At midnight on 31st December AD 406–1st January AD 407, the Vandals, the Alans and the Sueves crossed the upper, and the Burgundians and the Alamanni the lower, Rhine, the whole river being frozen. Within a few years they had spread themselves through France and Spain as far as Gibraltar, and Rome had been sacked by Alaric (AD 410). In AD 425 the first Vandals crossed from Spain into Africa.

Throughout the fifth and sixth centuries AD new peoples settled in the lands of France, Spain and Germany. Gladly accepting

Roman civilisation but merging Roman ways with their respective tribal predispositions, they produced each their own individual variations of that civilisation. In the end the Roman empire in the west was simply swamped and transformed by weight of numbers, by geographical and demographic forces, and by pressures that came irresistibly thundering out of the north.

The earliest stimulation to Greek and European civilisation had descended round about 2,000 BC or thereabouts from the north. From the same point of the compass came also the final overwhelming and dissolution of the Roman empire in the west, and with it that titanic transformation of Europe that scattered the Ancient World and brought history to the threshold of the Middle Ages.

40

The Ultimate Three Minutes
(Passover AD 33)

Salvation History, 1,800 BC–AD 33

During those four thousand years, while the northern boundary was pullulating with pressure from invaders, although pierced also with long periods of peace; while the Aegean was expanding as a centre of culture and commerce and then falling back again into nostalgic neglect; while the principles of civilised community living were working their way steadily from east to west, there was also at work a fourth dynamic. It was pursuing a pre-planned programme towards a meticulously calculated climax.

Late in the Bronze Age (3,500–1,050 BC) was formed the myth of Orpheus the lyre-maker, testifying to the instinctive and emotional response of humanity to the appeal of music.

Similarly in the Egyptian Middle Kingdom (2,040–1,674 BC), stands the figure of Abraham, round about 1,800 BC, representing the universal curiosity provoked in the human mind by the teasing problem of existence.

Standing apart from all the cultures and speculations that whirled about in his day, the sceptical Abraham resolved the problem of existence for himself and his descendants by believing in one sole creating and communicating power. Abraham's grandson Jacob (also called "Israel") then, about 1,710 BC, followed his own sons, Joseph and his eleven brothers, down into Egypt.

430 years later, in about 1,280 BC, Moses gathered together the descendants of these original pioneers, now amounting in number to twelve tribes, and led them back to the border of the lands from which their ancestors had previously descended.

Moses taught them that they were God's Chosen People. To Moses also is attributed a large and lasting body of law and liturgy.

Foremost within the liturgy was the Feast of the Passover, the hasty supper and the re-enactment of the flight from slavery in Egypt. In the centuries that followed, the worship of the God of Abraham, Isaac, Jacob and Moses came to be established centrally in the Temple of Solomon in Jerusalem (940 BC) and, following innate musical instinct, to be celebrated in heartfelt song.

Israelite life and Jerusalem Temple worship were rudely interrupted in 586 BC when the city of Jerusalem was sacked by Nebuchadnezzar, and the cream of its inhabitants carried away by him into exile in Babylon. Born into Babylonian exile, but steeped by exilic teaching and worship in the traditions, history and song of Israel, the anonymous poet known today as Second Isaiah voiced an interpretation of the enigma of existence which, at its heart, foresaw an awesome and solitary figure who in unaccompanied and unsupported lonesomeness must achieve a mysterious but redemptive triumph.

Near the beginning of his stunning poetry, the prophet Second Isaiah had coined the summons, "The voice of one crying in the wilderness, 'Prepare ye the way of the Lord'" (Isaiah 40.3).

560 or so years later, in the period of long Roman peace established by the providentially favoured emperor Augustus (63 BC–AD 14), John the Baptist (about AD 28) personified the "voice of one crying in the wilderness," and took up within his own generation the summons, "Prepare ye the way of the Lord" (Mark 1.3).

John the Baptist was not the only one to take up the torch of Second Isaiah. Jesus of Nazareth, whom John introduced as the "Lord" whose way he had been appointed to prepare, also took up language echoing down from the prophet of the Babylonian exile, and before him echoing from as far back as Moses (1,280 BC). Jesus took up the simple, passionate, loaded formula "I am." "I am the bread of life: he that cometh to me shall never hunger, and he that believeth in me shall never thirst" (John 6. 35).

Nevertheless Jesus of Nazareth, in spite of delivering this and comparable messages, was not welcomed with universal joy – but condemned to die!

At the moment of his final arrest, leading to the two trials of Jesus, St. John reports that Jesus three times, interrogating his captors, repeated the religiously resonant formula "I am he" (John 18. 4–8). The awesome, mysterious Servant/Redeemer was marched away in unaccompanied lonesomeness to be tried, flogged and crucified. At a poignant moment in the proceedings, even Pontius

Pilate, the Roman governor, declared of him, "Behold, the man!" (John 19. 5).

The last three minutes of the earthly life of the lone and crucified Jesus of Nazareth were the ultimate three minutes – the Ultimate Three Minutes in the labour of the Redemption of a fallen universe.

Salvation Language

In Bronze Age times, the marvels of nature and the press of events besieged the human mind with such unified intensity that the most creative imaginations felt that it was in the language of legend, myth and parable that they could most impressively deliver the impact of experience.

During the Ultimate Three Minutes and the Ultimate Six Hours which lead up to them, as on the Cross the Lord suffers and draws near to man, and man in fascinated and trembling curiosity draws near to God, the still primitive ingenuity of modern human beings can only register the impact of the experience by the same innocent Bronze Age technique – the Parable of the Attendants behind the Door; the Parable of the Target; the Parable of the Doppler Shift; and, mirroring Paul Gauguin, a Parable of Everyman.

First comes the Parable of the Attendants behind the Door, a rusted and implacably locked iron door standing at the end of a gruesome, high-walled cul-de-sac. Skeletons festooned with cobwebs testify to the millions who have entered this dead end and knocked at the door in vain.

Further to secure the door, in addition to the lock and the rust, no fewer than eight strong bolts on the further side guarantee that all access is impossible. Graffiti scrawled upon door and desolate walls provide the unneccessary information that this is indeed the dead end.

Now however, for the first and only time, eight attendants, one each allocated to the stiff, rusted bolts, take up their position behind the door. Their response to the signals and exertions of the Ultimate Three Minutes will see the door perform an entering function never ventured or achieved before!

THE ULTIMATE THREE MINUTES

The Ultimate Three Minutes

Five and a Half Hours to Go

At an early stage in the Crucifixion of our Lord, the soldiers detailed to inflict the capital punishment had taken the cloak of Jesus of Nazareth, his final earthly possession, and leaving him naked, had gambled for possession of it. What these soldiers did not know was that they were falling into a previously described fold of destiny, "They parted my garments among them: and cast lots upon my vesture" (Psalm 22. 18).

With this correspondence between Psalmic blueprint and historical actuality, the attendants now spring to their posts, waiting for the signals for each of the eight bars, bolt by bolt, to be withdrawn.

Three Minutes to Go

Five hours and twenty-seven minutes passed. Then Jesus gave the cry, "I thirst" – the thirst not only of a dehydrated victim beneath a burning Middle Eastern sun; he had emptied himself to endure the privations of space/time dehydration in order that the injured victims of the wounds of time, being redeemed, might never thirst again. Therefore with the signal "I thirst," the first attendant draws back the first bolt of the immovable securing set.

Two Minutes and Forty Seconds to Go

The second signal was the application, either in mockery or in mercy, of vinegar to the lips of the thirsting Jesus. Whatever the human motives, according to the economy of redemption, the vinegar was applied in fulfilment of Psalm 69.22, "They gave me gall to eat: and when I was thirsty they gave me vinegar to drink." The second bolt of the final set that remains behind the iron portal "The End," is slid back.

Two Minutes and Twenty Seconds to Go

The third signal was the unpromising cry of Jesus, "My God, my God, why hast thou forsaken me?" Yet like the gambling away of his garments, the cry was a second fulfilment of Psalm 22 (verse 1). The third bolt of the rusted set behind the frowning iron doorway is drawn back.

Two Minutes To Go

St. Luke's witnesses then heard Jesus say, "Father, into thy hands I commend my Spirit" (Luke 23. 46) – a prayer first found at Psalm 31.6. The fourth bar of the remaining set that secured the door of the dead end is drawn back.

One Minute and Forty Seconds to Go

St. John heard Jesus utter a cry, "It is finished" (John 19.30). The cry may be supposed to have rung from Jerusalem to the ends of the earth, from beyond the Pillars of Creation in the constellation of the Eagle to the light year at the furthest corner of the universe. But it meant that the fifth bar was now pulled back.

One Minute and Twenty Second to Go

All four accounts of the death of Jesus Christ, the Anointed Redeemer, then record that Jesus "gave up the ghost" (Mark 15.37; Matthew 27.50; Luke 23.46; John 19.30). Jesus had the liberty at any time, of his own accord to quit the torment of this time-space existence; now was the moment when, under the discipline of obedience, he was released and given leave to do so. The sixth bar was heaved back.

One Minute to Go

"And the veil of the Temple was rent in twain from the top to the bottom" (Mark 15.38). In the Jewish religion the "veil of the Temple" was a symbolic equivalent of the Iron Door. Its "rending" is the visible proof that Jesus Christ's redeeming death has been universally and victoriously effective. The weary, painful labour of the Incarnation and the Crucifixion has been crowned with the ultimate triumph of Redemption. The seventh bolt behind the iron portal of death is thus drawn back.

Forty Seconds to Go

"When the centurion who stood over against him, saw that he so cried and gave up the ghost, he said, Truly, this man was the Son of God" (Mark 15.39). The first person whose eyes were open to recognise the Son of God was not a member of the Chosen Nation but, on the contrary, a Gentile. Truly then, the highway of full Redemption, the access to the holy, living God, has by the victory of the Crucifixion been thrown open wide.

Back rattles the eighth, the ultimate, bolt on the yonder side of the portal of estrangement and alienation, of annihilation and death.

Twenty Seconds to Go

With groaning resistance the impenetrable gate grinds open inch by inch. Glimpses of paradise flash through.

"God forbid that I should boast, save in the Cross of our Lord Jesus Christ, by which the world is crucified to me, and I unto the world" (Galatians 6. 14).

41

The Parable of the Target

"Where Do We Come From? What Are We? Where Are We Going?"

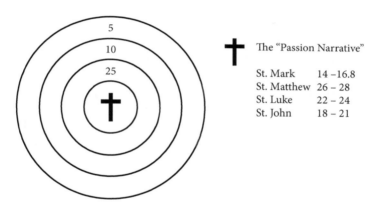

The "Passion Narrative"

St. Mark	14 –16.8
St. Matthew	26 – 28
St. Luke	22 – 24
St. John	18 – 21

From the Old Testament (the first major section of the Bible), read any book and you are on the track towards an answer to Paul Gauguin. Allow yourself five points.

From the New Testament (the second major section of the Bible), read any book from the Acts of the Apostle to Revelation, and you are growing warm. Allow yourself ten points.

Read any one of the four Gospels from the beginning of the New Testament (the second major section of the Bible), and you are almost there. Allow yourself twenty-five points.

Read the "Passion Narrative" in any one of the four Gospels (chapters given above), and your have hit the bullseye.

42

The Parable of the Doppler Shift

Nature and the Bible

In the study of any work of literature, an examination of the simple words "as" and "like" does not seem to promise a very exciting expedition. Nevertheless, in the Bible such an enterprise supplies an unexpected and gratifying yield of deep and charming nature images.

"They shall mount up with wings as eagles" says the prophet Isaiah (40.31) of that devotion that "waits upon the Lord."

Of anyone who "exercises himself in the law of the Lord day and night" the author of Psalm 1 declares that "He shall be like a tree planted by the waterside: that bringeth forth his fruits in due season."

"Thy righteousness standeth like the strong mountains: thy judgements are like the great deep" (Psalm 36.6).

"Like as the hart desireth the water-brooks: so longeth my soul after thee, O God" (Psalm 42.1).

Jesus in the Sermon on the Mount (Matthew 5–7) has twenty-seven nature images, including sun and rain, pearls and rust, sheep and grass, wolves and grapes and the contrast between rock and sand.

More usually, the imagery drawn from nature is less flattering to the human race and more candid about the human condition. For all his comparison with "eagles' wings" (40.31), the prophet Isaiah has many more similes on the transience and frailty that characterise mankind – "dust" (40.15; 41.2), "stubble" (40.24; 41.2; 57.14), "chaff" (41.15), "tow" (43.17), "smoke" (51.6), "wind" (41.29) and the yielding of garments to moth (50.9; 51.8).

The prophet Amos likens the sins of humanity to a farm cart or haywain heavily burdened and weighed down with sheaves (2.13).

"My people have committed two evils," says the prophet Jeremiah commenting on the follies of mankind. "They have forsaken me, the fountain of living waters, and have hewed themselves out cisterns, broken cisterns that can hold no water" (2.13).

A singularly resonant nature image of the frailty of man, that of grass, stands to the credit of the prophet Isaiah (40.6–8; 51.12). His mournful comparison, "Surely the people is grass; the grass withereth, the flower fadeth" is coined by one who has seen the searing effect on tender vegetation of the savage sirocco. "Grass" is taken up from Isaiah by the author of Psalm 103 (15–16) and in the New Testament by St. Peter (I Peter 1.24).

From nature, the most common Biblical image of all is that of "sheep."

"All we like sheep have gone astray" confesses Isaiah in 53.6. "I have gone astray like a lost sheep" repeats Paslm 119. 176. "The Lord is my shepherd" is the theme of the well-known Psalm 23, echoed in Psalms 95 and 100.

God himself takes over from the unworthy shepherds. "I will seek out my sheep and deliver them out of all places where they have been scattered in the cloudy and dark day" (Ezekiel 34.12). Jesus in the New Testament performs this exact searching function (Luke 15. 3–7) Incidentally, Jesus in the Sermon on the Mount takes recourse to the nature imagery both of grass and of sheep. Elsewhere, he is the "Good Shepherd" (John 10. 1–18); the "great shepherd of the sheep" whom "the God of peace brought again from the dead" (Hebrews 13.20); and "the chief shepherd, who will appear" (I Peter 5.4).

In other passages outside the Sermon on the Mount, Jesus in his parables frequently draws upon the nature imagery associated with the agricultural life and calendar: ox-ploughing (Matthew 11. 28–30); sowing (Matthew 13. 1–23); harvesting (Matthew 13. 24–30); storing (Luke 12. 16–21); general labouring (Matthew 20. 1–16) and the weather (Matthew 16. 2–3). In the Parable of the Vineyard (Luke 20, 9–18) and the Parable of the Talents (Matthew 25. 14–30) Jesus seems to liken himself to an absentee landlord, who one day will return to see how things on the estate are going.

However, throughout the Bible, as also throughout the ancient world, no individual was ever able to travel faster than the speed of a galloping horse. Therefore one image derived from nature that is never found in any reference or text, is the "Doppler Shift."

The Doppler Shift

To understand the Doppler Shift, it is best to visualise a remote country bridge over a silent railway line on a still summer morning. It is a Sunday, and the track beneath carries only one express train every two hours.

Long before the moment designated on the railway time-table there is a faint and distant hum and an anticipatory vibration along the rails. With a high-pitched scream the express thunders towards the bridge and rattles through beneath. Immediately the tone of the receding locomotive drops to a low rumble. This rumble continues to quiver along the railway line even when the express is now far away.

This change in pitch from the high scream to the low rumble is the "Doppler Effect," also known as the "Doppler Shift."

Inherited from the ancient Greeks, modern science possesses both the curiosity to examine every phenomenon of nature, however apparently insignificant, and the determination, in pursuing researches, to leave no stone unturned. Towards mid-nineteenth century the physicist Christian Johann Doppler (1803–1853) set himself to examine this strange and unexplained property of sound.

Doppler discovered it to be a universal law of nature that, relative to a stationary observer, the wavelength of sound changes in accordance with the direction of motion of the body emitting the sound. What happens therefore under the Doppler Shift, is that the wavelength of sound of (for example) the express as it approaches the bridge and the passers-by upon it, has to be different from the wavelength of the sound of the express as, having passed under the bridge, it speeds away from it. This is perceived by the observer as the high pitch shifts immediately to a low rumble once the train has passed through.

Since not only sound, but light also, is on the spectrum of wavelengths, Doppler proceeded to discover that light obeys the same rule. The wavelengths of light shift towards violet if a source of light is moving towards an observer, and towards red if a light is moving away.

The principles of the Doppler Effect are applied daily within the science of astronomy. It has been through the study of the Doppler Shift in the furthest universe that the motions and directions of different stars have been capable of measurement; that nebular and galactic redshifts have been investigated and proof has been established that the universe is expanding.

"The kingdom of heaven may be likened unto ....." is a formula with which Jesus begins a number of his parables. The "Ultimate Three Minutes," in their preparation and their consequences, may be "likened unto" the succession of phenomena that combine in the Doppler Shift, to form a twenty-first century modern nature parable on the origins, person, work and progress of Jesus Christ.

The Doppler Shift as Nature Parable

After seventeen centuries (3,500–1,800 BC) of settling agriculture and evolving civilisation, a faint but distinctive hum is first heard echoing along the passageways of history. It is Abraham, standing for the first renunciation by the human mind of the fantasies concerning creation and existence, of humanity's childhood; and his advocacy of a simple adult system of belief that a single force, power or God stands behind all existence.

Five hundred years later, (1,300–1,200 BC) Abraham's thought amplifies as it rolls nearer. To Moses it is revealed that there is indeed a single principle behind all existence, whose name bears the redoubled force and intensity of "I am that I am." Moses is, in addition, commanded to institute the religious feast known as the Passover, which centres upon two of the most basic needs of all humanity – eating and drinking!

With the work of Second Isaiah some seven hundred or so years later (538 BC), other mile-posts are passed. The whole created existence owes its origin to God's "Word" (Isaiah 55. 10–11). Creation is sustained in existence by him from moment to moment because God imparts "being" to it from his own substance, as a freely chosen form of self-expression of his own.

Yet the universe has within it inadequacies which are in need of redemption, just as the inadequacies of God's Chosen People, exposed by their lamentable history, are in need of restoration and redemption. So specialised a task is this redemption that it is ignorant folly to assume that human beings can achieve it of their own resources. It can be achieved only by one single suffering figure, and by him suffering alone.

As the Psalms annually carry the Passover and daily sing of the Creator and long for his Redemption, the on-going process of preparation for such Redemption speeds towards the high pitch of its climax.

During the providential period of Roman peace, early in the era of the emperor Augustus, consistent with traditions and beliefs that derive from Abraham, Jesus is born in Bethlehem. In the first decades of the period of history which we call "AD" the process which redeems and reveals meaning for mortal life and human existence now thunders through.

The Rumble of the Sacraments

In the forty seconds between "My God, my God, why hast thou forsaken me?" and "It is accomplished!" the frequency shifts from high-pitched expectation to the deep-throated satisfaction of fulfilment. It leaves behind to rumble for ever afterwards, through every passage of events, "sacraments" – religious features unknown to human experience or mentality before and unique to the Christian religion alone. Simple, commonplace elements like water, bread and wine, are to convey, and even to personify, unique and all-embracing redemptive truth.

There are two sacraments inseparable from these Ultimate Three Minutes – Baptism and the Eucharist (or "Holy Communion"). At every Baptism and at every service of Holy Communion, in the re-enactment and in the remembrance of Jesus of Nazareth and his redeeming death, the suffering and significance of the same Jesus, and his transforming work, continue to rumble along the rails of human experience and resound about the landscapes of human history. Between the birth of Jesus Christ in, notionally, AD 1 and his death and resurrection in AD 33, a process parallel to the climax of the Doppler Shift passes through human history, resolving its dilemmas and transforming its anguishes into vision and positive hope.

The preparatory hum of this process had arisen with and within the culture, history and song of the Chosen People, rising to its heights in the prophets of Israel, of which the last and latest was John the Baptist.

Its departing reverberations are reviewed and renewed from day to day through the centuries in the immersing beneath the surface of water – the symbolic drowning which is Baptism – and the repeated re-enactment of the Last Supper, which is the Eucharist.

The time-table of the long sequence of events is clear, logical and symmetrical. Having taken its departure in about 1,800 BC in Middle Kingdom Egypt, this is an express train which is still running and will not need to come a second time.

"Where Do We Come From? What Are We? Where Are We Going?"

There are three questions fundamental to the mysteries of human existence within a time/space continuum. The answer to these questions is to be found in Jesus Christ, the preparations for his coming, the good news of his creative death, and the reverberation of his abiding presence in his sacraments.

At the very centre of this whole long process stand the central Ultimate Three Minutes – the central vortex and all other associated properties of the fourth decade of the first century AD (AD 31–40). We find our meaning in those events of that decade that lie between the teaching of John the Baptist in its first year and the preaching of St. Paul in Syria and southern Turkey in its last.

Yet these first and last messages of these two such contrasting characters, at their heart concentrate down upon the life and ministry of Jesus, his Last Supper, his Crucifixion, his Resurrection and Ascension; upon the descent of the Holy Spirit and the founding of the Church.

Central to it all John the Baptist and St. Paul focus upon Jesus Christ and the four phases or aspects of Jesus Christ as carpenter of Nazareth; as crucified Redeemer; as risen and ascended Lord; and as for ever risen and present in the corporate Body of his Church.

Epilogue

This attempt to place in context the Ultimate Three Minutes in the history, life and experience of the human race should end, as it began, with a parable of Everyman.

Rosemary Wilson booked herself a return flight from Heathrow to Hong Kong on a first class ticket. As the plane took off, she noticed that only a small scattering of other passengers were travelling first class that day.

Part-way through the journey the pilot, out of respect for her first class status, invited her up to his cabin and to his observation deck. He explained to her his controls, instruments, computers, automatic pilot and safety procedures. Together they looked down as the continents passed beneath them. He identified the cities, the rivers, the landscapes, the mountain ranges, the endless Siberian forests.

When he had finished his guided tour, Rosemary Wilson did not spit in his face. She did not tear his flesh with her nails. She did not return to the first class saloon to slander him, or to conspire with other passengers to contrive for him a painful and humiliating death.

When she realised with what solicitude her Pilot was protecting and conducting her through every minute of her perilous journey from the place where she had come from to the place to which she was going, Rosemary graciously thanked him.

Almighty God, Father of all mercies, We thine unworthy servants do give thee most humble and hearty thanks for all thy goodness and loving-kindness to us, and to all men; We bless thee for our creation, preservation, and all the blessings of this life; But above all for thine inestimable love in the redemption of the world by our Lord Jesus Christ; For the means of grace, and for the hope of glory. And, we beseech thee, give us that due sense of all thy mercies, that our hearts may be unfeignedly thankful, and that we shew forth thy praise, not only in our lips, but in our lives; By giving up ourselves to thy service, and by walking before thee in holiness and righteousness all our days; though Jesus Christ our Lord, to whom with thee and the Holy Ghost be all honour and glory, world without end. AMEN